Accolades for Phil's *Nam-A-Rama*

Publisher's Weekly,
(Starred review).

Nam-A-Rama   Phillip Jennings

"This highly entertaining, provocative lampooning of the Vietnam War is reminiscent of *Catch-22* and David Mamet's *Wag the Dog*. In this wonderfully irreverent novel, evocative of vintage Max Shulman, hearty belly laughs contrast with chilling insights into high-level political machinations."

The New York Times
James Parker

Nam-A-Rama   Phillip Jennings

"At its best Jennings's humor comes down like lightning, fully charged, from some higher and more vital realm; at its least effective, when the page is crowded with pratfalls, improbabilities and silly names, it invites the use of that wilting word "zany." Additionally, some estrangement seems to have occurred between the merry jester responsible for the book's best lines and the distinguished veteran gravely blessing America in the afterword. But this is Jennings's problem, and not the reader's.

Kirkus Reviews

Nam-A-Rama   Phillip Jennings

(Starred Review) Tall tales of the flying war in Vietnam mix successfully, for the most part, with adventures both amusing and hair-raising in Southeast Asia. Oliver Stone confirmed that war is evil. Joseph Heller made the case that war is nuts. First-novelist and Marine aviation veteran Jennings suggests that war, even the war in Vietnam, could pretty much be fun. It was hell too, of course, and the battle scenes here are tough, fast, and frightening. But episodes of wackiness predominate in a story premised on secret orders from the nameless, though unmistakably Lyndonesque president. The orders send pilot Jack Armstrong and his fearless, wild-and-crazy buddy Gearheardt (first name seems not to have made it across the Pacific) into the Marine air wing with almost-captain rank and a mission to go to Hanoi and assassinate Ho Chi Minh-General Giap, too, if the opportunity arises. Success of the mission seems to depend on the powers of distraction associated with parachuting into Hanoi the luscious nude star of the film Barbonella (make your own connection), who is keen to have a go with the Hanoi anti-air battery. Gearheardt and Jack have a terrible time getting away from South Vietnam.

Real war keeps intruding, and the pilots constantly have to fly real missions. When they finally do slip away, Gearheardt promptly loses the orders somewhere over the jungle, and their plane is shot down by irritable rice farmers well short of Hanoi. The naked movie star does drop, and the lads do make it to the North Vietnamese capital. But Ho turns out to be an awfully good drinking companion, and the orders to execute the communist leadership may actually have been orders to set up beer distribution agreements. Hmm. Bring on the bar girls.

"Set during a pivotal time in U.S. history and populated by a bizarre cast of characters, Phillip Jennings' zany novel is cynical, fast-paced, irreverent, thought-provoking and thoroughly entertaining."

-**Bob Kerrey**

"Just when you thought it was safe to stop reading novels about the Vietnam War, along comes Phillip Jennings with Nam-A-Rama. . . . a wild, original and often hilarious ride from its opening sentence to the last. . . . [a] weird, painfully funny, wonderful book."

-**Christopher Buckley**

"Nam-A-Rama is a dazzlingly inventive novel of an epic American adventure abroad run totally amuck, a work that demands your full attention from start to finish."

-**Nicholas A. Basbanes**

"Jennings has done a big service to all of us Vietnam vets and anyone else who was touched by that conflict. He has written a book that hacks its way through the dark tangle of the Vietnam War with a blade that flashes with comedy. One of the most bizarrely profound aspects of the human condition is the way horror and hilarity can intimately embrace. To capture that truth in fiction may be the toughest stunt of all. Phillip Jennings does that and does it brilliantly."

-**Robert Olen Butler**

"Nam-A-Rama is a wild piece of work, a sustained vaudeville soft-shoe on the most rollicking, ugly topic. Very, very funny, ribald, raunchy and smart."

-**Stewart O'Nan**

"The story rips up and down like zippers in a Saigon whorehouse… His lampoons… are miraculously funny. But what moved me the most were the pages in which he goes beyond satirizing venal leaders to write fiercely and humanely as a man who was there."

The Washington Post

"Has enough surprises, manic laughter, and grisly just-born newness in it to earn comparison to Hunter S. Thompson's *Fear and Loathing in Law Vegas* and….to Joseph *Heller's Catch-22.*"

The New York Times Book Review

"Marries searing satire with bone-on-bone despair. It's hard to tell the difference between madness and truth here, and perhaps that's the most memorable aspect of the book. It is born from chaos and never attempts to moralize the horror or the hilarity."

Los Angeles Times

"Accomplished with madcap grace… refreshingly irreverent…. Jennings limns his japes with a tribute to the men who fought in Vietnam, especially to the Marines, in words so beautiful they brought tears to my eyes. Rarely does a novelist storm the emotional ramparts so decisively."

The Wall Street Journal

Gearheardt for President

"These may be tough times to poke fun at the military. But Vietnam vet Phillip Jennings, a former pilot and CIA man, follows in the footsteps of Catch-22 and M*A*S*H with Nam-A-Rama, which includes a naked starlet parachuting into Hanoi. It all begins in the White House where President Larry Bob Jones hatches the Vietnam War over pizza."

New York Post

Phillip Jennings

Gearheardt
for President

A Novel

Phillip Jennings

Phillip Jennings

An Intellect Publishing Book

Copyright 2022 Phillip Jennings

ISBN: 978-1-961485-24-2

www.PhillipJenningsAuthor.com

Cover design by Michael Ilacqua

www.cyber-theorist.com

FV-13 Ingram

All rights reserved. No part of this book may be reproduced in any form or by any electronic, mechanical, or other means now known or hereafter invented, including photocopying or recording, or stored in any information storage or retrieval systems without the express written permission of the publisher, except for newspaper, magazine, or other reviewers who wish to quote brief passages in connection with a review.

Please respect Authors' Rights.

To contact the Author:
phil@jenningsphil.com

Intellect Publishing, LLC
www.IntellectPublishing.com

Dedication

"If you pick up a starving dog and make him prosperous he will not bite you. This is the principal difference between a dog and man." **Mark Twain***

For **Margareta, Jason, Alison, Coleman, Leslie, Jake, Henley and Sawyer** for bringing joy and meaning and excitement into my weird life.

And for **James S. Robbins**, a scholar and a gentleman, who restored my sanity and energy for writing.

---

* A special thanks to VM, TL, EJ for going above and beyond. You know who you are. And have to live with it. Memento Mori.

Phillip Jennings

Foreword

This is the last in the three-book series begun years ago. It is, again, satire. The first book, *Nam-A-Rama,* came out in 2005. It was a satirical view of the war in Vietnam, of which I was a happy participant. The dual protagonists in the book were Jack and Gearheardt.

Goodbye Mexico was published in 2007. A black comedy featuring the same central characters, now employed by the Central Intelligence Agency operating in Mexico. I attended graduate school in Mexico.

Now *Gearheardt* completes the series. Jack and Gearheardt are still ostensibly working for either the government, Wall Street, or the CIA. The difference eludes them and probably the reader. (I am here to tell the reader it makes little difference). And their theater of operations is Wall Street and its annex, Washington DC.

Aside from the boys, the main characters are eerily similar to former occupiers of the White House who remain anonymous but were probably employed previously in high positions in rural America. Probably.

It could be said that my political opinions differ from many people in government like New York Cheesecake differs from baboon diarrhea. Long live the Republic.

I am perhaps casting aspersions on some who have diligently attempted to run the country. I do that primarily in the search of a good laugh. I include these ad hominem attacks because I am sick to death of the childish, horrific, personal attacks on politicians. I don't feel sorry for many of the bastards. It's just keeping good people out of the arena. Granted, **psychopaths** and **morons** are actually doing a fairly good job (assuming the description of America as a skid-mark in the underwear of history is their goal) but these **P**'s and **M**'s are infesting institutions beyond just the three branches of government--Silly, Venal, and Redundant.

As to the overall themes of the Jack and Gearheardt series, they are largely autobiographical as to philosophy and geography. But certainly not down to the last antic and tirade. And that's all I will say about that. The books mirror what I see as the deterioration of a once exceptional nation. It *was* quite exceptional, and it might still be. The American exceptionalism debate is drowning in a sea of "self" elevation. Everyone is a hero. So there are no heroes. Everyone is racist. So there are no racists. We are dumbing down. Not to the mean but below the mean, although on its face that seems impossible. Poverty is fashion, torn jeans and all. Yet wealth is nirvana—the driver of opinion and judgement. Everyone hates the rich and will kill to be among them.

A reader would benefit from reading the descriptions of *Nam-A-Rama* and *Goodbye Mexico*. The author (me) can be credited with near God-like prescience having realized that America as he knew it was flinging itself headlong into insanity. Watching it happen, as I have, was as painful as taking a broken-glass enema with both hands emersed in the French fry boiling oil at a Burger King. (Don't try this at home).

As you should be aware, satire has been eclipsed by everyday life.

Looking out at the landscape of wonton destruction, senseless killing on a Biblical scale, hate, envy and the other five or six things not to do, plus the worship of goat art (understandable), I had an epiphany. This is the world I would make if I were God. It seems I bore easily and am rather a jackass at times. I'm not suggesting He suffers from those afflictions. He probably made thousands of other civilizations in His image and sat on His throne bored to tears. So when he made earth and its people, He had kind of a "What the hell?"* moment and just emptied a bottle of craziness into the human gene bowl. He might watch those other civilizations during the day when He's supposed to be working, but in the evening I can almost guarantee He grabs a beer and says, "I gotta see what those morons on earth are up to."

Phillip "Goatman" Jennings

- *God is allowed to say Hell.*
- *Nickname courtesy of Major General Larry S. Taylor USMC (ret)*

Gearheardt
for President

Phillip Jennings

Chapter One

Which is Actually About An Earlier Time

Gearheardt wasn't invited to Jack's mother's first funeral, but Jack wasn't surprised to see his grinning-jackass face when he stepped out of the funeral car behind the hearse which bore her coffin.

Gearheardt had known Jack's mother for almost as long as he and Jack had known each other. Which was when they met at flight school in Pensacola, Florida. From the outside one could assume that Gearheardt's missions in life for the next fifteen or so years was trying to get Jack killed and being his best friend.

"Jack," he would say, "sometimes I have to make tough choices."

"You mean all those times you almost got me killed you had other choices?"

And then he would say what he always said when he wouldn't or couldn't answer. "It's not that simple, Jack."

Which explained nothing. Not that they hadn't had some good times, exciting times. And sometimes did important things. Like trying to stop the Vietnam War and not assassinating the president of Mexico, although they almost did both.

Now Gearheardt was lounging in one of the folding chairs alongside the rectangular hole. Smoking a cigarette, which he threw into the grave as he saw Jack and stood up.

"Jack," he said loudly as the few dozen mourners left their cars and streamed toward the grave, "I thought I might find you here."

He tried to steer Jack away from the grave by putting his arm around Jack's shoulders. Jack resisted, which led to them half-wrestling graveside as the casket was being put into place above the open grave.

"Jack, I just need a few minutes. Give me just a minute. We have things we have to do. Things we've been planning for years. It's now...."

"I haven't seen or heard from you in two years, Gearheardt." Jack took a deep breath and noticed they had attracted the attention of most mourners. The Reverend Thomas stood by the grave, bible in hand, and a look of serious consternation on his face. He shrugged as if 'Oh well, what the hell' and began reading out of the bible. The few family members took seats, the gaggle of mourners moved in, and Gearheardt steered Jack a few yards away.

"It's my mother's funeral, for God's sake, Gearheardt. This is no time…."

"It's the perfect time, Jack. Who would suspect that two spies would be planning…?"

"Not that crap again, Gearheardt. I'm not a spy. I was never a spy. I don't want to be a spy. And I don't want to hear about some idiotic plan you and your friends have dreamed up." Jack paused. "My mother is dead, you jackass."

"We can thank God for that, Jack. Burying your mother alive would be—"

"It's not the place to….wait, what did you say?"

"I just said that to calm you down, Jack."

"You are truly insane, Gearheardt."

The silence from behind indicated that Gearheardt and Jack were not quite far enough away from the listening mourners. Jack managed to shove Gearheardt away and stepped back to graveside and dropped into a folding chair. When he looked back at Gearheardt, he was grinning.

The burial ceremony took on a look of normality with Jack's mother's sisters and half-brother finally able to weep loudly and dramatically. He gave a small wave at Gearheardt, who, after all, had been his mother's favorite of all Jack's Marine pals. Jack saw him wave to a thuggish man standing half hidden behind a tree.

An incredibly loud burst of dozens of fireworks went off. As the mourners sat and stood in shock, a flowered wall of colorful explosions spelled out "Good Luck Mom."

Jack dropped his face into his hands. Only Gearheardt could have been so unaware of the craziness of wishing Good Luck to someone in a coffin.

So, he laughed. Pretended to cry. But he couldn't help realizing he was glad to see him. That damn Gearheardt.

Continuing the Chapter One (above) After the Funeral

The funeral was over. Gearheardt had been asked not to throw cigarette butts in the grave, and he had agreed. The fire from the fireworks spreading from grave to grave had been extinguished. Only a few of the more elderly mourners still lay on the grass being attended to after the unexpected display of explosives.

"Let's take a drive, Jack."

Walking toward the gate, Gearheardt started to reminisce. "Jack," he said, "that chapter's over. Everybody has a mom who dies. Except me. Never had a mom that I remember." He paused, a pensive expression with his eyes focused on something unseen. "I was raised by the CIA, you know," he finally said.

"Actually, Gearheardt, I knew that you were an orphan. I'm not sure when the CIA intervened." I knew the story and didn't want to hear it again.

"They didn't make me kill anyone or overthrow a government until I had a driver's license."

"Gearheardt, I just buried my mother. What the hell do you want?"

"Jack, the Mohicans believe that dead mothers reappear as Shingala Warriors in the next life."

"No, they don't, Gearheardt. What damn looney task are you distracting me away from? In all the years we've known each other through flight school, Vietnam and the Marines, Air America, then Mexico, you have never leveled with me. Never."

"This is just another of those times, Jack."

They had reached the gate of the cemetery. Gearheardt waved at someone outside and moments later a black Mercedes pulled up. The driver came around and opened the back door for them to get in the car. Which they did without ceremony and definitely not aforethought. Jack was in another of Gearheardt's schemes to make the world a better place. For himself primarily as it turned out.

The Mercedes pulled away from the cemetery with the thuggish driver honking continuously at recent graveside people trying to get into their cars. Gearheardt laid out the plan which put Jack running a bank for the government. Which government Jack wasn't sure of. The

Russians were often mentioned and a couple of Okies who had exhibited greed at a record-breaking level.

"Jack, it should be no surprise to you that our government has screwed up royally and has, through my Agency bosses of course, asked me to unscrew it. And this time," he looked over at Jack "you can't fail like you did when we were tasked to stop the Vietnam War."

"I won't even respond to that statement, Gearheardt. But I will remind you that it was you who lost our plans out the window of the helicopter when we were heading for Hanoi. Let's knock off the bullshit and you can tell me what the hell you want. And by the way, you might point out to your driver," he nodded toward the front, "that I'm pretty sure the speed limit around here is not 105 miles an hour."

Gearheardt laughed and spoke to the driver sounding Russian or Eastern European. The driver turned and scowled at Jack but slowed down to a relatively safe 85.

"I might suggest you not piss off the driver, Jack. And I didn't come all the way out to wherever this place is to just say hello."

Jack sighed and there was a pause. "Okay, why did you come all this way, and we're in Kansas for your information."

"Kansas? Well, I'll be damned. Anyway, Jack, I need your help." He had turned toward Jack and worked a bit of emotion into the statement.

"No."

"Seriously, Jack. Ever since I jumped out of that Turkish airliner, which was on fire of course, with just a towel wrapped around me, I've worked on this special assignment. I couldn't tell you earlier."

Jack just looked at him, thinking he might see some reality. "Gearheardt, that was the story the CIA spread to disappear you when you screwed up taking over Cuba, for God's sake. It's not…"

"But what if they're right? What if I did die in a Turkish airliner crash?"

"Then we finally know for sure that hell has telephones, Gearheardt."

"Very funny, Jack. But as an employee of the Central Intelligence Agency, you are pretty much contractually bound to help me. And you seem annoyed that I would remind you of your past CIA mission failures." He suddenly smiled.

"Remember when that old, half-blind Ukrainian sniper tried to shoot you in Mexico City, Jack?" Gearheardt asked.

"You mean the old half-blind Ukrainian sniper *you hired* to shoot me?"

"Nothing personal, Jack. I was just making sure you were committed to assassinating the president of Mexico but actually were not committed to assassinating him. No need to get upset about things like that?"

Gearheardt's main personality attributes were his soaring intellect and an absolute inability to make sense. Jack had been with him through flight school, in the squadron with him in Vietnam where they didn't kill Ho Chi Minh, and two years ago in Mexico City where his scheme to assassinate the president of Mexico, blame it on the Cubans, and use that as an excuse to take over Cuba for either the Pope or a place where Gearheardt's international cadre of intelligence gathering whores could retire in safety.

When queried him about the madness and irrationality of that scheme, Gearheardt said, "It's all in the perception, Jack."

"Gearheardt, the most dangerous thing about you is not your incredibly insane plots and plans, but that you can make them all sound reasonable. You are a genius of disinformation and distraction. An evil, but friendly, asshole."

"You're in the CIA, Jack. That's what we do."

"*You're* in the CIA, Gearheardt. I'm just an agent. A lowly contractor who they can disown if it suits them. And even if I had been in it, I'm out now."

"You don't get out of the CIA, Jack. The CIA couldn't have people just wandering about society with all those secrets, and the...."

"I don't know any secrets, Gearheardt."

"Of course, that's what you would say, Jack. Res judicata." He smiled.

"Okay, Jack, let's get down to business."

"No."

"I'll have to kill you then. Now that you know my plans."

"First, go ahead. Second, I seriously doubt you have a plan. Third, you've shown me nothing." Jack scoffed. "That is, unless this is your normal *plan* where we run around trying to not get shot before we figure out what we're supposed to do."

"Sure, but this time it's not guns and bombs, invading squalid crapholes we didn't really care about, or saving the lives of people who don't even speak English. This time it's about money." Gearheardt paused, then spoke succinctly, as if imparting something of importance. "Facta non verba, Jack," he said.

"Oh, knock off the Latin crap, Gearheardt."

"It means...."

"I know what it means, Gearheardt. Stop talking and get off my ass. You don't need that pretentious bullshit....."

"It's not pretentious. Latin is used because it is precise. And I'm dating a lot of Latin American women."

"Who do not speak Latin, you prick."

"You always make fun of my education, Jack. Remember, I went to Princeton."

"Where you were escorted off campus at gunpoint. This is becoming an Abbott and Costello show.

Meaningless jabbering about spies and killing people and doing things for your country."

"That's one way of putting it, Jack" Gearheardt looked out the windows, slowly and deliberately, squinting as he tried to see in the distance.

He turned back and leaned close, in sotto voce he said, "I need you to run a bank."

"Did you just look around the countryside to make sure no one was listening while we're screaming down a backroad in rural Kansas?"

Gearheardt didn't change expression.

Jack went on, "And by the way, I'm not sure I even heard or understood what the hell you just said. But pretty sure I don't want to know."

"Jack, I'll go straight to the point. I repeat, I need you to run a bank for us."

"Us? As in US?" Then it dawned on him. "The CIA?"

"I don't work for JC Penny, Jack. Of course, I mean the Agency."

Jack couldn't help but groan. "So, you're telling me this bank job is actually for the agency? The CIA is into banking now?"

"The CIA is banking, Jack. After it bought Wall Street in the forties, right after it was formed out of the old SAS or whatever they called it----"

"SAS is an airline, Gearheardt."

Gearheardt scoffed. "Sure, and the agency knows nothing about airlines does it, Jack. Or should I say former Captain Armstrong, Air America, Inc.?"

"It was OSS, Gearheardt, not SAS."

Gearheardt laughed. "And you said you didn't know any secrets, Jack."

Jack thought of jumping out of the car. But that might be why the giant who was driving kept the speed pegged at eighty-five miles an hour.

"You'll be at the center of things, Jack. We need someone with a good head on his shoulders. That's why I persuaded the Director to let me get you into the game. And anyway, everyone else had turned me down."

"Well, that's encouraging. But I'm not moving to New York, Gearheardt. The Agency, assuming I even take the job, has a per diem that would mean I lived on the street and ate out of trash bins."

Jack couldn't believe he was sounding like he might consider it. He was entertaining the idea of signing a contract with the Agency again. But then he had no wife. His mother was out of the picture. And truth be told, it was always exciting to work with Gearheardt. New York was expensive, but truly the center of the financial universe.

"I'll consider it, Gearheardt, but some department or division or the outright thieves in the Agency has to come up with a decent allowance."

Gearheardt dismissed my concern with a snort. "Not a problem, Jack. No worries. All set up." He looked around the countryside again to make sure some foreign agent disguised as a Kansas farmer wasn't alongside the car running roughly eighty-five miles an hour.

"You'll be running a savings and loan in Anadarko, Oklahoma. I've been there and I can assure you things are rock bottom cheap. And before you do your usual pissing and moaning, you'll be there for maybe two months. Three tops."

Seeing that Jack was gob smacked to speechless quiet, he continued. "And you actually don't have to run anything. We'll put you in as a bank examiner. You can nose around and check things to your heart's content."

"In Anadarko, Oklahoma."

"It's not far from Duncan, Oklahoma, Jack," Gearheardt said. As if that made things better.

The White House two years later

(not that we were at the White House two years earlier)

Gearheardt was awakened at five AM by a blood-curdling scream. His own, evidently, as a quick survey of the bedroom revealed only a still-sleeping redheaded woman in bed and a calm Bull Terrier beside the bed. Getting out of bed and stepping in a foot-discovered pool of dog pee did nothing to put him in a better mood.

"Patton, you bastard," he said to the dog, "for the last time, quit peeing on the damn floor." Nude, except for soaked socks, he padded to the bathroom to wash his feet, sans socks, in the tub.

When he returned to the bedroom, the redhead eyed him warily as she peeked from under the pillow she had clasped over her face.

"Were you yelling at the dog?" she asked, a slight tremor in her voice.

"Did you just pee on the floor?"

"Of course not."

"Then I was yelling at the dog." He pointed to the black and white animal munching on a two-hundred-dollar negligee, a gift Gearheardt had bestowed on the redhead about five minutes before he had yanked it off and thrown it onto the floor. Where it was handily sopping up dog pee and drool while undergoing canine devourment.

Gearheardt relieved the dog of the pink garment and tied it modestly around his waist. He sat down on the side of the bed and reached for the phone. Punching in a number he knew by heart, he turned to the redhead.

"Elizabeth, do you suppose you could make some coffee?"

The redhead lowered the pillow. "My name is Jennifer."

"What happened to Elizabeth?"

"There was no Elizabeth. Why are you...?"

Gearheardt held up a finger, shushing her.

"Jack!" he said into the phone as he pushed the speaker button. "It's Gearheardt."

A sleepy, grouchy voice responded. "It's four A.M., Gearheardt."

"Not here, Jack. Already five. But that's not why I called."

"Damn it, Gearheardt." Jack sighed and there was a pause. "Okay, why did you call?"

"Who else could I call, Jack? I need your help."

"No."

The redhead not named Elizabeth handed Gearheardt a cup of coffee. He smiled up at her and motioned her back into bed. She looked down at the negligee wrapped around Gearheardt's waist.

"Is that……?"

Gearheardt removed it and handed it to her. It was a flimsy, slobber and pee-drenched rag. She threw it back toward the dog where it draped over his head.

Gearheardt laughed.

"I'm hanging up, you jackass."

"Whoa, Jack, I was just laughing at Patton. He's got a two-hundred-dollar negligee wrapped around his head and….."

"Goodnight, Gearheardt."

"Jack, I didn't call you at five A.M. to……"
"It's four A.M."

"…. discuss contract terms. Which, by the way, have burial benefits. You *were* put in Oklahoma for a reason, you know."

"*You* were behind me taking over this bank in Anadarko, a town, by the way, whose major cultural feature is a 1957 Ford up on an Indian burial platform with Indian artifacts hanging all over the place."

Jack sighed. "Let's go back to you *sending* me to Anadarko, Oklahoma. This place needs a CIA bank examiner like Superman needed tits."

Gearheardt laughed. "They'd look dynamite in that tight suit. But as for getting you to Oklahoma, you can thank me later, Jack. Look, I didn't call to just chew the fat over old times or hear about the pleasures of living in rural Oklahoma. I'll be blunt. Hold on a minute."

Gearheardt turned. "Jennifer, could you excuse me for about ten minutes?"

The redhead known as 'not Elizabeth' seemed more than happy to excuse Gearheardt for the rest of her life as she grabbed various clothing items and padded out the door. Arms filled with clothing and beauty accoutrements, her hip closed the door with a gentleness that dislodged a painting on the wall.

"Okay, Jack, let's get down to business." Gearheardt moved to the desk, lit a cigarette and leaned back in the desk chair.

"No."

"Jack, lighten up. Your country needs you, buddy. We've faced crisis be---"

"We've *created* crisis before, Gearheardt."

"Jack, you're equivocating. Will you help me? We risk having to use salt wheels for currency if we don't do something."

"Gearheardt, you asshole, here's what I do know. I'm in a moldy smelling bed in a cheap apartment in Anadarko, Oklahoma, at four AM---"

"It's five here, Jack."

"Shut the hell up and listen to me!" Jack took another deep breath and continued, "--its four AM and in about four hours I have to be at a savings and loan run by idiots who are borrowing money from the Federal Reserve indirectly and loaning it to frog farm developers in southern Dog Patch and listening to you tell me I'm part of the CIA controlling all this and you need my help because Wall Street is in trouble."

"It's not that simple, Jack."

Jack slammed the phone down.

But he answered it again thirty seconds later.

"Yes," he said.

"Jack," Gearheardt said, "you know you're not in Anadarko, Oklahoma, because it's important to anyone."

"Not hard to believe. Why am I here then?"

"Because you screwed up, Jack. The agency doesn't like screw-ups."

"And that would be....?"

"Jack, you totally botched the Stop the Vietnam War mission."

"That was you, jackass."

Gearheardt went on, "And you didn't get the president of Mexico almost killed so the CIA could take over Cuba."

"That was you too, super-jackass." Jack was getting angry. "And I *did* get him almost killed. And, by the way, that was the most bizarre damn mission the agency ever thought up. No one had a clue what they were doing."

"They shouldn't have done it then."

"But--," Jack hesitated. This was Gearheardt's forte—confusing the issue beyond any logic with meaningless comments.

"You even pissed off the Pope, Jack. Quite an achievement for someone who didn't know what he was doing."

Jack was silent and let the moment pass.

Finally, "So why are you calling for my help?"

"The Russians have taken over the savings and loan industry, Jack. The agency wants us to straighten things out. Get the Fed under control, replenish the FSLIC funds and screw the Wall Street boys in the butt, if you'll pardon my expression. And not literally of course."

"Of course," Jack said absentmindedly. He was thinking more about how his best friend had screwed up his Marine Corps career, his potential CIA career, and his marriage.

"Don't you have other friends, Gearheardt?" he asked. "Someone who is more deserving of being led into a ten-car train wreck by a madman?"

"Is it cars or trains, Jack?"

Jack sighed again. "You are the most annoying son of a bitch in the world, Gearheardt."

"Thanks, Jack. But let's get back to the mission. By now we have convinced the brass that you're a witless pencil pusher scruffing around in the dredges of the savings and loan industry...."

"My turn to say thanks, Gearheardt. I'm pretty sure I know who I owe that impression to."

"......and the powers-that-be have finally agreed that action should be taken. And I mean real action. Guns and stuff. Not legal mumbo gumbo..."

"Jumbo."

"......but serious, straight forward, military style action."

"You have never been involved in anything straight forward, Gearheardt and neither has the CIA. Just give me the bottom line. The Russians are in the savings and loan business and the CIA wants to take over Wall Street, which, by the way, you told me they already owned."

"Wall Street has gone rogue, Jack. They're so far into this making-money crap that the Federal Reserve can't *give* money away. Wall Street packages loans and forgives them their debt--that's biblical by the way--before the ink is dry."

"How do they make money?" Jack asked with no hope of a sane answer.

"The government guarantees the loans."

"Of course. The government guarantees their own loans."

"The government, in this case the CIA, has every right to take whatever it wants if— "

"No, it doesn't."

"—if people like the Wall Street guys begin using the tools of democracy to enrich themselves."

"But that's exactly what the system is set up to do, Gearheardt. And if they try to keep all the money, then the public, the market, can— "

"Go f--k themselves?"

"Gearheardt, "Jack said, "what is your point? I can't figure out who is doing what to--"

"Jack, you laugh about my time at Princeton, but before that incident with the professor's daughter and her mother, I did finish a degree in economics."

It was true, and Jack looked out the window and thought of a world where Gearheardt had used his degree rather than working for the Central Intelligence Agency. He somehow knew it would have been a better world, certainly for his own careers.

"Jack," Gearheardt said, as if reading his mind "I had a conversation with my advisor at Princeton asking him what he felt was the best career path armed with a Princeton degree in economics. He said, 'if I knew that I wouldn't be sitting in this shitty little office talking to shitty little students like you'. That was almost discouraging to me, especially when he started crying."

There was silence on the line while Gearheardt lit his third cigarette and Jack rubbed his face and through the window watched a cowboy on his horse in the parking lot. The horse dropping a huge pile of horse manure next to Jack's car. At four in the morning. Anadarko, Oklahoma.

"You have not said a damn thing that makes any sense whatsoever, but I'll still listen. You mentioned actions and military, etcetera. What's that all about?"

"The plan—and don't worry this line is secure—is to arm the Federal Reserve employees to the teeth and attack Wall Street. Catch 'em during trading hours when they're all gathered in serious money-making mode."

"And..."

"Kill 'em. Every broker, dealer, loan package maker." Gearheardt's voice had risen an octave and sounded breathless. Like he was looking forward to all this.

"Right."

"I'm serious, Jack."

"Uh huh. And what about the Russians?"

"The Russians?" Gearheardt raised his eyebrows.

"The ones who have taken over the savings loan industry."

"They've WHAT?" Gearheardt responded.

"I truly hate you sometimes, Gearheardt. You sucker me into these completely looney conversations and then deny you said things and then...."

"We kill *them too*, Jack. But they're not actually Russians. Just good old American loan officers and tellers and folks like that. We just *say* they're Russian. I seriously doubt we could get Federal Reserve employees to kill American loan officers. But every kid who has bumped his head ducking under his school desk in an atomic bomb drill is willing to shoot a few Russians. And actually, they really are Russians. But they'll be fighting California. I'll fill you in later."

"Clears that up. And exactly what role do you have in mind for me in all this financial bloodbath, Gearheardt?"

"We want you to find the chairman of the Federal Reserve, Jack."

"I don't have the faintest idea how to find the Federal Reserve Chief."

"No one does, Jack. In fact no one seems to know who actually runs the Federal Reserve."

Jack allowed himself one deeper sigh. "Your pseudo government at work. "

"Jack, get your gear together and meet me at the Willard in DC next Monday. I'll go over everything. I'll introduce you to the Special Ops team. A couple of the guys you already know. I've got Frank Cox for artillery and...."

"Artillery? For God's sake, Gearheardt...."

".....and Finn is running air ops for us. Hold on, Jack. I have a call on the other line." Gearheardt punched a button. "Good morning, Evelyn. You're up awfully...."

"The president would like you to advance your departure, Mr. Gearheardt."

"He's up?"

"He's been up since the senate majority leader called him just now. You might know him as Jennifer's father."

"So the president suggested...."

"In the vernacular, he said to tell you to get your skinny ass out the side door and he would fix your bleeping wagon if you ever showed up again. The rest was too painful for me to repeat. But testicles were mentioned."

"Did he seem angry?" Gearheardt asked.

"Goodbye, Mr. Gearheardt." A polite knock at the door in Gearheardt's room, then a head stuck in. "May I help you pack, sir?" the head said.

Gearheardt nodded yes and indicated a pile of clothing resting comfortably beneath the bull terrier. He punched the blinking phone line.

"Jack, gotta run. Be here by Monday. And I was kidding about you running the Federal Reserve. Eddie Johnson put the Ki-bosh on that idea."

"Who is....?"

"I need to run, Jack. Look, I know it seems crazy, but sometimes you have to destroy a financial system in order to save it."

He hung up.

Chapter Two

All Hell Doesn't Break Loose Yet

An American Airlines redeye from Dallas put Jack into DC the following morning and in the lobby of the Willard Hotel just before noon. He had stopped by his office at Countrycommunityside Savings and Loan just long enough to leave the Chairman (son of the founder and arguably dumber) a note that read, "You are so screwed. Balance the books for once and find out how much", then driven like a madman through southern Oklahoma and northern Texas and arrived at DFW well before the smell of horse crap on his shoes had dissipated. The car rental agent had complained but Jack told her he had "been in Oklahoma" and she grimaced and checked him in.

"Jack!" Gearheardt shouted across the lobby. "Get your skinny butt over here."

Jack decided it was good to see the smiling buffoon. History told him that he was, at most, days, if not hours, away from life-threatening shenanigans with his best pal. But the country once again needed them. If for nothing else than a few good heart-stopping crises or rib-splitting bar tales with the agency guys.

Jack had met Gearheardt when he was going through flight school in Pensacola. As young Second Lieutenants they both lived on the white sandy beaches of Santa Rosa Island on the weekends. In the Schooner, a popular hangout, Gearheardt was holding court (with half-sloshed ensign and second lieutenant flight students) about his time in the CIA when he was only twelve years old. The Junior CIA, he called it.

Gearheardt had recruited Jack into the CIA, the real one he said, in a back booth of the Schooner after a day on the beach with beer and young, eventually elusive, women.

"It's your patriotic duty, Jack."

"I'm in the Marine Corps, Gearheardt."

"All the more reason."

Gearheardt had called for silence in the Schooner at which the crowd to a man completely ignored him. "Raise one of your hands, Jack. And repeat after me."

Gearheardt then assumed a sober face, his dignity only marginally marred by the bright red circles the well-beered, but ungrateful women, had drawn around his eyes with lipstick.

"Fue de joie. Fille de joie," he said solemnly.

"Few something and feeble saw," Jack repeated in syllables floating out of his mouth on moist beer fumes.

Later Jack learned the French Gearheardt surprisingly knew, had nothing to do with the CIA and much to do with saluting prostitutes. By then it was too late, and he was working for the CIA. When Gearheardt and Jack were kicked out of the Marine Corps for screwing up the Vietnam War, the Agency started paying him and sent him tickets to go places and told him things to do when he got there. Even after Gearheardt was killed the second time.

He was the Acting Chief of Station in Mexico City before he didn't kill the President of Mexico and was kicked out of the country along with the other CIA staff and some unlucky bystanders. Some of whom were just delivery people who happened to be in the U.S. Embassy, and were living in places like Olathe, Kansas, wondering what the hell?

The Agency had sent Jack to a banking training camp in the Utah desert where he ate lizard sandwiches and learned mortgage lending, along with a smattering of banking regulations. After a number of applications, he was allowed to change his name back to Jack Armstrong. Somewhere along the line, Jack now knew, the very alive Gearheardt got him transferred to Anadarko, Oklahoma, where he was to 'keep his powder dry' and try to keep the Countrycommunityside Savings and Loan from sucking more money from the feds. Then Gearheardt had called him. And now Jack was in the lobby of the Willard Hotel in DC and Gearheardt, smoking a giant cigar, was walking toward him.

"What do you think, Jack?" Gearheardt asked as he swung his arm around, indicating the crowd of men in the lobby.

Jack took a closer look at the group. Spread throughout the elegant furniture of the large hotel lobby the men were a varied lot. From pin-stripe suited Ivy League types to suspicious looking thugs grazing on the table decorations and plants.

"I'm not sure how to answer that, Gearheardt. I guess it depends on whether we're electing Lion's Club officers or assembling for an attack on an army of Mongols."

"Just so, Jack. Just so." Gearheardt smiled as if pleased at the description. "We'll need all kinds for this mission. All of the guys on Wall Street aren't just effeminate pussies if you'll pardon the expression. In fact, most of them are tough, heartless sons of bitches. I've seen them melt people down just for the tallow if they missed a margin call."

Jack looked skeptical and Gearheardt took him by the elbow and drew him close to the window.

"Look, Jack, I know this crew seems a bit motley, but we need a solid and committed crew to do what we gotta do. Sure, everyone wants to kill stockbrokers, but who actually carries through? There's not a swinging dick in here who didn't buy stock in Beanie Babies or Barratt Salt Mining. We need to stoke that anger to save America. And wimps won't do it."

"What about those guys over there in gray suits holding coffee cups with saucers?"

"Mostly defrocked bankers and con-men. Wall Street isn't all dart boards and ping pong balls with numbers on them. We have to have guys comfortable with numbers and records and all that backroom stuff. The conmen are just to watch the damn bankers to make sure they don't cook the books before we can figure out what's going on. We're not burning Wall Street down, that's un-American. We're taking over. The day the CIA can't take something over and run it....."

Gearheardt's voice trailed off and he blushed, averting Jack's eyes. After a moment, he spoke, "Sure, we've made some mistakes. But this is the country's future we're talking about, Jack."

"Gearheardt," Jack said, grabbing his friend's shoulder, "do you have any idea what you're doing? If you're really serious about taking down Wall Street, which, by the way, is actually a street and not something to be 'taken down,' but if you're serious, why not let the government do it legally?"

Gearheardt wasn't listening, having spotted a gaggle of what seemed to be hookers entering the lobby through the front door.

"What was that Jack?" he said, turning back to the conversation.

"I was saying if Wall Street is in need of *taking down*, why doesn't the government just deregulate it and let the whole damn thing disappear in a frenzy of trading, gouging and grand larceny?"

"The boys of New York are smarter than to let that happen again, Jack. That's how the banks and regulators got rid of the savings and loan business in the eighties. Damn good show if I might brag a bit."

"What did you have to do with....?"

"Jack, Wall Street is as American as apple pie. It's the backbone of our democracy. If the founding fathers hadn't thought of selling pieces of paper rather than actual things, we would still be stuck screwing the Indians for corn and blankets. Is that the America you would want to see, Jack?" His gaze, through crazed eyes, had shifted back to the hookers. Over his shoulder he said, "And, Jack, for the last time we're not *destroying Wall Street*, we're taking it over."

As Jack started to reply, Gearheardt abruptly broke away and walked rapidly toward the well-dressed and coiffured street women who were beginning to pair up with Gearheardt's assembled band of thugs and gentlemen. "Get those women out of here," he shouted at the surprised concierge. "Get some damn bellhops or the kitchen help and get those women out of the lobby."

He rushed around the women making shooing motions and noises. A number of the men protested but Gearheardt intimidated them into silence with a look that conveyed his disgust. The women regrouped and backed slowly toward the revolving doors, then out into the street. Gearheardt locked the revolving doors over the loudly expressed wishes of the front desk manager.

"Mr. Gearheardt, you can't lock the doors. There's a fire code and....."

Gearheardt turned on him. "I'll fire *your* code, desk dick. Who do you think is paying your salary? You can unlock the doors when I tell you to unlock the doors."

He then climbed onto the center table in the lobby, knocking over a very lovely and probably expensive flower arrangement of epic proportions. He kicked at it again to disengage his shoe from the rhododendrons.

"Everyone into the ball room, gents. Let's all get in there and get this show kicked off."

Jumping off the table, he walked through the press of men heading for the ball room and stopped in front of Jack.

"Quite a show, Gearheardt," Jack said. "Who the heck *does* pay their salary?" He speculated that, knowing Gearheardt, he had a deal with the owner or *was* the owner.

"How the hell would I know? Let's head in, Jack. I've got to brief this mob and get some structure going. I didn't ask you to fly all the way up here to participate in a group thumb-up-your butt."

"Elegantly put, as usual, Gearheardt. But let me ask you a question. I'm afraid I must be remembering a *different* Gearheardt. I've never seen you chase away a whore, stripper, hippy chick or, in fact, a horny housewife. What the hell was that all about?"

Gearheardt slapped Jack's shoulder, drew into him and whispered. "They weren't whores, Jack. Those women were wives and girlfriends of Darkman Darkman executives."

"Wait a minute, you mean....."

"They're on to us, Jack. Wall Street is already sending out spies and provocateurs. By God, we'll have to be on our toes, Jack. I'll bet a dollar to a numbnuts that Son of a Bitch, Eddie Johnson is working both sides. That's the kind of crap he would pull."

"Who is the heck is Eddie.....?"

Chapter Three

Yank Your Own Doodle

Jack was always a bit surprised to hear Gearheardt in front of a crowd.. He was not a good speaker. Quick as a frog's tongue talking one-on-one or to small groups, he stumbled and wandered verbally all over hell and back in front of a crowd. He had climbed to a small stage set up at one end of the ballroom. The mob he had gathered stopped shouting and sat staring, smoking and scarfing the free booze on the table.

"Gents," he began, "we all know why we're here." He stopped and squinted at the ceiling. "Wait, that's what I'm doing up here, isn't it? Telling you why we're here. Although I guess some of you know, and some of you......" He trailed off, then stopped and visibly gathered himself and began again. He squared himself in front of the microphone, unbuttoned his exquisitely tailored suit jacket and placed his hands on his hips, exposing a pistol in a shoulder holster.

"First of all, I'm obligated to tell you that the Central Intelligence Agency has nothing to do with the operation upon which we are about to embark. And they will be watching closely."

Gearheardt

Several of the men at a table down front laughed and Gearheardt stared them down.

"It goes without saying that our mission is vital to our nation's survival. Elements of a foreign nation have infiltrated critical segments of America's economic system. The last time that happened, we had to bomb Japan to keep from bankrupting the country."

Jack grimaced as he realized that Gearheardt was segueing into complete BS in order to confuse and distract anyone in the gathered mob who might question the mission. He was a master at dissimulation. He had only a vague understanding of the word—although using it often to dissimulate.

Some of the suited gentlemen had puzzled looks and even mouthed 'what the fuck is he talking about?' to one another. Among the less informationally-endowed a restlessness stirred.

"So how does that bring us to why we are here?" Gearheardt asked, rhetorically as no one could possibly have deduced squat from his talk so far.

"Marxist Keynesian theory has eaten away the very fiber of our banking industry, particularly in the Savings and Loan industry, which, frankly, has been run by cretins for the past few years. The Russians have taken advantage of this disarray and now own roughly sixty three percent of all home mortgages in the country. They were, and are, aided and abetted by Wall Street!"

A grumble grew to a roar in the room, led by what Jack was sure were Gearheardt stooges.

"The borscht-eating bastards!" yelled a man jumping to his feet and theatrically shaking his fist. The more thuggish in the crowd rose and spouted venomous nonsense toward Gearheardt. At the table of the suited and well-tied, borscht recipes were exchanged along with addresses of excellent Russian restaurants in DC and New York.

Gearheardt quieted the group by whistling and pounding a gavel on the makeshift podium. He was grinning.

"That's the spirit, men. We might have let the Russians screw the Krauts, but they've gone too far now. Owning a home is every man's dream. That and a Swedish nurse. But that's another story. Take your seats and let me go over the basics of the operation. Memorize it, and then forget it. Wait a minute..." he paused, "that doesn't make much sense. Anyway, the Operation is named "Kill Every Bastard on Wall Street and Send the Russian Savings and Loan Owners Back to the Urals Along With Their Marxist Keynesian Theories.""

A number of the men had risen to their feet in anticipation of chanting the mission's name. They stumbled over the first few words and then sat down, embarrassed and a bit pissed at Gearheardt.

Gearheardt had the room darkened and launched into a slide show illustrating his overall plan of attacking Wall Street. The charts and graphs, with pictures of naked women sometimes thrown in, were hard to follow but seemed to indicate that the failure of the Savings and Loan industry would produce sufficient chaos in the financial system, not to mention a lot of pissed off Russians, to allow the Federal Reserve troops to establish a beachhead on the southern tip of Manhattan Island.

During a break, Jack cornered Gearheardt coming out of the men's room. He grabbed his arm and led him, forcefully, to an alcove in the hallway.

"What the hell, Gearheardt? Do you honestly plan a physical attack on Wall Street? I had, hopefully I might add, assumed you were using combat euphemisms for planning a financial kind of challenge or maybe take over some offices, or—

"Jack, did you miss the part about our way of life, the American way of life, is at risk? If we let the damn Russians move into our commercial banking system, the average American will be eating grass and drinking ditch water by Thanksgiving."

Jack grabbed the front of Gearheardt's shirt, scrunching up the tie, and pulled Gearheardt closer. Through clinched teeth he said, "Why in the hell are we attacking Wall Street if it's the Russians who— "

"Wall Street is financing the Russians, Jack." He peeled Jack's fingers away from his shirt and straightened his tie. "You've been a spy long enough to know that your friends often turn out to be your enemies. And your enemies are by definition your enemies. So pretty much everyone is your enemy." Although partially true, that was actually a cover story for Jack's cover story. Another Gearheardt invention which confused everyone, Jack most of all.

"Which explains nothing, you jackass. And I'm not a spy. I work on contract for the CIA but I'm not a spy."

"Which explains nothing, Jack." Gearheardt smiled as if he had made a point. "Let's get a drink."

In the hotel lounge Gearheardt was well-greeted and attended. A staggeringly nubile cocktail waitress appeared with a drink as soon as he sat down.

"You're as steady as the damn sun coming up, Gearheardt." Jack shook off Gearheardt's grip and folded his hands on the table. "Speak to me, Jarhead. And it better be clearer than Russians who are really American savings and loan executives who we want the Federal Reserve folks to kill by telling them they're Russians even though they really are Americans and are in cahoots with Wall Street."

"More or less," Gearheardt said. He paused, lighting a Winston with a zippo that Jack recognized from their Marine Corps days. He knew it was engraved, *When I die I'm going to heaven 'cause I've spent my time in hell--the East End Club, Olongapo, Philippines.* An inside joke for those in the naval services who had been to the Philippines. At the East End Club which was posted on all ships as off limits evidently by the marketing department of the East End Club as it drew attention to sailors and Marines who were plumbing the depths of debauchery, things could get a little rough.

"Won't work this time, pal," Jack said. "Every time I try to outline a ridiculous plan you always say, 'not that simple, Jack' or like now 'more or less, Jack' and you expect me to threaten to kill you or storm out of the room. But this time, cowboy, I'm sitting right here until you tell me what you've gotten me into. Then I may kill you."

"You can take the boy out of Oklahoma, but you can't take Oklahoma out of the boy. What's this cowboy shit?"

"Start talking, Gearheardt. You have a hundred men staying in this hotel primed to attack an amorphous concept of Wall Street. You say you've lined up artillery and air support.

And knowing you as I do, I believe all of it. But what in the hell are you really up to? Who's behind all this? What's the end game?"

Betsy arrived with their drinks, smiling at Jack and not meeting Gearheardt's eyes. As soon as she left, Gearheardt leaned forward again with a lascivious smile.

"Get back to this assault on Wall Street, you bastard. I'm not saying it's a bad idea. But is this just some cock-eyed grab-ass nightmare you and the pygmy** dreamed up?"

"You don't like the pygmy do you, Jack?"

"The pygmy was trying to kill me."

"I would say that taints your character more than his, Jack. Someone must do something pretty terrible to have a pygmy** want to kill him. They're usually— "

"I swear I'm going to kill you, Gearheardt." Jack was reaching the end of his rope. Gearheardt could be the most frustrating S.O.B. in the world.

"Don't kill the messenger, Jack," Gearheardt said, patting Jacks' arm and dropping cigarette ashes on his jacket sleeve. "Drink up and I'll take you to see the man driving this goat wagon. You'll feel better when you know our support comes from the top. No one would be foolish enough to slaughter people on Wall Street without the blessings of... I'll just let you see for yourself."

**The pygmy was an actual pygmy who had infiltrated the headquarters of the Central Intelligence Agency and lived in broom closets and had nightly raids on the cafeteria, never cleaning up after himself. Over the years he learned sufficient

spy craft to formulate his own plans and by hacking the computers got Agency employees working for him. He became highly regarded in the Agency, the result of his willingness to accept blame for the failure of any mission—his own or someone else's. "They can't hurt me, "he would crow, "I'm a goddamn pygmy." He would then make clicking noises in his throat which Agency anthropologists claimed was pygmy talk.

There actually might not have been a pygmy but rather an invention of Gearheardt, or someone like Gearheardt—God help us—who, once the rumor was circulated, existed -as no one wanted to admit he was not a friend of the pygmy. Once he let everyone know he was available to take blame, even in advance for missions yet to come, no one had ever muttered even the slightest doubt that a three-foot tall semi-aboriginal man dressed in wolf fur roamed the halls at Langley, holding briefings, accumulating acolytes, and pretty much being a rotten little shit most of the time.

A mission that was backed by the pygmy was accepted in the same manner as those blessed by the Gods of the CIA who met and murmured endlessly, drinking coffee and smoking cigars, casting suspicious looks at the other sixth floor Gods and wondering what in the hell the rabble below them in the building would cook up next. They could spend days looking at maps and scouring documents thick with rumor and innuendo. On the occasions when the Director of Central Intelligence was let out of his office (he was rumored to be over one hundred and six years old) he would scream feebly for someone to 'get him the pygmy' which is why the Agency had a brace of dwarves available to entertain the old man until he was shooed back into his office. He had once prepared and sent out a memo declaring the CIA redundant and useless, as every bit of intelligence in the world was contained in the Encyclopedia Britannica. Afraid some asshole who didn't like revolutions and secret wars might replace him, he was protected and supported by the Agency and feared by the consecutive presidents who were the only ones who could have him replaced. No one was brave enough to call the old man's bluff which was, "if I'm fired, I'm taking the whole damn town down with me" and then rambling about the nuclear code he had memorized. Although no one knew what that meant. Meanwhile the rest of the Agency employees, those not clerks and menial laborers, planned and plotted and overthrew and ran roughshod over everyone, or country, that pissed them off. Amazingly the system mostly accomplished good deeds in the end. Being Americans, the CIA folks lost interest in those conquered or bewildered and left the remnants to sort things out.

Sometime in the late nineteen eighties or early nineties, a memo went out, to all employees, from the sixth floor, signed by the old man and 'seconded' by the pygmy that simply said, in bold type –**Damn it, we need to make some money**.

The Agency was forever changed.

Is It **Chapter Four** Already?

When Evelyn ushered them into the Oval Office, Jack clumsily stumbled into Gearheardt who had stopped just inside the room. They both heard the president before they saw him.

"Oh Lordy, Lord," he was saying. He was gripping the edge of his desk with his eyes closed moving up and down.

Gearheardt, for once, seemed nonplused. "Maybe we-"

The president jumped to his feet. He pointed at Gearheardt and bellowed, "Gotcha, you sonofagun. You otta see the look on your face." He laughed loudly and came around the desk, holding out his hand. "The Majority Leader's daughter? You sure know how to make friends, Gearheardt." He pumped Gearheardt's hand and put his other hand on his shoulder.

Noticing Jack with his jaw still slack, he asked, "Who's your pal, G-man? This the world-famous Jack Armstrong? Welcome to the center of the world, Jack. Any friend of Gearheardt's is a friend of mine, assuming he's not screwing one of my secretaries."

His grip was firm and manly. His eyes positively twinkled with sincerity. Never a fan, but Jack knew then why he had won over his party and the people of America. At least the majority of them. He tried to believe he wasn't impressed, but it wasn't working.

"My pleasure, Mr. President. This is an honor to be here in the Oval Office. All Amer— "

"You mean more of an honor than half a dozen Thai women in a hot tub?" The president laughed loudly again and pounded Gearheardt on the back.

He waved them to chairs in the center of the room and dropped into an easy chair, putting his feet on the coffee table.

"Evelyn!" he shouted, "have George bring up some barbequed pork rinds and three or four Coca Cola's."

He put his feet back on the floor and leaned forward, his voice conspiratorial. "G-man, did I ever tell you about the time in school over in Frog-land I thought I was about to be lynched? That's the problem when you're nineteen messing around in a foreign place and don't know all the habits and food and stuff. Never insult a chef, even if he's a prissy wimp looking guy. And don't put ketchup on *coq au vin*, or date pre-teen women."

The president laughed so hard Jack thought he was going to bust a gut. Gearheardt laughed. Jack politely chuckled.

The president suddenly sobered and looked at his watch. "Hold on, gents. I think I'm on a call in about five minutes." He pointed to a cabinet. "There's rum in there for those cokes IF THEY EVER GET HERE," he projected toward the door to Evelyn's desk.

Sitting behind his own desk he began punching buttons on a switchboard he had lifted from his credenza.

"I can't figure out how to work half the buttons on this gizmo. Hazel thought the red phone clashed with the room so she shit-canned it and this is my, my, hell I don't know what you call it. Does translations and secret stuff. I can order pizza or bomb Alaska on this thing." He put on a headset but left one ear uncovered.

"Hazel?" Gearheardt said.

The president pointed to his wedding ring and grimaced.

"Oh," Gearheardt said.

Jack was transfixed watching the president of the United States, his feet on his desk, resting a Jules Vern looking contraption in his lap, happily punching at buttons and adjusting small switches. His boyish mannerisms were juxtaposed on a strange aura of power and intelligence. Jack remembered the President was rumored to be a genius, although an extremely horny one.

A voice came out of the box, "Mr. President, please quit punching that button. You're opening and closing the White House garage door." It was Evelyn.

The president laughed. "She's shittin' me, boys. Just her way of telling me to quit jacking around and talk to some foreign minister or Secretary of the Congo Communist Party. You would not believe the folks I have to put up with just to keep the world in one piece."

He sat up and put the box on his desk.

There ensued a conversation with someone who spoke a precisely pronounced and classic English, as if it were not his native tongue but learned in a British school. Evidently an event of considerable danger was imminent, and the caller was asking the President for American help, both financially and, potentially, militarily.

Jack was not sure about Gearheardt, who had found the rum after the Cokes were delivered, but he felt almost frozen in awe, sitting in the Oval Office listened to a highly intelligent and serious statesman, our President, calmly debate another Head of State. That is until during a long, elegant plea by the distraught Head of State, the President caught Gearheardt's eye and comically lifted his eyebrows. "Dumb as a f-ing stump," he mouthed, pointing at the phone. He pumped his fist up and down, imitating masturbation.

After he hung up, the President held up one finger, as in 'just a moment' and called the Secretary of Defense.

"Roger, looks like things are heating up in the region we discussed yesterday, Spicville or some shit. I may need you to put get some folks airborne and ready." A pause. "Nope, just a show of force at the moment. State is going to try to bargain with the opposition and maybe loan money— "He paused again. "No, we'll loan to both sides. Not quite sure which side we'll bomb yet. Call Larry over at State and coordinate with him so we won't be shooting the messenger so to speak."

He started to hang up the handset, then put it back to his ear. After listening, he spoke. "Do NOT talk to those boys at the CIA. They have ways of screwing up a wet dream. I'll brief them when we know more about what's going on. Thanks."

He smiled as he rose from behind his desk and retook his seat in the center of the room.

"Okay, boys, where were we? Shit like that happens all the time around here and Lord knows how much time I've got before peasants rush the food vault and some potentate feels like he needs us to bail his ass out." He shoved a handful of pork rinds in his mouth and leaned back in his chair. "Give it to me, G-man."

Gearheardt drained his rum and coke and leaned forward. "Yes, sir, Mr. President," he started, "let me hit the high spots and then we can go into detail as you wish. Jack here will be hearing some of this for the first time, but like I told you he's one hundred percent on board. Jack and I have embraced wars and whores together all over the world the past ten years."

Jack started to protest the 'whore' part which was almost exclusively Gearheardt but realized in this audience that was probably a plus.

"I like a man who will screw for his country, G-man," the president said through a grin.

Jack had been right.

"So here's where we are—can I call you 'Slick' like your pals do?"

"As long as we get rich and still run the country, you can call me anything you want in private. In public, it's still Mr. President. It's all about the dignity of the office, Gearheardt."

"Okay, Slick, here's where we are. Jack here has been more or less running the little Savings and Loan that you put us on to. We're solidly in control of that financial basket case and with that we have our hands on about fifty other S and L's who we can just take over with some 'wish paper' and help from the accounting firms and the Federal Home Loan Bank. They're desperate to kick dirt over the mess they were supposed to be over-seeing."

"You say we have our hands on, what does that mean? We got deals that--?"

"Don't need deals, Slick, they all traded participations in crap loans. So, we tank the first one, the one Jack is at, and that tanks a whole slew of them. We paper up the first one and merge in the rest. I would say that in a year or less we could own two to three hundred Savings and Loans without writing a single check."

"I like the sound of that, G-man. Those damn little shops can be like a money printing press if you got friends and a tad of larceny in your heart." He laughed. "Not that I have any of that, of course. But I know some boys in Mississippi...."

"Exactly, Slick. Then when— "

"I don't mean to jump ahead, but how in old Billy Heck does Wall Street get into this mess? I mean that's the big plan, right, take over Wall Street?"

"Yes, sir, and I'll get to that. But just let me say that we need the savings and loan shops so that we can have a national distribution system and we can get that for nothing. But Wall Street wants to control them. They make money hand over fist without any risk. They really don't have the welfare of America's financial system at heart."

"Those bastards," the president said, laughing. "How in the hell do they do that?"

"A bit complicated, Slick. But basically, since the FSLIC insures all of the deposits up to one hundred thousand dollars, Wall Street set up a system to loan the savings and loan what they call Certificates of Deposits for one hundred thousand dollars, so the savings and loans have billions to loan to rabbit ranches and cheap condos. They don't really give a rat's ass if the loans pay off. Wall Street is paid by the FSLIC if the banks fail. They're not really banks, but we call 'em banks. People are more comfortable dealing with banks."

The president chuckled. "You do know, G-man, that I know all about banks and financial institutions. And I've done some very profitable deals with those S&Ls when I was in office down south. I just wasn't sure what you were referring to as our 'plan.' So go on."

"We have the boys over at the Federal Reserve all primed. Some good troops over there. Most of them are tired of operating in obscurity their entire careers."

The president looked pensive. "Do any of them know *'come here'* from *sic 'em'* about fighting though? I mean actual combat?"

Gearheardt shrugged. "I kind of doubt it, Slick. Maybe a few veterans. But keep in mind that we don't expect them to actually accomplish anything. I would imagine they'll be slaughtered in the streets. The Wall Street guys are as tough as they come. And we're talking about separating them from their source of large estates and fast cars. Kind of like getting between a mother bear and her cubs."

"So, remind me why we're attacking Wall Street."

"Sir, you have to— "

He was interrupted by the door slamming against the wall as it opened with hurricane force. An apparition in red swept through the office scattering papers, knocking over lamps, displacing chairs and keeping up a constant chant of curses, accusations and warnings of certain death after castration. It exited and Gearheardt and I sat wide-eyed and stunned.

The president dusted himself off and picked up scattered papers, righted a lamp, and sat down heavily in his easy chair, sighing and muttering.

"I guess the little woman came by to say hello, boys." He yelled out to Evelyn, "Thanks for warning me, Evelyn! Find someone to come in here and straighten things up." He grabbed the bottle of rum from the coffee table and poured a quarter of a pint down his throat. After he grimaced, he looked back at the two of us and smiled.

"So you were reminding me why we're attacking Wall Street only to get Federal Reserve people slaughtered in the streets. I'm not saying I'm against the idea. I've got a lot on my mind and maybe I've missed some of the finer points."

The President suddenly straightened up and glared. "And before you go off about bombing and killing ever one in sight, which I don't personally worry much about, keep in mind that I ain't looking to spend eternity ass-end up on the bottom bunk roomin' with Hitler and Idi Amin."

Gearheardt had regained his poise. "No problem, Slick. Let's go back to the beginning. You wanted to nationalize Wall Street, right? And that word got over to the CIA who thought they were controlling Wall Street. They caused a stink and since I was on the Wall Street oversight committee at the Agency, I saw an opportunity for you to have your cake and eat it too."

"Gearheardt, I like the way you talk. And I would like it even better if you did less of it. What the hell is the plan?"

Gearheardt was not to be distracted, even by a president. "I'm getting there. So, in short, we send the Fed Reserve folks into lower Manhattan. They're mowed down, and if some make it inside an investment bank or two, so what? At this point you order in the Marines— "

"Not sure I can trust those assho- "

"We're Marines, Slick. And you can trust us."

The president blushed. "I just don't want those bastards turning on me and keeping Wall Street for themselves. But wouldn't it be easier to just have the Marines go take the damn place without the Fed troops, Russians or whatever they are, going in and— "

"That actually *is* the plan, Slick. We just can't tell anyone the real plan because the real plan has to be secret. Any plan worth its salt is secret, I think you'll agree. And don't worry, we have a plan for the Fed troops, Russian or not."

"Secret, I suppose?"

"Secret as a baby's dreams." Gearheardt continued, "So now we have the Marines secure all the investment banks and lock up the officers. Then Slick Savings and Loan—that's us, Mr. President—takes over the Federal Reserve Bank. Now we control a retail outlet, the savings and loans, the investment community, and the Central Bank."

"What about the regular banks, those run by half-way smart guys. Won't they raise a stink?"

"We run the Federal Reserve, Slick. The banks won't give us any trouble."

Jack actually had only the vaguest of ideas about what the Federal Reserve did. He assumed that Gearheardt didn't know either. But he was the best 'bluffer' he had ever met. He also assumed that the president knew exactly what the Federal Reserve did, and in fact had a working knowledge of the entire banking system. Like a lot of Gearheardt's superiors, he probably thought it best not to interfere with a plan, no matter how stupid or venal, if the end result was enriching him.

"Sounds like we need a shitload of paperwork, G-man," the president said, "I mean to get all this stuff legal and past the GAO, the IRS, and all those other worthless dipshits."

"My idea is to go ahead and get everything under our control and then figure out what kind of paperwork we need." Gearheardt looked at his watch. "You might have to sweet talk Congress and throw a bone to the FDIC." He stood up. "I probably should run, Slick. I have to get down to Quantico and talk to the Marines."

The door opened slightly, and Evelyn stuck her head inside. "Mr. President, you have the Bolivian Ambassador here for his appointment."

"Aw for Pete's sake. The little pissant is probably collecting for the damn Bolivian charity fund, or what they call a government down there. Money runs through their grubby little brown fingers like piss out of a horse. And they send that Ambassador prick around to suck up. Remind me who the president of Guatemaran is, Evelyn. He the one married to that white woman?"

Jack could see the Ambassador behind Evelyn trying to act as if he couldn't hear the president. Evelyn stood steadfast through the president's tirade, never changing her slightly disparaging countenance. She had been with the president since she 'was old enough to screw' according to the way Slick had earlier described her.

The president turned to Gearheardt and Jack. "You boys scoot out that other door. Give me a holler tomorrow afternoon and let me know how things are shaping up. And for God's sakes, don't let the H-woman get word of this."

He slapped Jack on the back as he passed by and asked Gearheardt, "You ever had any Guatemalan poontang, Gearheardt?"

Jack didn't hear Gearheardt's reply above the president's booming laugh and greeting.

"Como esta, Senor Ambassador. Mi amigo! It is an honor to welcome you to the White House. La Casa de White-o."

Just before the door closed, a young woman slipped out, nodded at them, and disappeared again through the private kitchen. Jack looked at Gearheardt who shrugged.

On the way to Quantico, I commented on Gearheardt's fancy car. "Didn't you say you had an Agency car, Gearheardt?" I asked. "This, if I'm not mistaken, is an Aston Martin."

"I do have an Agency car, Jack. This is a Chevrolet Malibu."

"It's an Aston Martin, Gearheardt."

Gearheardt looked over at me, dangerously taking his eyes off of the traffic we were weaving through. "It's a Chevrolet, Jack." The discussion was over. He had somehow gotten an Aston Martin on his expense report, listed as a Chevy, and for all practical purposes, as far as the CIA was concerned, it was a Chevy. And somewhere in some God-forsaken jungle there were troops out of bullets.

Somehow that thought made Jack melancholy. He leaned his head back on the headrest and watched the Reagan Airport go by. He wanted to catch an airplane and go back to somewhere. He wasn't quite melancholy enough to want to go back to Anadarko. But Washington was getting weird.

Everything was about money. Everything. The country spent money like it was on heroin with a crack cocaine chaser. He remembered a 'white paper' Gearheardt had sent him in Anadarko. Gearheardt was proud to have been a co-author. The basic thesis was that America needed to begin acting like a leader in the world. In this case, taking land and other assets from countries that had crap for armies and which even the communists didn't like. According to the paper, we were going to have to quit spending or start spending other people's money. If we went broke, the world would go to hell and we owed it to the world not to let that happen. As usual with Gearheardt zany ideas, it was dangerous because he could make it seem to make sense. Jack was thinking 'damn right' halfway through reading it before he realized it was talking about becoming the exploiter of the rest of the world that Europe and Africa accused them of being.

Chapter Five

The Chapter Known as Five

Gearheardt pulled up to the gate leading into Quantico, home of the Marine Corps. After we stopped, nothing happened. Inside the guard shack we could see a man in an indistinct uniform staring straight ahead. He did not acknowledge our presence.

"Hey, numbnuts," Gearheardt shouted through his window, waving his identification card. "Are you going to check us out to let us in?"

The man stood and turned toward us. After opening the door of the guard shack, he tapped his way to the side of Gearheardt's Aston Martin using a long white stick.

"May I see your ID," he said to the air over the top of the car. He continued tapping his white cane, now rapping the Aston's hood, fender and door.

Gearheardt was a genius at handling awkward situations; this one with a blind gate guard telling us we needed an ID.

"Hey cement head, that card you just knocked out of my hand with your cane was a pass from the President of the

United States of America." Which of course was not even close to the truth.

"Oh, for God's sake, Gearheardt. He's not hurting your car." Jack leaned over the center console and looked up at the gate guard. "Sir, we're here to see the base commander."

"Why didn't you say you wanted in?" the man whined, turning to go back to his perch in the guard shack. "How am I supposed to know what every visitor has on his mind?"

He began punching buttons, muttering and cursing until the crossbar began rising.

Gearheardt burned rubber accelerating through the gate. Giving the gate guard the finger as he passed.

"He's blind, Gearheardt."

"Whoever had the damn bright idea to outsource gate guarding and security to the lowest bidder should be drawn and quartered. Anyone could just drive through and— "

"He stopped us."

"Did you notice that Russian accent, Jack?"

They reached the main campus and Gearheardt parked in the space reserved for the Base Commander. They saw few Marines, maybe half a dozen all together. Inside the building our footsteps echoed down a deserted hallway following the yellow-on-red signs indicating the Base Commander's office lay ahead.

At the door, Gearheardt knocked loudly and then opened it. Inside amid a row of unattended desks, was a single female Marine, busy on a desktop computer. She looked up.

"Yes, sirs, may I help you?"

"We're here to see General Fixture?" The implied question mark seemed appropriate in the mostly empty, very quiet office.

"Send 'em in!" came from an open door. We moved toward the sound and entering the office saw a Marine general lounging comfortably, feet upon desk, smoking a cigar roughly the size of a small baseball bat.

"Hello, gents," he said. "Take a load off." He pointed to chairs in front of his desk. "What brings you here when we're closed?"

"Sir, before we get to what brought us here, I don't quite understand the concept of the Marine Corps being closed. Is that some kind of— "

"We're just the Marine Corps on odd months, son. We're the Army every other month, and the Air Force on weekends. The Navy stays the Navy all year round, but they just get on their damn boats and float around wherever they feel like it. Don't answer the phone or do shit, far as I can tell."

Perhaps seeing the perplexed, and worried, looks on our faces, the General dropped his feet to the floor, carefully balanced the cigar on a stand beside his desk and leaned forward toward us.

"You boys are Marines, right? I mean I know you're CIA at the moment, but once a Marine, blah blah, blah, am I right?"

Gearheardt grinned. "Generals are always right, sir."

Now the general grinned. "Good answer, Marine."

"So, here's the deal. We are always Marines. Some damn Marine General was testifying on the Hill about how the Marines could do anything the Army or Air Force could do. Next budget round, they laid off the Army and Air Force. But you know what?"

"Still Marines, sir?"

"Damn right. And don't even think about us acting like those Air Force pussies. Sure, we crash a shitpot full of airplanes here and there, but that's just some snafu on getting our pilots clearance to fly Air Force planes. Right now, we just draw straws. And believe you me, you've never seen a monkey screwing a football funnier than a tank commander trying to get a helicopter airborne the first time. Maybe the idiots in the Pentagon are saving beaucoup bucks. But I can tell you this, the sequestration bullshit has to stop." He leaned on his elbows. "Damn Army not pulling their weight, I can tell you that. Never did if you ask me. Took the grandkids over to Arlington last week to see, you know that unknown soldier deal, wlth changing of the guard…"

Gearheardt piped up, "Yessir, very impressive,"

"….. and there wasn't a damn guard in sight. Army left a sign that said, 'His name was Bob,' and evidently hightailed it out of town. That supposed to be a damn joke?"

He looked at Jack, then Gearheardt, a more serious war face never seen. It was probably the thought of the idiots at the Pentagon. Then he relaxed and sat back in his chair.

"So, what is it that you boys want?"

"I'll jump to the bottom line, General. The CIA and the White House believe that Wall Street has been completely taken over by communists. We want the Marines to go in and clean them out."

The General's grin broadened. "Give me a minute to finish pissing in my pants, son! Wow. You mean to tell me the United States Marine Corps, Semper Fi, by the way, can pack up our gear and attack New York investment bankers? Free of any damn Rules of Engagement?"

"I actually didn't mention ROE, General. But basically, yes."

"What's the catch?"

"No catch, but aren't you interested in why the president— "

"You mean Slick?"

"Yes, "Gearheardt answered. "That's exactly who I mean."

The general held up one finger. "Hold on, let me get my G-2 in here. He needs to hear this." He rose, walked to the door and stuck his head out. "Corporal Phelps, can you find Colonel Edwards and have him in my office muy pronto?"

He returned to his desk and opened a drawer, pulling out a bottle of Vat 69 plus three small glasses. "This calls for a drink, fellas. Here's to putting the Marine Corps flag right up that Bull statue's butt."

"I'll certainly drink to that, General," Gearheardt said. Jack knew Gearheardt would also drink to any combination of words in any language at any time. Jack only sipped, feeling intuitively that he might want to keep his wits about him. Something about the General reminded him of Gearheardt. And Gearheardt commanding a division of armed and ready Marines was a scary thought.

Gearheardt and the General shared another couple of shots and then sat down to take a breather. Jack broke the silence, "I'm surprised at your willingness, or I should say eagerness to attack Wall Street, General. A personal issue or do you believe, as I do, that Wall Street has overextended its control of the financial markets and holds an unfair advantage in the marketplace with regard to non-institutional investors?"

The general drained the last drip of scotch from his glass and set it carefully on his desk before turning to Jack.

"Yeah, that and a garage full of fucking Beanie Babies! I just hope to hell I can make it to *Clevenger and Nolan* and shoot that damn broker myself."

The General and Gearheardt engaged in small talk, Marine style—heavy on the f-word and the joys of shooting people—for fifteen minutes before an Army Colonel, out of breath, joined us.

"Mother of God, Edwards, what the hell have you got on?"

"The General perhaps forgot that I am actually an Army officer. This *is* my uniform. Your command did not indicate I should go by my quarters to change clothes."

"Well, if I'da known you would show up here in a damn clown suit with gold buttons that can be seen from the moon, I mighta made the allowance. Never mind. Meet these two CIA guys, former Marines, by the way. Got bounced from the corps for screwing up in Hanoi and Mexico City."

It made no sense to explain the General's introduction, so they shook hands and, drawing up a third chair, seated themselves in front of his desk. Gearheardt gave a brief overview of the situation to the intelligence officer, who seemed to be a bit more sophisticated than his boss concerning the financial intricacies of the NYSE.

Edwards exhaled deeply and sunk into his chair, pursing his lips and looking at the floor. After a moment, he raised his head and looked squarely at me.

"I guess this is all about the derivatives, Jack," he said. "Someone has finally realized that Wall Street has bet the entire net worth of the United States on some esoteric combination of risk and reward combined with hedging and tom-foolerly."

"I'm not a financial genius, Colonel. But I can pretty well guess the tomfoolery is right."

"Give it some layman's language, Edwards." The General seemed to sense something serious was being discussed.

"Okay, General, let's say ten people are sitting at a table with a deck of cards. The dealer is about to turn a card face up on the table. So Gearheardt here bets it will be a red card. Jack turns to his neighbor and bets that more than half of the people at the table have bet he's right. So, the same transaction has now created a derivative. The second bet on the same transaction. Two of the guys at the table bet that Gearheardt bets more than five dollars. Two more bet that the dealer will screw up and turn up two cards rather than just one. And on and on. Each derivative creates another opportunity to bet. Different bets but on the same single transactions."

"So, what's the problem?" Gearheardt asked.

"Well, the guys at the table all work at the same bank. So, the bank is not taking a *single* risk, but *multiple* risks and there is no reasonable way to figure out if the best outcome is a red card or a black card until the card is turned over and the bets begin to be settled."

"So, Wall Street—" Jack started.

"And hundreds of lesser Wall Streets around the world," the Colonel added.

"—has a risk of unknown proportions."

"Yes is a simple but accurate answer."

"And if all the bets go the wrong way.....is that possible?"

"Theoretically it could even out. But the fact is that if only one or two or a few banks have concentrated losses, it affects the whole system."

"So how much have the U.S. banks *bet* on this mystical hand?" Jack asked.

"No one is sure, but the best guess I've seen is two hundred seventy-three trillion dollars."

The room was silent as each level of financial intelligence tried to deduce the importance of that number. Finally, the General spoke up, "That seems like a hell of a lot of money."

"It *is* a lot of money. Fifteen or twenty times the entire annual budget of the United States. Maybe more." The colonel actually smiled.

The General slapped his hands on his desk and stood up. "That will be all, gentlemen. I'll leave the economics to you boys." He turned to Gearheardt. "Do you happen to know when I might be getting orders, and from who?" he asked.

Gearheardt shook his head. "I would imagine it will be directly from your Commander in Chief. Who else would have the balls to order the Marines to establish a beachhead in southern Manhattan?"

"You're sure Slick is behind this?" the general asked. "Hell, I know Slick. Hold on and I'll see if I can get him on the line and get right to the horse's ass."

"Sir, I don't think you should— "

But the general already was.

"Slick," he said when someone on the other end of the phone answered. "This here's the Oklahoma draft board. We need to talk." He paused and grinned at Jack and Gearheardt. "Naw, just shitting you, Mr. President, Bob Fixture here."

I actually felt we were being bullshitted. Even Marine generals didn't pick up the phone and talk directly to the president.

The general had sat back down and was grinning as he listened.

"No, sir," he said, "I don't know why the astronauts went on strike."

After a moment listening with a silly grin he laughed. He looked up at the three of us in front of his desk. He covered the receiver. "He says it's because they got no Poon in their Tang."

It definitely was the president on the line.

"Yessir, well I was just checking if you had some orders for me regarding the operation some gentlemen have described to me." He looked at Gearheardt and me. "Are you men Gearheardt and Armstrong?"

We shook our heads-yes.

"Yessir, and the only other person in the room is Colonel Edwards. No, he's not a Marine. He's the Intelligence Officer seventy-seven thousandth airborne motorized infantry or some damn thing. I can't figure out how the damn Army—yes, ours—keeps track of their units. Oh, yessir, you can come down to Quantico if that's your preference. At the O Club. Yessir, I'll see if she's still working there. Give me just a minute and I'll have that information for you, Slick."

He looked up at the Army Colonel. "Colonel, would you please ask Corporal Phelps to step in here."

"Yes, General, "she said from the door.

"Corporal Phelps, can you tell me when we get the Marine Corps back?"

"Next week, General. But we are the Marine Corps for only two weeks. We have to be the Air Force because they have that golf tournament and they've scheduled the Marines to handle the logistics and security."

"Well they can't expect to use the whole damn Marine Corps for that."

"Sir, that kind of decision is above my pay grade."

"Evidently mine too, Corporal. I don't know what the hell we're going to do if we ever get a war started." He dropped his head into his hand and noticed the phone lying on the desk. "Holy shit," he picked up the phone, "are you still there, Mr. President? Thank you, sir. I do apologize. I beg your pardon. Oh, yes, sir. But I believe she's married."

Corporal Phelps shook her head yes. Jack suspected that she had been through this before.

"Well, gents, I'm sure we'll be back together soon. Please leave your contact information with Corporal Phelps. And if you get any more information yourselves, I would appreciate you getting in touch. Carry on. And Semper Fi. Except for you, Dogface."

The Army Colonel accompanied us to the entrance.

When we stopped at the door, I asked the colonel, "Why didn't you just tell the General what a derivative actually is? That card and bet thing was more confusing than the real answer."

"Which is?" the Colonel said, a smart-ass smile on his face.

"Well, let's start with this-- A financial instrument whose characteristics and value depend upon the characteristics and value of an underlier, typically a commodity, bond, equity or currency."

Gearheardt laughed. "Learned that between lizard sandwiches did you, Jack."

"Yes, I did, Gearheardt." Jack laughed at his own statement and at the look on the Colonel's face.

"I don't know how you happened to learn that dictionary definition. But the answer to your question is that the General probably doesn't know a financial instrument from a hole in the ground, and I didn't want to waste my time."

He turned to leave, not quick enough to escape Gearheardt's hand digging into his neck.

"Let me tell you something, Dogface. That Marine back there lost his toes and gained a Silver Star carrying his wounded troops at Chosin Reservoir in Korea. And his funny arm movement, I saw your smirk when he dropped the phone, is from an AK-47 round through his shoulder at Khe Sanh where he got his second Silver Star, to go along with his five purple hearts."

By this time, the Colonel's face was bright purple, and his breathing looked as strained as someone who had an iron fist squeezed around his windpipe. Which he did.

"And I can assure you he doesn't give a flying fuck about derivatives or your financial instruments. He's just concerned that some dickheads in New York are making about twelve million dollars a minute screwing the taxpayers, which includes his troops who make about twelve bucks a day, Kemo Sabe." He relaxed his grip.

"And let me tell you this, you dogface bastard."

"Gearheardt," Jack said, nodding at Corporal Phelps who had appeared beside us, "just hold it down, pal." The Colonel took the chance to leave.

Corporal Phelps smiled a lovely smile and handed a folder to Jack. "I know you both were Captains, and I never correct my superiors." She smiled again. "I've been through boot camp, Gentleman. As the General said, carry on."

Once outside the building, Gearheardt and Jack were surprised to see the Army Colonel waiting. He was rubbing his throat and backed down the stairs as we approached him.

"Look, Marines, I didn't mean anything by my comment about the General. He's not a bad guy as a matter of fact, as Marines go. It's just damned unnerving to one day be with the Army and then the Marine Corps. I was even sent over to the Air Force one weekend and they tried to make me fly a C-130. I taxied the damn thing all over the parking lot till someone finally shot out the tires and blew up an engine. I had no idea where the frigging runway was. And— "

Gearheardt held up his hand, palm toward the Colonel. "So, what do you want from us?"

"I want to help. If you're trying to take over Wall Street, I know a lot about the financial markets. I was a bond salesman for *Tidewater Goatman* until the crash. The judge gave me the choice of joining the Army or going to jail. The Army made me a general because they were Marines the day I got to Fort Mr. Rogers— "

"Where the fu— "Gearheardt interrupted.

"Let him finish," Jack said.

"—and the Marines thought it would be funny to start off as a general and then keep busting me in rank until I was a private. They told me that if I got busted from private to a civilian—they called it a puke—I could go home."

"So, you actually know some shit about Wall Street?" Gearheardt asked.

"I know everything about Wall Street. I once sold a blind grandmother, living on fifteen hundred dollars a month social security, fifty-eight thousand dollars in bonds backed by the credit of a bank that had failed in 1956."

"Nice," Gearheardt said, smiling and shaking the colonel's hand. "Welcome aboard."

Jack wasn't sure he liked the guy and was surprised that Gearheardt seemed friendly. Gearheardt was a womanizer, a gambler, and an all-around sexist pig—his words—but he almost always stood up for the little guy, the underdogs of the world.

Granted, his theories of 'standing up' were sometime strong on logic but weak on common sense. He had once explained to me that during a war, if the local populace went to the agonizing trouble of turning their women into prostitutes, it would be pretty damned callous to not screw them, leaving them sitting in dark bars wearing cheap perfume and tawdry gowns with no income.

"That makes no sense at all, Gearheardt," Jack had said.

"Thanks, Jack," he had replied, patting my shoulder.

"By the way, Edwards, you look familiar. Ever been out to Langley?"

"Where?" Edwards asked.

But now they were three and they hopped in Gearheardt's Aston Martin Chevrolet and headed back to DC. They stopped at the colonel's (he was pretty sure he would be at least a major once they found out he was missing) quarters to pick up his gear.

"That was one happy woman," he said as he climbed into the back seat. "She's married to a Lieutenant in the Navy, but the Marines made her be my wife 'for the time being' as they put it. We never really hit it off." He closed the door and dropped his bag on the floor. "Hey, is this an Aston Martin?"

"Chevrolet," Jack said, not looking back at him.

Gearheardt peeled away from the curb. He had one of the general's huge cigars in his mouth and a determined look on his face. As they approached the gate, Gearheardt floored it and burst by the guard shack with horn blaring. A white cane flew toward them, landing far behind.

"It might be a Chevrolet," the colonel said, rubbing his hands over the polished wood on the door and fine leather on the seats, "but I'll bet a Chevrolet like this would take the fees from three widows, the crippled children's fund, and a side deal with an Arab bag-man to pay for this baby."

He and Gearheardt laughed and Jack felt a bit of a chill in his chest. Once, in Laos, Gearheardt had abandoned a perfectly good helicopter to scramble over and pull his skinny butt out of a soon-to-be flaming pile of helicopter parts (courtesy of a North Vietnamese .37 millimeter). It seemed like the world made sense then.

Chapter Six or Maybe Seven

They pulled into a parking garage attached to the Hilton near the White House. After Gearheardt directed the colonel to grab three rooms and meet them later, he motioned for Jack to follow him.

"Now where?" Jack asked. "I thought we were supposed to be at the Federal Reserve building for a briefing and weapons check or whatever you called it."

"I just passed that word to screw up anyone following us, Jack."

"I'm the only one you told, Gearheardt."

"It worked, evidently. Get a move on. We're due back at the White House. Slick sent word he has some plan changes he needs to brief us on."

The White House guards waved us through and before Jack could figure out how the President, Slick, had sent word, they were ushered through a door into a room marked 'Secret Operations'. They stood aside to let two young women exit, giggling and adjusting non-WhiteHouse-looking clothes. Unless costumes Jack had last seen on women working in the Purple Fox in Tijuana were considered White-House-looking.

"Hey, Gearheardt and…. your buddy, what took you so long? You just missed the damndest briefing I've ever had." He grinned, max-toothy, from his semi-supine position on a chaise lounge. He was bizarrely attired in what Jack believed was called a dressing gown. Rising to greet them with outstretched hand, he said, "I see you're oogling the duds, Jack isn't it? Hef gave me a damn closet full of stuff. Mrs. President doesn't approve but she's thankfully barred from the Secret Operations room. My pals over at the FBI keep flunking her on her security check." He winked.

"Grab a couple of chairs at the table there and let me show you something."

He ducked behind a bar/cabinet and they heard what had to be safe cogs spinning. When he sat down at the conference table he slammed down a three-inch-thick folder.

"Gold," he said, looking at Gearheardt. "Pure gold."

Gearheardt reached for the folder but the president slapped his hand away.

They sat awkwardly for what seemed like five minutes. Finally, the President spoke.

"Aren't you going to ask me what's in the package?" he said, dropping his grin and looking a bit disappointed.

"What's in the package, Slick?" Gearheardt asked.

"Let me tell you a story first, Gearheardt. When I was President of Oklahoma— "

Jack decided to let that pass.

"—some old boys from Tulsa or somewhere up there, had me over a barrel for a misunderstood lake front property deal. No need to go into details but I can tell you I didn't need a lot of publicity about lake front property deals."

"I can imagine not, Slick," Gearheardt said.

The president looked at Gearheardt like he was probably sorry he told Gearheardt that he could call him Slick. He kept his hand on top of the folders.

"So anyways," he went on, "I was about to think that there ought to be a few missing Okies when a loyal aide sashays into the office and lays a package on my desk not unlike the package we see before us."

"And what was in THAT package, Mr. Former President of Oklahoma?" Gearheardt seemed to already know.

"An eight by ten glossy of Bud Wilson mounting a goat."

Gearheardt laughed. The president laughed. Jack managed what was probably a sickly grin.

"Let me guess, Slick. Bud Wilson was in the lake front property deal."

"Good guess, Gearheardt. And he stayed in the lake front property deal for about fifteen seconds after I invited him over to chat about goats." He sobered. "But this package is about a whole lot more than lake property and goats."

"I'm not sure I understand you, Mr. President." Although Jack was afraid he actually did.

Gearheardt grabbed the folders and pulled them toward him. The president didn't move to stop him as he tore open the seal.

"Jack, if that's your real name, you and your troops are going to take over the banking system as soon as you get off your ass and get some attacking started. But that's not enough. Bottom line is that the system ran best when we had the gold standard. I'm suggesting, and a president suggesting something is pretty damn sure to get someone's attention, that we adopt a new standard." He looked up and raised his eyebrows as if expecting a response.

"I'm not sure I get it, Mr. President. We're going back to the gold standard?" Jack asked.

"Jack, we have no gold to set a standard by. We traded our gold to the Arabs for oil long before I got here." He frowned at me. "You don't believe Ft Knox is full of gold, do you?"

Jack wasn't sure what he believed and didn't respond.

Gearheardt was happily going through the contents of the folder. "Holy shit," he said. "Is this who I think it is?" He held up a black and white photo which even in the far reaches of pervert hell would be offensive.

The president grinned and shook his head. "That was before he was Prime Minister."

"Who are the women?" Gearheardt asked, not taking his eyes off the photo.

"Let's just say they're probably not his wives," Slick answered, snickering.

"Mr. President, I'm not following," Jack broke in, "we have no gold in Fort Knox. You want to go back onto a gold standard. We're trying to attack—"

"I didn't say I wanted to go back to a gold standard, Jack. I just said that a financial system works more efficiently and is more sound if there is a basis to control the fluctuations and manipulations of unscrupulous sonsabitches like old Bud Wilson. Who was a banker, by the way."

Jack sat and stared at the president's cluelessly cheerful face. He looked at Gearheardt who was completely and gleefully absorbed in reviewing the material.

The president was also watching Gearheardt. With an avuncular smile. Finally, he said, "You know how big Fort Knox is, Jack? I can tell you it holds about seventeen thousand four hundred sixty-three files the size of the one Gearheardt's holding. On just the first floor."

Now Gearheardt looked up. At Jack. Who the president was also looking at.

"Are you telling me, Mr. President, that the new financial system you're asking us to bring about is based on the pornography standard?"

"Prudery is the root of all evil, Jack," Gearheardt, the grinning bastard, said.

"That's not even a misquote, Gearheardt. You mean to tell me— "

"Jack, this is America," the president began, "and as the leader of Americans I have an obligation to not only preserve our freedoms and all that other stuff, but to promote and enhance fair trade, capitalism, and economic domination over the rest of the world."

"With all due respect, assuming some is due, sir, the idea of blackmail as the foundation of a financial system is insane."

"First of all, Jack," Gearheardt broke in, "it's not blackmail to simply remind someone of their previous indiscretions in order to get their attention. And— "

"Yes, it is, you damn nut."

"Hold on, Jack," the former King of Oklahoma interjected, "Gearheardt is just trying to put this in perspective. How sane is it to dig up a bunch of yellow iron and tell folks they can't have any of it unless they give us stuff? You tried eating gold lately, Jack?"

Condescension was piled thick on top of barely disguised disgust as he lectured. "You call it sane to tell people they can have pieces of paper that mean they can theoretically exchange for some gold— which they can't—if they lose confidence in the paper?"

Of course, Jack had no answer. What answer could there be to madness and incredible vulgarity disguised as a financial system? He looked over at his best pal, former Almost Captain Gearheardt, USMC. Former Case Officer Gearheardt, Central Intelligence Agency. Former absolute through and through American patriot. A fighter for all good causes. A defender of the hookers he frequented—well, that was pretty vintage Gearheardt. But he always, *always* had a good heart and a good sense of loyalty. Now? Had he sold out? Given up? Gone looney? He had always been on the edge of looney of course.

WHAM, BAM, Rattle, Scream, BAM, BAM.

"I think Hazel is at the door," the president said calmly. He grabbed the package away from Gearheardt and starting shoving photos back into the folder. "Think up some Secret Operations shit in case she breaks the damn door down, guys. I need to stash this."

When the president bent down behind the bar to open the safe, Gearheardt leaned toward Jack. "Hazel was in some of those photos, Jack. I may have to have an eye transplant."

He laughed and Jack saw a man who enjoyed the chaos, the wars, the whores, the assassinations, the general disorder and disarray that our well-intentioned forays had created and exposed them to. But Gearheardt winked and said, "Just play along, Jack. Just play along."

Jack wanted to believe they were still on the right side.

"Okay, gents, I think they've dragged Hazel back upstairs. And I heard you, Gearheardt, yes we have the goods on her too. I'm just waiting for the right minute when I need to get myself out of a jam before I use those photos." He smiled wistfully. "But I have to tell you, I'm not sure she wouldn't like the publicity. She has ambitions far beyond just running around screwing up everything she touches."

Gearheardt stood. "If that's all, President Slick, Jack and I need to grab some chow and then head up to New York and lay some groundwork."

"I hear you on the 'lay' part, Gearheardt. She got a sister?" The president laughed and poked Jack in the side. "But before you leave, I got a message you need to get to Langley. And that's if that fucking pygmy doesn't get out of the White House muy pronto, some heads will roll. He's scaring the help, leaving chicken bones in the hallway, pissing in the corners, and generally disrupting every damn meeting I try to have with the cabinet or an intern. Tell Langley to get his ass out of here."

"I'll pass the message, Slick. I'm not sure Langley actually controls the pygmy, but— "

"Who the hell does?

"I think he reports to Eddie Johnson. But I've heard rumors that he *IS* Eddie Johnson."

The president grabbed Jack's upper arm and squeezed hard with a laugh to make it seem a friendly gesture.

"That little turd is upsetting the whole plan. Three D took two years to set up and he's pissing on the campfire while we're trying to roast our marshmallows."

Jack and Gearheardt looked at each other. The president noticed.

"You boys just do what I tell you to do. If we can pull this off we'll be feeding on a life-time banquet."

He began shooing them toward the door.

Jack had to ask. "What happens if we fail whatever we're supposed to do?"

"Still get that lifetime buffet. Your particular life will be about half a second."

"But we're hunting the—"

"Son if I wanted to play twenty questions I could have not run for the president and everyone question ever damn thing I say." He sighed, went to his desk and plopped into his chair. He spoke without looking up. "Gearheardt knows what we need from Mr. Pygmy."

"I'm sorry, sir, but what about the pygmy?"

"Kill him," the president said. "And bring me his stubby little toes."

Chapter 7 or So But Who's Counting.

On their way back to the parking garage Jack queried Gearheardt incessantly about plans, who was involved, what was 3 D, why were they doing anything at all.

Finally, Gearheardt stopped and turned to Jack.

"Jack, you know I would tell you if I could. I can tell you one thing. The operation is meant to distract the public and even most of the government. That's what the three Ds stand for. Distraction, Distraction, Distraction."

"Distraction from what? It must be one hell of something that you need that much distraction."

"I can't tell you that."

"Why not?"

Gearheardt smiled. "They've forgotten which one was the real problem they were trying to cover. Remember this is the government. Everyone is on "need to know" restriction with serious consequences. So they can't talk to each other about 3 D."

"Surely the president knows?"

"Who's going to ask? Everyone just carries on with their objective and hopes its sorted out soon." Gearheardt turned. Through with the conversation.

As Gearheardt stepped into the street, Jack didn't move. "So we're really not at war with Wall Street." There was a touch of relief on his face.

Gearheardt continued walking. Over his shoulder he said. "I think a few 20 Mike Mikes into their boardrooms might change things, Jack."

The good news, thought Jack as he joined up with Gearheardt, was that Gearheardt always lied and exaggerated. This time he had outdone himself. Something was up, but not killing American bankers. Their mission was to find the pygmy. He would worry about it then.

"Come with me to reconnoiter the battlefield, Jack. Let's get our gear out of the car and head for the train station."

Jack stopped as they turned the corner in the alley.

"To go?"

"The Big Apple, Jack. Hey, Apple Jack, that sounds like…"

"You have the attention span of a gnat, Gearheardt. I assume you mean we're heading to New York."

"Specifically, to lower Manhattan, my boy. We need to know what kind of defenses they could throw up quickly if our initial landing force got pinned down in Battery Park. Artillery can be ineffective if they've got steel reinforced concrete bunkers."

"Last time I was in that area, I didn't notice any. Gearheardt, are you actually, really planning on militarily attacking Wall Street? With air support and artillery supporting ground troops? I hear you, but I tell myself you're just using euphemisms or maybe I'm just insane. Or, hopefully, this is a bad dream."

Gearheardt nodded, yes.

They had reached Union Station. Gearheardt got tickets and waved for Jack to follow. They boarded a crowded car and found seats on either side of a chubby guy reading a newspaper. He didn't look up as they stood over him.

"Pardon me, sir," Gearheardt said, pushing aside the top of the man's paper. "My pal and I need to sit together. I hope you won't mind moving to another seat. I think there's some in the next car."

The man shook his paper back upright and began reading again. He did not know Gearheardt like Jack did and was about to be worse off for that unfortunate circumstance.

The fire at the bottom of his newspaper quickly engulfed the entire sheet and, evidently, from the man's reactions, scorched his face.

"Sorry," Gearheardt said. "My pal and I really do need to sit here." Gearheardt was helping the shell-shocked fellow out of the seat by pulling upward on his tie. The man wisely said nothing, brushed the ashes of his newspaper from his lap, and shouldered between them and off down the aisle.

"Why are you such an asshole, Gearheardt?" I said as we settled in. "The poor guy— "

"Jack, maybe you don't take the future of America's financial system very seriously. But I do. The mission needed these seats." He leaned his head against the window and closed his eyes. While Jack sat staring at him, he began to snore lightly.

"He was a Russian thug," Gearheardt said, without opening his eyes. "Are you chickening out? Did you fall into a honey hole?

"No, Gearheardt, I haven't been gotten to and I haven't fallen into a honey *trap*. I might add that since you would screw anything on two legs and would be proud to promote it, a *honey trap* would be useless on you." Jack knew he wasn't going to get anywhere by talking seriously with Gearheardt, so he leaned his head back and closed his eyes.

"I do limit it to bi-peds, Jack."

By dawn they were on Ellis Island, looking across at lower Manhattan. From the train to Ellis Island was a blur of Gearheardt ordering, asking, cajoling, and intimidating drivers and guards while Jack just zoned out and went along.

"Just look at that skyline, Jack," Gearheardt said, looking at the World Trade Center and the lesser buildings surrounding it. "Or, as my arty guys call it, the ultimate aiming stake."

"Arty as in artillery I presume."

"Can't attack Wall Street with pussywillows, Jack. I know you're afraid of a little bloodshed so that we can get this country on a sound financial footing again— "

"Yes."

"But I think it was Nate Arnold who once said, 'The cost of money comes at the price of liberty and justice for those with it.'"

"No one said anything like that at all, you dick. I don't know whether you make that crap up to bug me or if you really think someone said the sayings you're always screwing up."

"Jack, I'm not saying it's because you went to that cow college in bumfuzzle Oklahoma, but sometimes I think you just don't get it."

Jack didn't even turn to look at him. They stood on the pier, Jack marveling at the New York skyline and Gearheardt pacing back and forth, checking his watch every ten seconds. The cry of the seagulls circling and the water shushing up against the pier in random small waves lent an air of adventure and mystery to the scene.

What the hell am I doing here, Jack said to himself?

"We'll give him another five minutes and then push off. That boat will take us close to Battery Park and then we'll swim ashore."

"No, we won't, Gearheardt. We're in suits and there is absolutely no reason we can't dock at one of the places provided for boats." Now Jack looked at him. "And who, pray tell, are we waiting for?"

"That fellow just coming out of Liberty's toe. The tall one dressed like a refugee from Nagasaki."

The refugee approached them, grinned through a layer of camouflage face-paint, and stuck out his hand. "Good to see you again---Jack, isn't it?"

"Yes, Mr. President. It's Jack."

"Hey, Slick," Gearheardt said.

The president frowned. "Didn't I tell you---"

"I mean, hey, Mr. President. And by way, sir, although we are honored to have you join us in getting the lay of the land— "

"And she better be cute."

Jack had no idea if the president was making a joke or was expecting a babe to be discovered. He suspected the latter as the joke was too weak for him to use twice.

"—we, as Jack recently pointed out, are not in combat attire and you would, if I might say so, stand out like a sore thumb pooping and snooping around lower Manhattan in that getup."

"Was I supposed to know that pooping and snooping garb would mean Brooks Brother suits and Princeton ties? Hold on, I'll have my numbnut aide get some decent attire. Be right back." He turned as he walked away. "Try not to make a f--king fool of me more than about once a day, Gearheardt."

Within a few minutes, the President returned, tricked out in a blue suit and regimental tie. He wore a fedora, pulled down practically over his ears, and sunglasses. Jack saw a Secret Service man sneak away in underwear.

The three of them, plus two Secret Service agents, gathered near the boat which would take them to Wall Street. Gearheardt retrieved a map from the boat and spread it on the ground. They kneeled.

"We land here. But the attack forces— "

"When is D-Day, Gearheardt?"

"Still classified, Mr. President. We will take a look around today, feed the information into G-2, that's the intelligence section, Mr. President, and come up with the final strategy. Based on the strategy, we can start to make those kinds of decision."

"Who's we? Am I not the Commander in Chief of all the military?"

"Yes, you are, Mr. President. When would you like to launch the attack forces?"

"I don't have the foggiest idea and you know it, wise-ass. Just give me the first look at all the intelligence and let me give some kind of speech to those boys going ashore. Always wanted to do that. We'll fight on the beach. We'll fight on the…place behind the beach. We'll kick 'em in the nuts til their noses bleed. We'll ga— "

"Very inspiring, Mr. President."

"Thank you, Jack."

He actually thought Jack was serious.

As Jack was beginning to not like the guy, and as Gearheardt was busy instructing the boat driver, he engaged the President.

"Were you in Vietnam, sir? You seem to be about the right age."

"Yep, all over that damn place. But mostly under cover. I had this ROTC guy stop me from volunteering. He was tasked with finding someone who looked like he was going to Vietnam but was too smart to actually waste his life over there. Fit me to a tee if I do say so. And I do. We put out the word that I was deferred and sent me to Vietnam as a sniper-spy. I spotted them and I shot them. That was my motto. Spot and shoot." His voice kind of tapered off. He looked at the ground as if he might have gone too far.

"I kind of thought you went to Europe or some place. Maybe it was— "

"So you don't think you can go to Vietnam from Europe, wise-ass? You ever hear of a place called France? They had guys down there left and right. I don't know why people are so damned interested in how I got to Vietnam! Did Harry Truman ever go to Vietnam? Damn right he didn't."

Jack started to push him further but a commotion in the water got the attention of all of them.

An enormous waterspout had appeared, churning the water and rocking the boats tied to the dock. The morning sun shone through the misty spout, turning it bright red.

"Jumpin' Jesus Christ on blue rubber crutches," the president yelled. He stood up and then dove headlong into the bottom of the boat. "It's that damned 'H' boys, run for your lives."

But he was giggling and aiming at the apparition with a .45 pistol he had pulled from his jacket.

As the water calmed, Gearheardt put away his maps and indicated our team, the three of them and the Secret Service guys, needed to hop aboard. We settled in for the short ride and Gearheardt smiled at me, and then the President.

"Did you know the president was in Vietnam, Gearheardt? All over the place evidently. He was one of those sniper spies. I think his motto was," Jack looked at the smoldering president, "something like 'shoot and shit.'"

The president aimed his .45 at Jack, but after a moment smiled and returned it to his shoulder holster. "That Jack is a laugh a minute, Gearheardt. I hope he doesn't have a lot of dependents who are missing him. Him spending a lot of time away."

"Nope," answered Gearheardt innocently, "Jack's pretty much a loner. Does 'H' have a boyfriend?"

Even the president laughed at that one and they all seemed to relax for the moment. Battery Park was near, and they were soon ashore.

They strolled through the streets of lower Manhattan for the next hour. Unnoticed, after they made the president rub off his face camouflage, they were able to take photos of all the entrances and exits of the subway and the larger office buildings. The Secret Service finally took the President's gun away from him after he continued to twirl it on his finger as they walked along. He seemed to be enjoying the anonymity.

At lunch, a diner near the Brooklyn Bridge, Gearheardt planned the afternoon. Listening to him, Jack remembered that the guy was an experienced war planner and strategist. On his map he made notes of potential targets for the aerial attacks, areas of particular avenues of danger for advancing infantry— no easy exits and little shelter along the sidewalks, first and second story windows which could expose the troops to rifle and machine-gun fire—and descriptions, down to the foot, of entrances to *Goldharm and Savage*, along with other major investment banking firms in the area.

Jack had a thought and asked, "Weren't we supposed to meet the Colonel, now Major heading to Captain, at the hotel in DC last night?"

Gearheardt looked up. "Oh shit."

Jack had hoped for a different reply. "Do you want me to try to get hold of him?"

Gearheardt marked an X on a street and put his pen away. "He has the keys to the Aston Martin. I would imagine he's heading hell bent for Mexico by now. Too bad, I kind of liked the guy."

Who, as it happened, walked into the diner.

"Thanks a lot, boys," he said. He saw the president, up close he was pretty recognizable, and stopped. "Sir, I...." He stammered and looked at Gearheardt with a 'what the hell' look on his face.

"Meet the president, Major."

"Captain," he said, genuflecting to the president. He obviously had met few presidents in diners, or elsewhere. Now one was balancing a waitress on one knee before him.

"Hello, Captain."

"Hello, Mr. President. An honor to meet you, sir."

"You're Edwards, right?"

"Yes, sir. I am in the Army and seconded to the Marines at the moment. If I may, sir, I would like to take this opportunity to— "

The president held up his free hand, palm toward the Army man of questionable rank status.

"But sir, I would like to— "

The dope thought he could appeal his case directly to his Commander in Chief, and not have to put up with Gearheardt's crap, or that of the Marine Corps. Gearheardt had dropped his maps on the table, and sat with folded arms, a slight grin on his face, watching the Army guy begin to grovel. The President didn't give him much of a chance.

"Didn't I just sign some damn commission or something making you a general, Edwards?"

"That was just the Marines jerking me around, sir. The fact is— "

"The fact is that you're beginning to piss me off.... what the hell rank are you anyway? Is the whole damn army like you?" The president stood, dumping the anxious-to-get-away-anyway waitress onto the floor. "What in all that is holy in Oklahoma is going on in the Army, Edwards? I can't seem to get a straight answer from anyone at the Pentagon. I keep getting the runaround when I try to invade some piss-ant backwater so that I don't have to invade some big-ass backwater. So maybe you—"

He paused, ran his fingers through his full head of hair, then looked over at Gearheardt. "Where the hell was I going with this, Gearheardt?"

"I think you've covered it, Mr. President." He stood and began folding his maps and notes. "Jack, why don't you split off and take Edwards with you. See if there's a natural barrier we could use between here and Little Italy. Those damn Italians will come running to a fight. If we could block off a couple of streets, channel them down a single street, we could handle them with a squad or two. Maybe set out some free vino, pasta, and autographed photos of Sophia Loren. Give 'em a place to set in the sun and bullshit one another."

"There is no stereotype off limits to you, is there, Gearheardt? Please don't describe your method of preventing folks coming down from Harlem." Jack grabbed Edwards by the arm—he was still pleading with the President—and started dragging him toward the door of the diner.

Which was about to become jammed with people who had heard the President of the United States was having coffee and a donut inside.

"Gearheardt," Jack called back, "better get Slick out the back door."

But Slick had caught the smell of adulation, a scent he could congenitally not ignore. With a wide, dental exam smile he began greeting his people.

"Great to see you, pardner. Hey, is this beauty your wife, you lucky dog? Come on in and get some free coffee. Happy to meet you, pal. There's a sweet woman. Crowd on in here and let the folks in back shake hands too. Whoa, sorry ma'am. I thought I was kissing a little bald baby-head poking out. Heh, heh. Put 'er there, pal."

He went on for ten minutes, hardly stopping to breathe. The diner was packed. The secret service guys were gamefully keeping the growing crowd under control, although the owner of the diner was swept away while watching the mob munch through everything not made of metal.

The president's grin began drooping and became grotesquely false. His responses to those who appeared before him, hands outstretched, were down to "Hey, Yeah man, Good, Yes, yes", and finally, "Nice tits" and after that things began to degenerate.

"Let's get him out of here, boys," Gearheardt said. He began squirting ketchup and mustard from plastic containers toward the crowd. The presidential supporters, however, seemed to appreciate the free ketchup and mustard and pressed harder.

"Give me my f--king gun, "the President said to Gus, the senior agent, "these silly bastards are squeezing my gonads and picking my pockets." He seemed genuinely distressed, and surprised, that the mob was beginning to turn on him.

Gus, instead, pulled his own weapon from its holster and began firing through the roof of the diner. Jack heard an anguished groan from the diner owner above the din and the roar of the presidential admirers. Finally, the last of the admirers were swept out into the parking lot. Save one angry thug who clung to the doorframe, refusing to go even though the agents were beating on his fingers.

"What the hell, Gus? Shoot the sonofabitch. He's endangering the President of the United States. What the blaz—?

"That's his wife you've got your arm around, Mr. President. With your hand down her dress. He's just— "

"Oh, my golly, this little lady here?" The President was looking at the clearly distraught woman as if she was a prize he had found in a box of Cracker Jacks. "Mighty fine-looking woman, sir." He pulled his hand from her dress top and shoved her toward the door with a pat on her bottom.

Edwards and Jack headed toward the door. "Gearheardt, I'll take a look at Little Italy like you suggested. Maybe grab some pizza and see you back in DC tomorrow morning."

Gearheardt grabbed Jack's arm and pulled him aside. "You're still not taking this seriously are you, Jack? I'm telling you that we are attacking these bastards on Wall Street who are bleeding our country dry. Dry as a Sudanese refugee woman's teat."

Jack's mind, as Gearheardt knew it would, tried to wade through the twisted analogy to formulate an answer. Over Gearheardt's shoulder he could see the President at the counter, his hat pushed back on his head and his sunglasses hanging from his ears, devouring a pecan pie with vanilla ice cream.

"It's just too bizarre, Gearheardt. Slick over there, seems almost insane. Is this pornography thing an actual—?

"Pure bullshit, Jack. It's a ruse to throw the dissenters off the trail. The President, whatever else he may be, is a smart guy. He knows what will work in this country, and what won't. He knows our financial system took a beating in the last decade and needs revamping. And he knows he needs to make a whole lot of money while he's in office. A whole lot. He has no skills other than politicking. But he's world class at that, you have to admit."

Jack was beginning to understand. The motive, if not the operation. It was about making money, controlling money, and then making more money.

"You mentioned dissenters. You mean the Federal Reserve guys—?"

"Oh, hell no," Gearheardt laughed. "Those pricks don't do dick and they get paid for it. Why would they want to change anything? No," he looked around and lowered his voice, "it's those bastards in congress. They hate the president. And his wife. Probably hate his kid too. They think he's just a loud-mouth, draft dodging, Oklahoma cracker with a slew of college degrees and the tongue of a Roman orator."

"Well— "

"Yeah, but they don't like to be pushed around. They have their own financial well-being to look out for. Everyone doesn't have a land deal, Jack."

"Why doesn't congress just, you know, exercise their congressional powers and— "

"Jack, the congress is about as functional as a guy trying to stuff a turd back up his ass. Monkeys in a circus, Jack. Running for congress is like trying out for 'Who Wants to be a Millionaire?'

Glancing up, Jack saw the President, a forkful of pecan pie halfway between plate and mouth, looking intently toward him and Gearheardt. His eyes squinted a signal. He didn't trust us or the horse we rode in on.

"I think I should make contact with someone in the Senate, Gearheardt. This whole plan seems bogus. It's obviously insane, but that hasn't stopped good men before. I have a couple of college buddies in the sen— "

"Don't even think about it, Jack. If the congress got wind of this, it would be a typhoon piss storm. We have the Federal Reserve, the Administration, the CIA and the military. We don't need those clowns over on Capitol Hill."

Chapter 8 Unless I Miss My Guess

Jack was not happy. Not by a long shot.

Safely ensconced in the DC Hilton, room service dishes with non-eaten remains outside his door, he finally had a chance to lay back and think about what was going on. The problem was—he didn't have a clue. Gearheardt, his best pal and companion since USMC flight school, was completely looney, and the only truly freethinker that Jack knew. In Gearheardt's wild and outrageous schemes lay the seeds of honest realizations of the problems and frustrations of American life, with dubious yet practical solutions to most of them. Contradiction, thy name is Gearheardt.

So far, the plan was to use thugs to invade Wall Street and kill all the investment bankers who were Americans disguised as Russians disguised as Americans.

But the thugs were being shipped off and the Marines were taking their place surreptitiously because invading Wall Street with Marines might worry the citizens about a possible coup.

All of America's money seemed to have been lost in the derivative market (no one was sure how much that was) and the invasion of Wall street was to distract the American people while the government and the head of the Federal Reserve figured out a scheme for bilking the holders of American debt. But the Chairman of the Federal Reserve, a pygmy suspected of being Eddie Johnson was one step ahead of them. The pygmy had locked the double-secret shrink wrapped laptop computer and only he knew the code that could open the computer so they could print more money.

The actual killing of the Wall Street investment bankers was murky. When the Marine Corps asked for volunteers to clean out Wall Street there was 100 percent participation. Jack was unsure that the government could stop the slaughter of bankers if things got out of control.

"Are you suggesting that we let millions of people go hungry just to save the lives of a few hundred investment bankers?" Gearheardt asked Jack.

"That's a non sequitur, Gearheardt," Jack said. "And a serious one."

"Well, Jack, find the damn pygmy and stop the slaughter."

Jack rubbed his eyes and bowed his head. Then looked up at Gearheardt who was brushing pecan pie from his shirt sleeve. "And where does the Savings and Loan thing fit in. I assume it's part of this idiotic plan."

"The president wants to own them when he's run out of office. All of them."

"Well, I can certainly see the logic in that." Jack shrugged.

When the then president of the United States, Larry Bob Jackass as Gearheardt called him, had tasked Jack and Gearheardt to end the war in Vietnam, Gearheardt's idea of offering Ho Chi Minh title to one of the Hawaiian Islands and a quarter of a billion dollars seemed, on the surface, much more reasonable than dropping a billion bombs in neighboring countries. The bomb idea was chosen.

Faking an assassination of a Mexican president and blaming it on Communist Cubans sounded more reasonable (and a lot more fun) than a half-assed boat invasion to overthrow the evil rogues—half-assed boat invasion carried the day and Gearheardt and Jack were ostracized.

In so many cases, ethics, morality, and basic goodness, prevented us from embracing the practical solution of killing the sons-of-bitches who caused us so much grief and ruled with a bloody hand over legions of suffering human beings. And this pissed Gearheardt off.

Was the Ugly American aka Gearheardt really so bad? Was Jack, Mr. All-American boy, worse— pro-longing the agony and angst beyond the nasty, brutish, and short solution favored by great-thinkers of the past?

True, some of Gearheardt's most outlandish schemes were not, in the light of day, outlandish. Replacing the Central Intelligence Agency with a global network of prostitutes made a great deal of budgetary as well as humanitarian sense. (See *Goodbye Mexico*, Forge, 2007)

Unless it served to entice young women into prostitution. Or the CIA. There again, Jack struggled with the moral issues. When he had tried to discuss the situation with Gearheardt, Gearheardt had seemed to give a thoughtful pause, even wrinkling his brow, before he replied, "Jack, in all my years with the Agency, I've met exactly *two* case officers I wouldn't mind screwing. As to whores—"

"You're an idiot, Gearheardt," Jack said. The scheme had floundered in any event, with few hookers willing to risk being outed as employees of the Central Intelligence Agency. State secrets and information whispered or screamed in maximus extremis were lost into walls of sordid hostels in shameful abandon by the millions.

Jack's reflection was interrupted by the phone. "Armstrong," he said.

"Jack, it's Edwards. What say you and I pow wow in a few minutes. I'm just down the hall."

"Captain, I'm not sure—"

"It's Lieutenant Edwards now."

"Sorry to hear that, but if Gearheardt—"

"He just left. Said he was headed to the Willard to screw some Darkman Darkman folks. I've got to hand it to him. He works long hours."

"No, he meant it about the Darkman people. So okay, see you in the lobby bar in ten minutes." Jack hung up and swung his legs over the side of the bed. Putting on his shoes, he felt a slight twinge of disloyalty.

In the bar, Edwards signaled him to a table in the corner. Away from the noisy tables crowded with almost important Washington DC workers and almost important elected people.

When they had ordered drinks, Edwards leaned forward.

"Jack, what do you know about this taking over Wall Street operation? Gearheardt, to tell the truth, seems to be just playing it by ear. Making it up as he goes along." His face showed concern.

"I've got some good news and bad news for you, Edwards—you're right."

Edwards slumped back into his chair and sighed. "That's what I was afraid you would say, Jack."

He rubbed his forehead and then looked at Jack. "So, what do we do now? The whole attack thing and derivatives crisis is…what?"

Jack took a sip of his scotch and water while he thought for a minute. And he decided he could trust Edwards. "Unfortunately, both of those things are probably on the table. Gearheardt does not make idle threats, nor statements he has no way of backing up."

"So, he's telling the truth?"

"The truth as he sees it. He used to tell me 'I'm an honest man, Jack. If I say I think it, it's because I really think it.'"

Edwards took a long drink of his dark rum. "That makes no sense whatsoever."

"He's also the guy who once told me he always lies because no man *never* lies so the only truly honest man lies all the time and admits it." Jack shrugged his shoulders. "Yes, I know it makes no sense."

"He should run for office."

"He thinks it's beneath his dignity."

Edwards smiled. "I'm told he once pissed on the president's desk."

"The president was barely splashed on and Gearheardt defines dignity a bit differently than most. He's a Marine officer."

"That says it all," Edwards said sarcastically.

Jack held up a finger, his gaze steady into Edward's eyes. "Gearheardt also told me Nietzsche's statement that truth is ugly and a moveable host of metaphors, metonymies, and anthropomorphisms' is the proper response to a discussion of truth."

Edwards's glass had stopped midway between the table and his lip. "I have no idea what you just said that Gearheardt said, Jack."

"I'm just saying not to underestimate Gearheardt. He's a madman, but he was escorted from his Princeton graduation at gunpoint."

"I say again," Edwards said, "that says it all."

Jack and Edwards both contemplated their drinks, silent in the din of the surrounding guzzlers and hustlers. Edwards tapped his plastic swizzle stick against the table. Jack studied him and saw what he thought was an honest, squared away military man who was caught up in a bizarre world. A world that favored guys like Gearheardt who operated at the bizarre level in the straightest of times.

"So, what do we do, Jack?" Edwards asked, looking up. "The way I understand it, we are putting together a plan to attack the financial institutions on Wall Street because they and the Russians have taken over the U.S. mortgage market. Right?"

"It might seem—"

"Let me finish," Edwards held up his hand. "And the real reason we're attacking Wall Street is to cover up the governments exposure in the derivatives market which is somewhere north of ten trillion dollars."

"You know more about that than I do, Edwards. But that sounds like what I've been hearing. And, by the way, I think Gearheardt and the president have a scheme to take over the U.S. banking system at the same time."

It was the first time Jack could remember betraying Gearheardt. The surprise—it didn't bother him for some reason.

Meanwhile Chapter 9 Happened

"Gearheardt," the president started, carefully setting his cigar on the end table without losing the two-inch ash, "I'm not sure about your boy Jack. Seems a bit of a pussy to me." He looked up and raised his eyebrows. "And not the kind I like."

It was late at night and the two were in the White House, the president's private suite.

"He's okay, Slick," Gearheardt replied. "Jack is just kind of...honest or something." He was not completely sober and chose his words less than carefully.

"Hmmm." The president was lying on his back on the sofa. "Well, I damn sure only like honest people around me."

Gearheardt violently expelled beer through his nose.

The president lifted his head off the couch pillow and looked at Gearheardt.

"Is that beer dripping out of your nose an insult?"

"No, Mr. Presidnetness. Just took too big a swig." He used his handkerchief to wipe his nose and chin. "Look, I would much appreciate if we could go over some of the details of our—"

"My."

"—*your* plan. It might help if you put on some pants too, Mr. President."

"I think better with no pants on, G-man."

"I'm not sure history will agree with that, Mr. President, but we just need to get serious about launching this plan you call Flags to Riches. That's right, isn't it? Flags to—"

"Told you umpteen times, G-man. I wuz sitting there in the chair in the Oval Office and looked back and saw the American flag on one side of me and the President flag on the other and my chest just swelled up. I thought to myself, I can make some money on this deal."

Gearheardt internally flinched but said, "And no one deserves that more than you, Mr. President."

The president lurched to his feet with a groan and padded to a closet. His pinstriped boxer shorts matched his wife-beater shirt with '*Do you Cabo*?' written on the front over a picture of a Mexican Day of the Dead figure. He scratched his butt and then put on a long blue robe. The presidential seal flashed impressively over the breast pocket as he returned to the couch and dropped down heavily.

"Let's go over it again, G-man," he sighed, taking the sheath of papers Gearheardt had produced.

Gearheardt gobbled two white pills and chased them with the remainder of his beer. He took a deep breath and shook his head, then looked back up at the president.

"Right," Gearheardt said, "first the ostensible plan, that is, the one we're spreading around—"

"I know what ostensible means, piss-ant. I went to the sorbet for Pete's sake. You don't—"

"I think you went to the Sorbonne, Mr. President. Sorbet is—"

"Did I say sorbet? I just know there was more damn French folks than you can shake a stick at on the campus." He reached for the now extinguished cigar, slapped his robe pockets and then accepted Gearheardt's proffered match. "Thanks. Let's get on with it."

Gearheardt took time to blow out the match and look for an ashtray. He was struggling to forget he had a splitting headache while trying to stay alert enough to *read* the president.

Billy Nickel Costain, now known as President Costain, played the country fool as well as anyone had ever played it. He was known to be highly, very highly, intelligent but used a folksy, slightly goofy persona to trap unsuspecting politicians, and nubile women, into thinking they had the upper hand. In each meeting since the president had summoned him to the White House, Gearheardt was hard-pressed to stay ahead of what the president really had in mind. He knew the president didn't believe he went to Sorbet University. But he had no clue as to why Billy Nickel (a name his alleged father had given him for reasons unknown) said he did. Or why he pretended to know nothing about the Federal Reserve.

Two possibilities had occurred to Gearheardt. One, that the good-old-boy goofiness gave 'plausible denial' to things he said or did. "Aw, I was just funnin' ya. I never meant I'd vote against killin' babies."

Or two, and this was a tricky one, the 'dumb blonde' syndrome had taken over permanently as it had with a number of women Gearheardt knew. They had played the dumb blonde for so long that they became a dumb blonde. And found it more and more difficult to *play* the sharp intelligent woman they might really have been.

In this case, Gearheardt had decided, it was probably number one—plausible denial. The challenge was exacerbated by the insistence--by the president-- that it was *his* idea to gob smack the Federal Reserve. Each element of the plan being hatched by Gearheardt had to be planted in the president's thick ego and then dragged out of him as a unique, and clever, idea. When the Director of Central Intelligence had mistakenly blessed Gearheardt's idea of taking over the global financial system, his only caveat was that the idea had to come from the White House.

"If we fall on our ass on this one, Gearheardt, I'll be back to combing through garbage to find out if the Russian commies use Chinese Kleenex. The country can tolerate losing a country to the communist bastards every once in a while. But there's hell to pay if the rich folks running the show get hit in the pocketbook. So, mind your peas and carrots."

Gearheardt, being the CIA's most ardent patriot and best bullshitter, didn't argue with the 'White House idea' requirement at the time. He had assumed that the current president was as un-creative and solidly uptight as the majority of his predecessors.

Billy Nickel Costain was anything but. In fact, he had been unavoidably drunk when during his inauguration day interview with the outgoing president. And while trying to look up the dress of the outgoing president's secretary, had completely missed the last-minute advice the old man had given. Something about Vietnam and another country he was only vaguely aware existed. The drunkenness was unavoidable as there was a great deal of free liquor in the White House and Billy Nickel Costain was a raging, yet fully functioning, alcoholic. Given the mind-numbing formality and decorum required in the change-over, combined with alcohol and an all-hands near-nervous breakdown, it was no surprise when the outgoing president stood, held out his hand to the new boss, and asked if he had any questions, Billy Nickel asked if the president's secretary 'put out.'

"Well, hoss, are we going over the plans or not?"

Gearheardt snapped out of his bourbon induced reverie and said, "Well, Mr. President, if there is any aspect or action of the plan of which you are unclear or don't understand, I'm happy to explain them to you again." A brilliant thrust, born of a splitting headache and rising nausea, which Gearheardt intuitively knew the president would not parry.

"What's complicated about attacking Wall Street with the Federal Reserve numb-nuts as the front-line troops and taking over the banking system while everyone with more than a pot to piss in is distracted?"

"So, in your plan, Mr. President, the Federal Reserve is on *our* side?"

"Gearheardt, when I was freezing my ass off in Korea, every once in a while about two or three million Chinese soldiers would start running and screaming and blowing horns whilst they ran in to get mowed down by us. But they were on the Commies side, right?"

"You were one year old when the Korean War was fought, Mr. President."

"And what the hell and horny toads does that have to do with my point, Gearheardt?" It was always G-man when he was friendly and Gearheardt when he was pissed. "My *point* was that those horn-blowing Chinamen running out so that we could shoot them were doing their job. The employees of the Federal Reserve bank can do their damn job too."

"Mr. President, you do know that Federal Reserve employees are technically not government employees."

The president narrowed his eyes and thought for a moment. "Do you know how many government employees there are, G-man? Well, before you have to guess, let me tell you it's exactly a shit-pot full. We got employees out the ying-yang. And if the country wants some of them to attack Wall Street...." His voice trailed off.

After a moment, the president sighed and stretched out on the couch again. "What time is it, G-man? I'm so tired I feel like its day after tomorrow."

"It's one thirty in the morning, Mr. President."

The President put his hand over his eyes. "Oh, Lord. You-know-who will be waking up to visit the lady's room any minute. You could set your clock by her bladder. I'm going to just go ahead and shoot myself, G-man. I can't face that woman, particularly if she gets word of what you've gotten me into."

"Sir, you've mentioned that a number of times. Your......*difficulty* with Mrs. President on occasion."

"Yeah, the occasion of every time I see her."

"So, I was thinking that maybe, and I've not thought this all the way through, we might just bring her in on the deal."

The president, who had been rubbing his eyes, stopped all motion, even breathing. The room was silent except for the

Budweiser Beer clock on the wall which made bubbling noises. The president said a salesman had given it to him and damned if he wasn't going to hang it where he wanted to hang it. It bubbled again.

The president dropped his hand from his face and turned his head toward Gearheardt, who was sorry that he was not armed at the moment.

"G-man, I gotta tell you something. You are not, evidently, as stupid as you look. Bring her in? A damn genius move. I don't know why I didn't think of it." He sat up and adjusted his robe. "Come to think of it, I *did* just think of it when you reminded me."

Gearheardt was not at all concerned that the president was stealing his idea. Somehow he knew that in the future whoever had thought of it was going to be incredibly sorry. He had suggested it only because he was certain the president would blow a gasket and throw him out and he could go back over to the hotel and get some badly needed sleep. It hadn't worked quite that way.

The president slid to the end of the couch and picked up the phone from the end table.

"Mary Lou," he said, "when the First Lady comes out of the pisser, tell her to come into the boy's room or whatever she calls it." He listened. "She calls it that in public?"

He hung up and grinned at Gearheardt. "Brace yourself, old pal Gearheardt. You are about to experience something like an orgasm if orgasms hurt like hell." He chuckled, stood, and pulled the robe belt tighter.

The door blew open and a short tower of fire entered the room. Gearheardt wished he had some of those glasses used on Artic exploration trips to prevent snow blindness—little slits to look through.

"There better be a damned important reason you got me out of bed, turnip-head." She turned to Gearheardt. "Who is this miserable creature. Looks like a damned spook."

"I'm not," said Gearheardt.

"He is," said the president.

"I'm Gearheardt, Mrs. President," Gearheardt said. He extended his hand, then thought better of it and pulled it back in, sticking it in his pocket for no good reason but awkwardness.

"I don't give a shit who you are, spook boy. What have you and Loony Tunes been cooking up in here?"

"Now honey, Mr. Gearheardt has come up with a plan to make us, you and me, a lot of money."

The First Lady smirked derisively and dropped into an armchair. She looked at her husband for a long, death-rattling moment.

"We're the damn president, jackass. We can just *take* the money. If you think I'm going to leave this place as broke as when I got here, you're just as stupid as you look."

Gearheardt was afraid to say anything. The president pointed his chin at the First Lady, as if he was about to rebut something, but he didn't. The beer clock bubbled.

Finally, Mrs. President sighed. "Is someone going to tell me exactly how we're going to get this money?"

"Actually, Mrs. First, it isn't so much about *getting* the money as it is *controlling* it."

Mrs. President turned toward Gearheardt who was on his feet, inching toward the door, surreptitiously he had hoped.

"Controlling how much of it?"

"All of it, ma'am."

"I like the sound of that." She almost smiled. She looked back at the president. "Does this spook have any idea what he's talking about?"

The President dropped back to the couch. A degree of tension had left the room.

"Well, honey, it's actually my idea—"

"Yeah, I bet it is."

The president's face clouded. "Hey, who was it come up with the idea of me being president? Huh?"

The First Lady scoffed. "Well, if memory serves me, it was that college girl in your ethics class you were tutoring the be-Jesus out of."

The First Lady motioned for her husband to move over and moved to the place beside him. "You," pointing at Gearheardt, "get your skinny butt in that chair and take me through this *controlling the money* scheme."

Gearheardt did as he was told. "Mrs. First, I just...I mean we...." He wasn't sure how much to reveal and the president was studiously inspecting his fingernails. Long moments went by without being able to catch the president's eye.

Finally, the First lady snorted in disgust. "You just want to do what the hell I tell you, Gearhead, or whatever your name is." She looked at her husband. "And both of you gather up any plans, diagrams, notes, or memos and bring them to my apartment first thing tomorrow."

Gearheardt looked at the president who smiled.

"You mean we should just take—"

"Did I stutter, spook boy?" the first lady snapped. "I don't trust this numbnut with any documents and if you're working with him..." waving a weak wrist at the president. "Look, you two peas in a pod just keep me informed. I'll find out what's going on tomorrow. Right now, I need my beauty sleep."

She rose and stormed (which I later realized was her standard mode) out of the room.

The president just smiled. "The first lady's quarters are at the end of the hallway. Where it says *'Lasciate ogne speranza, voi ch'intrate'* over the double door."

"Abandon all hope—"

"Yeah, the White House lawyers said she had to put it up there."

Gearheardt yawned. "Maybe we should—"

"Maybe you should give me that overview of the plan you promised me. I want to make damn sure you've understood what I outlined."

After a moment, "Right, Mr. President. But I need a chalk board or—"

"Easier done than done, Spook boy." He grinned. "I don't agree with the little woman very often, but I like that spook name."

Gearheardt was getting two-in-the-morning cranky. "Easier done than done? Don't you mean—"

The president lifted one of the three phones on the table. After a long moment, he said, "Who the hell is this?" Pause. "Well I don't usually wait all damn night for someone to answer. I need a chalk board up here muy pronto." Pause. "Well pardon me, Mr. Just Woke Up. Am I not the president all night or is that just a day job?" Pause. "Hell, I don't care if it's a chalk board. I just need something big you can write on." Pause. "Well thank you very much."

He looked at Gearheardt and smirked. "I picked up the wrong phone. That was the Vice President. He probably has half the town looking for a chalk board." He laughed. "I'm going to call him back and tell him I need colored chalk."

Gearheardt dozed in his chair while waiting for the board to be delivered.

Once, the president nudged his foot and asked, "Spook man, do you know any women we could get over here?" Then he laughed, plausible denial probably, and Gearheardt drifted off.

Finally, a hastily attired Vice President of the United States burst into the room, followed by workman carrying a six foot by four-foot acetate board. He placed the board on a stand, excused himself, sighing with relief.

The vice president stood with bed-haired attention and semi-genuflected to the president.

"I'm glad you felt free to call me at this late hour, Mr. President. It goes without saying that the gravity of the situation requires public servants to..be...uh, public servants in times like these." The vice president was edging toward the chair beside Gearheardt, his eyes on the president's face. He was obviously hoping to find out what the hell was going on.

"Well, thank you, Jimmy. But before you sit down, the First Lady would like you to stick your head into her quarters and let her share some information with you."

The vice president looked like he had leapfrogged early symptoms into full-blown malaria.

"Yes, sir. Uh..." He looked at his watch, "it's almost, uh, awfully late to—"

"Naw, Jimmy, just stick your head in there and see what she was so all-fired anxious to talk to you about."

Looking as if he would just as soon drink a pig's vomit milkshake, the vice president scuttled out of the room.

"Mr. President," Gearheardt started. "I want to begin by—"

The president, grinning, held up a finger. "Hold on."

After a few minutes a loud crash was followed by the sounds of people running down the hallway. Doors were slammed and the president walked quickly to the window, motioning Gearheardt to follow.

A man ran out from the White House and jumped into a waiting limo, which burned rubber out of the circle drive. The president was busting a gasket laughing.

"That poor sonofabitch. I pull that on him ever so often and he falls for it. Looks like he would just hightail it out of here and not open the first lady's door." Suddenly serious and looking at Gearheardt, he said, "And he didn't learn a damn thing about my plan."

The Tenth and only Chapter So Named

The president flopped back onto the couch and let out a long sigh. "Where were we, Spook Boy? And why is there a chalk board in my private briefing room?" He looked at his wrist as he said, "It's getting to be past my…..Oh damn it to hell." He jumped up and moved to the door, jerked it open and spoke to an unseen aide.

"Was there a woman, not the first lady, that left here a bit ago who was wearing a solid eighteen karat gold President model Rolex?"

Gearheardt could not hear the response but the president slammed the door and stomped back to his couch and dropped heavily on it.

"Lord love a duck, Gearheardt. You would think someone who I went to a hell of a lot of trouble to sneak into the White House would have the common decency not to steal my watch. The damn thing was given to me by, what's his name, that guy from China. This country is….." He trailed off, rubbing the slightly lighter patch of skin where his watch had once resided. "Let's get on with it."

Gearheardt went to the white board and drew a circle in its center. Inside the circle he drew a dollar sign and a stick figure beside it. "That's the simple focus, Mr. President. You should end up controlling all of the money."

"Draw another little person and put a skirt on it, Gearheardt. The first lady sees this without her included and people in hell will be shaking in fear they'll have to come back to earth."

Gearheardt turned away from the white board and faced the president. He knew that the first lady was going to be a factor in everything he ever did with President Slick, former King of Oklahoma. "Why is the first lady so.....cranky all the time, Mr. President? If she's going to be a part of this, wouldn't we---"

The president looked almost thoughtful. "Well, G-man, the first lady doesn't know a whole hell of a lot. But she knows two things. One, that she's a hell of a lot smarter than I am and a hell of a lot more driven to control the universe. And two, she knows I can't resist a skirt. She uses those two bits of information to stick her damn nose into everything. And what she can't control, she screws up."

"On purpose?"

"Who knows? And no one I know has the balls to ask her." He had been lying with one hand thrown over the back of the couch and the other over his eyes. Now he peeked between his fingers at Gearheardt and snapped, "Can we get by the Dr. Phil shit and just tell me what the hell we're doing?"

"Got it," Gearheardt said. "Let me start by just listing the major players in your plan."

"I'm not so sure I want it to be *my* plan. What if it doesn't work? Presidents can be held accountable, you know."

"It's an unfair part of the job, Mr. President, but let me go on."

Gearheardt then wrote:

Federal Reserve—armed and frontline troops, loyal

Wall Street Investment Banks—the enemy, not loyal

U.S. Marine Corps—operational control, logistics, unknown loyalty

Savings and Loan Industry—dumb as stumps, broke

Commercial Banks—clueless and potentially adversarial

U.S. general population—Screw 'em

The president started to speak but Gearheardt rushed ahead. "No one will see this, Mr. President, except for the first lady of course, and I'm just making a note of your general statement that who controls the money in America, or the world, should be of no concern to the average Joe as long as he has beer, bed, and bacon. I believe that was your position."

"Well, it don't look quite as, let's say News Friendly, when you write it out like that."

"Just so, Mr. President, but let me continue. This briefing is close to interminable."

Gearheardt turned back to the white board and wrote:

Russian banks—dupes

European banks—make Russian banks look smart

Saudi Royal Family—must have

Nigerian Trust Fund—scapegoat

"Damn, Gearheardt, I don't remember inviting all those bullshit organizations into this party."

"I think the acronyms might have confused you, Mr. President. This is from the org chart I prepared and first presented to you out in Langley."

"The CIA knows about this deal?"

"Yes, sir. I believe Miss Beavers was showing you around the building when we went over the part about their involvement. I believe you had the three-hour tour. Keep in mind that I work for them and Jack works for me. Or the Pygmy at times."

"The little prick."

Gearheardt continued, speaking and drawing arrows, boxes, and various symbols emanating about from the center circle.

"On D-day, Mr. President, the Federal Reserve employees, disguised as Russians acting as if they are everyday American savings and loan employees, will stage an attack on lower Manhattan directly opposite the Statue of Liberty. Where we were today," Gearheardt said, turning around to see if the president was even listening. He continued.

"On that day, you will issue an executive order declaring a bank holiday and the nationalization of the savings and loan industry. As the day—"

"I'm gonna what?"

"We'll emphasize the holiday aspect, sir, and assume the industry leaders, all hoping that someone, somewhere, will bail them out, will not make much of a fuss."

"Okay, I'm going to just lay here and listen. We're never going to finish this damn briefing if you insist on interrupting me every damn minute."

Gearheardt wisely ignored the ridiculous jab. "Right. So, you have the players. And there are some cabinet members we can drag in if we need people to blame. Mr. President, if I can have your full attention for just a minute or two."

"I was just scratching an itch on the plumbing."

"Yessir. The invasion of Wall Street will commence as soon as you declare a bank holiday and nationalize the financial institutions. We'll have the Russians staged on Ellis Island the night before. The Marines, experts at this kind of thing, by the way, will point the Russian/Federal Reserve/Savings and Loan employees—"

"Damn it, which *are* they?"

"Yes, Mr. President, that's the point. But remember, the attack on Wall Street, which will be spectacular by the way, is just a diversion."

"The main course must be a doozy if a few thousand folks hitting Manhattan with artillery and infantry is the diversion."

"It is, and this is where you come in. When the blood starts flowing on Wall Street and the investment banks are rubble and body parts, you lower the boom."

The president sat up. "I like this part, but I don't see us getting rich yet."

"You follow up the nationalization of the savings and loan industry with an edict that all the S and Ls have to mark to market by the end of the month."

The president stared at Gearheardt. For a long time. Finally, he said, "That's the damn boom I'm gonna lower? That's your big plan. Doing this market marking deal?"

"Mr. President, the financial industries execs would rather feed their daughters limb by limb to rabid warthogs than mark to market."

"Let's pretend I'm not a genius, which I am, Gearheardt, and explain to me how this is to work." The president found a beer bottle on the coffee table, held it up to the light to see if it was empty, upended it into his mouth, and lay back on the couch.

"Yessir, but first let me explain the end game. Remember, we're taking over the savings and loan industry as a first step in controlling all the money in the world."

"I like the sound of that," the president said, not opening his eyes.

"Well, the problem we have at the beginning, when we offer to buy all the savings and loans, is that some folks might not want to sell."

"The unpatriotic bastards."

"Yes, you and I agree. But in short form, having everyone mark to market will make owning a savings and loan about as desirable as having that disease where you vomit diarrhea all the time."

The president raised his head and looked at Gearheardt. "There's a disease like that?"

"I'm not a doctor, Mr. President."

"Yeah, go on." He dropped his head and closed his eyes again. Across the elegantly decorated room a grandfather clock chimed three times. The president threw a beer bottle at it. There was the tinkle of falling glass and the clock gave out one more sickly chime.

"You know how much that clock was worth, G-man?"

"I have no idea, sir."

"Yeah, me neither. The White House is full of old crap like that. I think Harry Truman got it from Hitler or something." He sighed, "Go ahead."

"I kind of doubt that Mr. President. Okay, quickly, years ago savings and loans could only make home loans. And they had a formula for how much to loan and interest rates, blah, blah, blah. So, they got together and asked the government, which in effect guarantees their loans, to let them make commercial loans. Like on office buildings, hotels, and factories and things like that. So, they did, and got royally screwed by every borrower this side of Bangladesh."

"Why was that?" The president sat up and looked interested.

"Basically, you had three types of borrowers. Folks looking to buy homes. Big city types who knew numbers better than their mother's breasts. And out and out crooks who often came out of the savings and loan business. Of course, there were a few honest and reasonable real estate developers who actually thought their project would work."

"So, some of those, at least, worked?"

"Not many. See, all of them, crooks and not-so-crooked, were relying on the same formula, shall we say. You had guys in twenty-five-hundred-dollar suits sitting down with guys in polyester pants, white socks and short sleeve white shirts. The suits threw out numbers and statistics like a rotary grass spreader. The savings and loans weren't all crooked. They were just overwhelmed. And the suits had one basic deal point which could not be argued."

"Which was?"

"Which was that all real estate projects would increase in value every year and, at the end of so many years, there would be greater fools to buy the real estate so that *they* could hold it and sell it to another guy."

The president was now perched on the side of the couch, intently listening to every word Gearheardt said.

"Well," he said as Gearheardt paused to light a cigarette, "if that isn't' true, I've got some brokers and partners back in the great state of Oklahoma with some 'splainin' to do." He was pensive for a moment. "So, what's with the mark-to-market *bomb* I'm supposed to drop?"

"Simply say to the FSLIC and the FDIC that all financial institutions must examine every asset they have loaned against and mark the value on their books as what the asset is worth in the market at the present time."

"None of that greater fool, B.S. then, huh?"

"Exactly, Mr. President. And I have done some numbers which show the approximate write-down in value of the nationwide loan portfolio will be nearly a trillion dollars. A number actually greater than the total size of the industry."

"Whoa, Nelly. Why would I want to own that mass of odorous malignancy?"

"Well, first of all we could cut that loss to a manageable five hundred billion. Second, we make a deal with Wall Street—remember we should be in control in a short while—to loan us enough to recapitalize the savings and loan industry. Then—"

"And why would anyone, even us, want to do that, Gearheardt?"

"The U.S. government would guarantee the Wall Street loan to the savings and loan."

"Mmm Humm. Makes sense." The president was trying to re-ignite the cigar he dug out of the overflowing ashtray. "I got pals over in the House who would guarantee that water burns if I gave 'em a nickel." Successful, he leaned his head back against couch and blew a smoke circle.

"And even if the loans default by the millions, the government is only on the hook for the lost interest."

"Because--?"

"The way Wall Street gets the money to loan us is from selling the mortgage portfolios to European banks."

"And why in the hell would the European banks buy the loans on millions of home mortgages and half-assed real estate deals?" The president sat, his head resting on the back of the couch, his arms folded across his chest, staring up at the ceiling. He was obviously interested in Gearheardt's explanation of the plan. "And where do the Russians come in?"

"Well, and again, Mr. President, I'm only hitting the high points, the American bankers were at least smart enough to package the loans in tranches. So many good loans were A loans down to D loans which were highly risky."

"But you said that most of the loans are bullshit if they're marked to market."

"But the genius of the D tranche, the wildly risky loans sold at deep discounts, made the A tranche loans seem almost solid."

"And the Russians?"

"The European banks quickly realized they had been bamboozled. So, they repackaged the loans and sold them to the Russians."

"Who bought them because….."

"The European banks convinced the Russians that by *calling* the millions of home mortgages they could basically conquer America in foreclosure."

"There's a lot to like about those damn Russians." The president laughed and slapped his knee. "We'll never let those bastards foreclose on all the homes owned by the good people of America. I can see your scheme now."

"Well, actually we would, Mr. President. In fact, the Federal Reserve and the Supreme Court have already prepared a document allowing Russians to foreclose. See, the Federal Reserve handled all the financial transactions for the Russian central bank, and they've made a deal. The Supreme Court—"

"Ours?"

"Yessir," Gearheardt answered. "The Supreme Court couldn't find anything in the constitution to prohibit Russian banks from foreclosing on American homes."

"Well, I'll be damned. Are you telling me we've wasted about three jillion dollars on missiles so that the Russians could just walk in here with a deed of trust or something and plant their asses down in American neighborhoods. Seems the American banking system has outsmarted itself." He mused. "Not the first time I guess. Didn't they screw up the stock market a few years back?"

Gearheardt, his throat parched, inadvertently took a drink from the glass the president had been using as an ashtray. He spewed the beer and cigar ash mixture onto the floor.

"You have any idea what that carpet you just puked on cost the American taxpayers?"

Gearheardt wiped his chin. "I have no idea, but—"

"Well I don't either, but you can bet your ass the White House decorators didn't order it out of the Sears Catalogue." He lay back on the couch. "Is there a plan in this damn pile of dog manure that I'm missing? Everything you've told me leads me to the assumption that the dumbass bankers in the country have sold us out to the Russians. And I'm sure they took a mighty good slice of that pie as it went down the chute."

He sighed and straightened the presidential robe around his legs. "If I had wanted to sponsor a drunk-monkey-dance-and-intercourse-get-together, I wouldn't have needed you, G-man. Someone told me, and I think it might have been you, that you and your pal were topnotch deal men." He opened his eyes and glared at Gearheardt. "And I'm not too damn sure I want to own the whole damn savings and loan industry."

Gearheardt straightened his tie and spit one more batch of coffee tobacco juice into a cup. "Mr. President, it is true that we sold the mortgages on roughly 70 percent of American homes to the European Banks. And they sold the package to the Russians, who will shortly own the majority of the American neighborhoods. And after that, as the escrow agents for mortgages, Slick Savings and Loan, us, will send the Russians a real estate tax bill of approximately three point six five trillion dollars."

"Lord love a duck, Gearheardt. I like it."

Chapter 11 (Pun Intended)

Jack was skeptical.

"No, Jack, I'm telling you," Gearheardt said, "he thought the whole scheme was something he cooked up himself."

Gearheardt was shaving, a towel wrapped around his waist, and talking to Jack through the open door.

Jack stopped his pacing. "What the heck does that mean? This was the Agency's scheme, taking over the financial system, right?"

Gearheardt toweled the remaining shaving cream off his face and went to the closet near the hotel room door. "Jack, how do you think it would look if the CIA controlled the currency? Heads would blow up. Fear of some kind of exploitation would run rampant in the streets." Gearheardt stopped buttoning up his freshly ironed shirt. "You know, I've always liked that term—running rampant. *I think I'll run rampant today.* Is that what a guy says to his wife when he leaves the house?"

Jack sat down in the desk chair. "Knock off the jacking around, Gearheardt. I understand the Agency can't really operate in the U.S.—"

"Yeah, right," Gearheardt scoffed.

"But I also get it that they can't just blatantly take over the financial system. I realize that there is subterfuge to the subterfuge."

"You got that right." Gearheardt, now putting on suit pants, turned. "Jack, if plans were simple and required no sneaking around and double-crossing and back-stabbing, the Little Sisters of the Poor could run the CIA. But when it comes to government work, there needs to be people who aren't concerned about the why or what. Or worrying about what the hell is going on. Like you always do."

"Pardon me for simply seeking clarity, Gearheardt. Which part of the plan is actually a plan, the military-like attack on Wall Street banks, the porno-backed monetary system, the president's savings and loan network owning the bulk of the U.S. retail banking outlets, or the fact that the Russians are going to wake up, as you said to the president, owing us three point five trillion dollars in real estate taxes? And am I forgetting anything?"

Gearheardt hesitated in mid-tie-tying. "Jack, it's really-"

"If you say, not that simple, I will shoot you."

"It's really three point SIX five trillion dollars, Jack."

A fully tricked-out Gearheardt sat down on the bed and put on shoes and socks. "The Willard is a damn nice hotel, you know."

"Answer me, you jackass."

"All of it is true, Jack. Maybe not all the same priority, but all of those need to work like clocks on a wheel."

"Which isn't an analogy at all."

"If you say so. The genius, if I do say so myself, is to play off one institution's agenda against another where each becomes a diversion for the other."

"I wish I could believe you know what the hell you're talking about, Gearheardt." Jack paused and, looking out the window onto Pennsylvania Avenue, sighed deeply, then turned back to Gearheardt. "I guess this is where I either strangle you to put you out of your misery, or say 'gee, that's so crazy it just might work.'"

"You couldn't strangle a baby kitten, Jack." He stood up and held out his arms. "How do I look?"

"Like a million dollars. Which is what this hotel is costing someone. Who's actually paying for those hoodlums and bankers I met the other night?"

Gearheardt beamed. Looking good is worth it, he always said. Leaving the actual meaning a bit vague.

"I think Countrysidecommunity Savings and Loan is picking up the tab. You came here on one of their credit cards, from your consulting gig with them, and I kind of used that card to take care of the boys."

"I'm sure they won't mind. They're broke and living off kickbacks and other people's deposits anyway,"

Gearheardt moved in front of the door mirror and put the finishing touches on his tie knot. "They've got plenty of cash now, Jack. They've issued about a hundred million in jumbo CD's since you left. The government guarantees them, you know. Up to a hundred grand." One last adjustment and he turned back to Jack. "You ready to head out?"

Jack stood. "And that would be going where?" He frowned. "Wait a minute. Countryside community Savings and Loan is dead nuts broke. How are they doing the CD business? Wouldn't that be illegal?"

Gearheardt pocketed his room key. "Not unless they've made stealing illegal."

"Perish the thought. We're talking banking rules here."

"And we're heading to the United States Senate building."

"You said we we're not going to involve congress."

"And we weren't," Gearheardt sounded cranky, "until some ass at the Federal Home Loan Bank got hammered and passed on the rumor he had heard from his mistress that the president was taking over the savings and loan industry. And said mistress asked her other boyfriend, who is a gay senator and only using her for cover, if she should move her account to a commercial bank."

They stepped into the hall. "Can you tell me again about the Federal Home Loan bank and the FDIC and the FSLIC," Jack asked. "And by the way, I need to stop by my room and get my raincoat."

Waiting for the elevator, Gearheardt expounded. "The Federal Home Loan Bank is the governing body for savings and loans and the FSLIC is the organization that insures the savings and loans. The FDIC does the same for commercial banks. The FSLIC and FDIC are direct pipelines to the taxpayer so that a lending institution gets to spread its losses over all citizens. This is the American way."

The elevator door opened and released a small yappy dog on a chain attached to a petite matron's hand. "If that dog yaps again tonight, I'm going to break down your door and set fire to your bed," Gearheardt said to the startled woman. "And I'll roast 'yippy' there on a spit."

Jack and Gearheardt stepped in the elevator. Jack shrugged at the stunned woman as the door closed.

"Gearheardt, I know all that crap about the acronym institutions. I meant, where are they in this deal and why are we going to the senate?"

"Fizz-lick and Fed-dick, as they're called, will be out of business when Slick Savings takes over. They've already started lobbying for the senate to have us killed."

"I figured that was coming," Jack said.

Gearheardt laughed. "I actually thought you would be pissed, Jack. Seems like every time we get into some kind of a scrape, you're always worrying about someone killing you."

The elevator stopped and the door opened. Both men got out and Gearheardt followed Jack down the hall.

"Be honest with yourself, Jack. Has anyone ever killed you?"

Jack stopped and opened the door to his room, looking back at Gearheardt. "You're really the most annoying bastard in the world, Gearheardt."

"Thanks, Jack," Gearheardt said, pushing by him into the room. "Holy Toledo!" he said.

The room was a complete wreck. Bed tossed. Chairs broken. Mirror shattered. Bland, manufactured picture of a field of flowers slashed. Jack's clothes and toilet articles were spread about the room.

"Well, I don't like the looks of this, Jack," Gearheardt said, shoving aside a rumpled suit coat and sitting on the edge of the bed. "Who have you pissed off?"

Jack was poking through the ruins of his belongings. He stopped and looked at Gearheardt with death rays. "Didn't you just say someone was going to have me killed? Any chance this is connected to that, genius?"

"Always a possibility, Jack. But you might note that the message written on the wall spells America with a K."

Jack turned a chair right-side up and looked at the wall. "It also threatens to torture and murder my mother. My mother is dead."

"Well, thank God for that."

They sat in silence for a few minutes, surveying the damage and looking for other clues as to why and by who.

"I'm sorry to hear about your mother, by the way."

"You went to her funeral, Gearheardt."

"That was your *mother*?"

"Just shut up for a minute. I need to call the front desk and—"

"And they'll call the cops and you will tell them what? That some Russians tore up your room because we're screwing them in the mortgage deal?"

"So, what *do* we tell them?"

"We don't report it. There is no good reason for Russians to trash a guy's hotel room unless some kind of international monkey business is behind it." He paused. "You're not screwing some Russian guy's wife, are you?"

"No."

"That was the only other reason I could think of. And believe me, those bastards will do more than trash your hotel room if you screw their girlfriends."

Jack didn't want to ask how Gearheardt knew.

Gearheardt stood and began putting things in a semblance of order. Commenting frequently, and irritatingly, about Jack's poor taste in clothing.

Finally, they took a last look around and started for the door.

"Gearheardt, you mentioned that someone was lobbying the senate to have me taken out of the savings and loan deal."

"Actually, I said to 'kill you' but I understand your choice of words."

"But this appears to be the Russians work. Is there a tie between them, the Russians and the senate?"

Gearheardt paused at the door, turning to admire the professional trashing job. "The only connection I know in the mortgage deal, and this, I know for certain, is between the Russian oligarchy and the President's wife."

He took the 'Make Room Now" door hanger and handed it to Jack. "Better let the maids know this needs some tending to."

As he closed the door, Jack said, "So you think we just act like nothing has happened? That's your plan?"

"Well, it's not my room, Jack. And the credit card is not my credit card. No blood on the carpet and no fires started. The maid will be pleased."

Waiting for their transportation, Gearheardt gave Jack a lecture about dealing with Congress. "You know I was the CIA liaison officer to Congress at one time, Jack."

"I somehow doubt that, Gearheardt. Keep in mind that I actually know you."

"Well, it wasn't official, I'll give you that. It was more in the dirty tricks and intimidation area."

"That, I believe."

"The secret to talking to a Congressman is not to waste his time on anything unpleasant unless there's a law he can pass which gathers votes at home."

"Even for a cynic that's pretty harsh." Jack noticed a few well-suited and tied men nearby glaring at Gearheardt who was his usual loud self.

"Cynicism has nothing to do with it, Jack. Congressmen don't have a lot of spare time except for the half year they're not in session. Besides law-passing which other people have to follow, they've got to deal with feathering their nest. In modern times, not a single senator has retired to work at Burger Whopper."

"Amazing. Where's this car you said you arranged?"

Gearheardt lowered his voice and leaned into Jack. "Here's the point, Jack. We're headed to Congress just so they can't claim complete ignorance of what we're doing."

"What ARE we doing?'

"That's immaterial. Remember this is all about money. The central, THE central issue in running a government. Let me give you some history. You're heard the term 'reaching across the aisle' right?"

"Sure."

"The original saying was 'reach across the trough.' Money was poured in a large trough and each Representative, with the senior member at the front of the trough, could reach in and take what he needed by dropping in the description of a project he needed funded."

"Oh, for Pete sakes, Gearheardt."

"Seriously. And they were men of honor, so they only took out what they legitimately felt was defensible if caught. But in one session, the junior rep for Montana only found eight cents left in the trough for a sewer project and shot up the room. Now they divvy up the money secretly and leave town before the budget is revealed."

"Why are you telling me this?" Jack asked.

"Because we're about to hear a load of bullshit about the health of the U.S. financial system and I don't want you all teary-eyed when you hear the Senators sad stories and their sacrifices and devotion to the American people."

The car arrived. "And also, Jack," Gearheardt said as he climbed in, "there is a factor of complicitness which must be addressed before any action can succeed in D.C. I've got a Representative. I need a senator."

The chauffeured drive to the Senate building was uneventful. Gearheardt was not in a talking mood. And Jack still worried about the hotel damage. After a brief scuffle at the security point, Gearheardt not wanting to relinquish his pistol, they were escorted to the offices of Senator F.W. Sensor.

Who greeted Gearheardt like a long-lost brother-in-law who had returned to try to borrow money. "Good to see you, Gearheardt. I'm due on the floor in a few minutes but can always make time for you. Come on into my office."

The senator from Wyoming had decorated his office exactly like a stable. A saddle on a barrel was the centerpiece and, although the senator took a seat at a desk, Jack imagined that he often sat on the saddle and slapped his hat against his chaps. He looked like that kind of guy.

Gearheardt and Jack sat on tractor seats, singularly uncomfortable pieces of furniture if you could call them that. Gearheardt kicked away the straw so that his feet touched the wooden floor. "Senator, I think you know why we're here. As the head of the senate finance committee, you have the capability—"

"You have no idea of the responsibilities of that position, my friend. The financial fate of many a citizen often rests heavily upon this old cowboy's shoulders.

"—to bring attention to a potential foreign entity engaging in illegal financial transactions or, on the other hand, ignoring it completely.

"When I was in law school at the University of Wyoming at Elbow Ridge, I often pondered my future and without doubt committed my life to the service of this great country. And it is, as you say, within my purview to investigate irregularities of a serious nature in the, shall we call it the financial eco-system, the multitude of transactions which facilitates goods and services to all constituents, not just those of my beloved Wyoming. Yes."

The senator's phone buzzed. He picked up the receiver, holding a slim finger up to Jack and Gearheardt.

"Senator F.W. Sensor speaking."

Gearheardt looked at Jack. "Do you know why they spread straw on the stable floor, Jack? It's to make it easier to clean up the horse shit."

The senator spoke a few quiet words into the phone and hung it up. "They want me down on the floor, it seems."

"Let's get right to it then," Gearheardt began. "The word on the street is that someone is asking someone in the senate, namely you, to have Jack killed and pass a law preventing foreign entities from owning mortgages on American homes."

The senator smiled at Gearheardt and began trimming his fingernails with a Bowie knife he took from a drawer. "Let's say, for the sake of argument, that what you say is correct. How would you prefer I respond to such a charge?"

"Well, for starters, killing Jack is not a good idea. But I'm not worried about that right now."

Jack looked at Gearheardt but could not catch his eye.

"The fact is that there are a number of people who would prefer that any foreign entities or individuals, say like

Russians for example, can own any damn thing they want. If they're willing to pay for it." Gearheardt was talking to the senator in a firm voice.

"Out of the question. The ownership of a home is the bedrock of a great de—"

Gearheardt jumped up. "Listen, you gob of spit. I've listened to all the duck-billed platitudes I can stomach. You knew why I was coming over here. Just tell me what you want and then stay in your stall until we need you." He sat back down.

"Gearheardt," the senator's face was red and contorted, "you will not speak to me in such a manner in my own office. Even if you were to offer the CIA's agreement to redirect funding for secret agency functions to Casper, I wouldn't budge."

"Consider it done."

The senator rose and came around the desk. Gearheardt and I rose from the butt-pinching tractor seats.

"Russians have the right to homes too. Any good American doesn't want homeless Russians camping in the streets." The senator smiled.

The three of us headed toward the door. The senator rested one hand on Gearheardt's shoulder and grasped his hand with the other. "*One-Eyed Jacks?*" he asked.

Gearheardt smiled. "And don't kill Jack, either."

"Out of my hands, Gearheardt." The senator shook Jack's hand. "Sorry, son."

Through the security exit and outside, Jack stopped Gearheardt. "Listen—"

"Oh, don't worry about it. Have I ever let anyone kill you?" Gearheardt held up his arm to signal a passing taxi, which ignored him.

"Let's walk awhile, Gearheardt," Jack said.

They headed toward the mall, threading through throngs of ordinary citizens doing ordinary things. Like not getting killed by Russian mortgage gangs.

"Jack," Gearheardt began, "have you noticed that every time we work on a project together, you seem to attract Russians who are trying to kill you?"

"You have my apology, Gearheardt. Endangering your life by exposing you to ill-aimed attempts to shoot me is unforgivable."

"No need to apologize, Jack. It would—"

"I'm being sarcastic, you jackass. Believe it not, there are very few attempts on my life when I'm not around you and your hare-brained schemes."

Gearheardt stepped off the sidewalk into the path of a speeding taxi. Which blared its horn as it screeched to halt. The driver was upset, if screaming and hand waving were any indication, and the customer in the backseat had only begun to protest as Gearheardt strode to the door, yanked it open and said, "Government business."

The man protested as Gearheardt began dragging him out, pointing at Jack and saying, "Russian mortgage holders are trying to kill this man! You don't want to be involved."

We left the open-mouthed citizen standing and staring. Soon, he would begin to wonder how he would describe what just happened to his family and friends.

"The Pentagon, Mohammed, and don't spare the horses."

"Not Mohammed," the driver said over his shoulder, burning rubber into the lane without the semblance of a signal or rearward check to see what was coming. "No horses. F***ing American people think everyone Mohammed." He continued ranting and pounding the steering wheel in a frenzy of anti-American people *verbal jihad* as he skillfully threaded traffic and approached the fourteenth street bridge.

"Why do you have to antagonize everyone you meet, Gearheardt? We could just---"

Gearheardt pointed to the license in plastic handing from the back of the seat.

"This license says your name is Mohammed."

"License lie." He slapped the steering wheel again. "F***ing license."

"Calm down, Mo-man. A change of destination. Take us to the Hilton in Crystal City."

Where we were deposited five minute later. The driver apoplectic as Gearheardt paid him in Cambodian riels.

"So why are we not at the Pentagon?" Jack asked.

Gearheardt watched the taxi until it turned the corner and disappeared.

"Jack, would you prefer racing up to the Pentagon checkpoint at about sixty miles an hour with Mohammed shouting anti-America profanity while he was beating the hell out of the steering wheel?"

"Well, since you put it that way—"

"Let me find a phone and call my Pentagon guy. He can meet us. I don't like going into the Pentagon anyway."

"I'm sure the feeling is mutual."

After a moment, Gearheardt returned. "It's a good thing we dodged the Pentagon. My pal says it's a madhouse. The rumor is going around that there's going to be a major attack on Wall Street and that the president is either behind it or against it." He started into the lobby bar, then turned as Jack started to follow him. "By the way, we need to be in Manhattan tomorrow morning. I'm going to have the Marines fly us up there."

"When we used the helicopter yesterday, the Marines seemed pretty unsure whether or not we were supposed to be using it."

"How were we supposed to get back and forth between DC and New York?"

"I don't think that's the Marine Corps' problem, Gearheardt."

They sat in the depressing atmosphere of a morning bar, each nursing a beer and both seemingly reflective. Jack watched as a large fellow sitting at the bar gulped two Bloody Mary's and signaled for a third. His briefcase was on the floor beside him, his shirt collar open with tie askew. Getting ready for another day, most likely, of hawking goods to the military.

Five years after he had left the Marine Corps, Jack still missed it. He knew that there were 'civilians' who loved their job. Felt they were contributing to…..whatever. But all emphasis was on just making more money. The guy at the bar looked like a good guy. But throwing down half a bottle of gin to face the day just seemed sad.

Jack noticed that Gearheardt was sitting with eyes closed, his hands folded on the table before him. His countenance peaceful and Jack wondered---

"You know what I think would have been a good idea, Jack," Gearheardt said, coming back to life. "If a woman's breasts were on the other side. You know, on her back. Then you could squeeze them every time you hugged. And the babies could just sit in little back—"

"Oh, for Pete's sake, Gearheardt. Is that what you've been sitting there thinking about?"

"Studies show that a man thinks about sex an average of—"

"Shut up, Gearheardt," Jack said, "just shut up. Can we not focus on the situation at hand? We're meeting some bozo from the Pentagon. Who and why?"

"This *bozo*, as you call him, happens to be the first cousin of Mrs. President. His name is Bryce Rogers, and he's a GS 59 or something like that. He handles weapon sales to NGOs and small pissant countries who aren't likely to turn around and use them against us."

"So, he's in the *pissant country* section of the Department of Defense?"

"I don't think there's an actual section that—oh, you were being sarcastic." Gearheardt smiled. "But basically, this guy knows every out-of-date, overstocked weapon in our inventory and gets great prices. I've used him before."

Jack started, "I'm sure you have. Wait, did you say out-of-date? Is that like, defective weapons?"

"Only when they misfire or blow up, Jack. Right now, they're perfectly fine." He paused and looked up from thumb-scraping the label from his beer bottle. "Did you think we would be using the newest weaponry in the U.S. arsenal to attack our own people?"

"I guess I never thought about it, Gearheardt."

A hand-grenade hit their table, shattering Jack's beer bottle before bouncing under the table next to them.

"Incoming" someone shouted, laughing at the same time.

Gearheardt dove across the table, shoving Jack aside, and in one motion scooping up the hand grenade and drawing back to toss it through the front window. Then paused and inspected the object in his hand and dropped the fake grenade onto the table.

"Rogers, you son of a bitch. You scared the crap out of everybody."

"Ha, ha. No one ever forgets the first time he meets Bryce Rogers," he said, looking at Jack.

"But everyone wishes they could," Gearheardt said, sitting back down.

"I assume this is Jack?" Rogers pointed at Jack as he drew up a chair. He was a large man, had a bowl haircut, an outlandishly painted tie, light blue polyester suit and white shoes.

"No, that's *Roy* Rogers, your brother."

"Ha ha, good one, Gearheardt." He stuck out his hand, which Jack shook.

"Nice getup, Rogers. You know light blue polyester suits and white shoes went out of style, assuming you call hillbilly outfits a style, ten years ago." Gearheardt signaled for the waitress to bring three beers.

"I guess I'm living proof that's a lie, Gearheardt. Ha ha." Rogers pulled a sheath of papers out of his thin briefcase and spread them on the table. Soaking up what remained of Jack's beer. "Shit," he said. After brushing off most of the beer and wiping the papers on his pants, he started again. "So, let's get down to tass bracks."

Jack leaned forward. "Down to what?"

"Rogers thinks it the height of hilarity to reverse the first letters of word in a phrase. He means brass tacks."

"Thanks for the edumumcation, Gearheardt."

Gearheardt groaned. "What have you got?"

"First, I've *got* to wring out my pants." Rogers rose and lumbered off toward the lobby.

"Does this guy actually have a line on something we need, Gearheardt? He seems goofier than a drunk bat."

"Not sure bats are big drinkers, Jack. But I know what you mean." He looked into the lobby at Rogers lurching toward the men's room. "Rogers was one of the shitter-dwellers, Jack. I've told you about them. Guys who were stationed in the various government office bathrooms who listened to the chatter all day and developed substantial intelligence about everything from love affairs to nuclear first strike contingencies."

"I thought you were just making that up."

"Nope, guys will stand together at the pissers and chat about the meetings they were just attending. Sharing amazing dope as they whiz. The shitter dwellers are usually standing at the urinals or camped out in the stalls, some with advanced listening devices. Rogers' cousin, Mrs. President, got him one of the choice shitters. Three different men's rooms in the Pentagon."

"So, this guy, this Rogers, is over in the Pentagon restrooms? That's who we're dealing with?"

Gearheardt laughed. "Rogers has had his own office suite and staff for years now. He spent five years on shitter detail and became one of the most powerful guys in the Department of Defense. Learned enough that he just moved into a vacant suite one weekend, assembled a staff, and began attending meetings."

"Five years?"

"He says if you follow some basic shitter rules, it's an easy living. First, always have your plumbing displayed. No one, and I mean *no* one, approaches a guy with his tool hanging out. Second, whistle *Somewhere Over the Rainbow* if anyone looks at you suspiciously. Finally, wear a lanyard around your neck with a nametag and random acronym printed on it."

"That's it?"

"Rogers was elected *Mr. Howdy* in the personality contest the Pentagon held last year." Gearheardt looked over Jack's shoulder. "Speak of the devil."

Rogers flopped back into his chair. "Where was I?"

Gearheardt tapped the papers. "Hopefully you were about to show us an inventory and price list for the weapons we need."

"Yep, and if I remember your request, you will be fighting in an urban environment. With little armor and no air cover. Will you have artillery or Gaval Nunfire support?"

"A little artillery and no *Naval Gunfire*. But we would like to leave the buildings intact as much as possible. We need mostly anti-personnel weapons and maybe some non-lethal gas."

"And you need these when?"

"Monday."

"Delivered where?"

"TBD. But most likely New Jersey."

Rogers' head snapped up. "Jew Nersey? As in New Jersey?"

"That's the one."

"Hmmm. The pygmy know about this?"

"Is this *Twenty Questions*, or a weapons purchase?" Gearheardt looked into Rogers' eyes without blinking.

Finally, Rogers looked back at the papers on the table. After smoothing out a beer-soaked corner he said, "Fifteen million dollars. FOB New Jersey. No refunds. No credit for duds. You sign a release and indemnity."

"You said five million on the phone."

"You didn't tell me you were domestic. Every Joe Blow you kill will have a family with an attorney before the old man checks into the Pinewood Hotel."

"Gee, Rogers, did you put a little something in there for yourself?"

"This is America, Gearheardt. I'm suspicious of anyone who doesn't overcharge."

"I got it. Just seems...unpatriotic to overcharge me for attacking our own citizens."

Rogers set his jaw. "Fifteen million, Gearheardt. And I need the first half tomorrow if I have to deliver to Jersey on Monday." He pointed to a signature line on the bottom sheet and offered Gearheardt a pen. Gearheardt signed.

"Nice doing business with you, boys." He looked at his watch. "The Shitter Squad alumni have lunch today if you guys want to come along. I'll be expecting the first seven point five million in my account by close of business today." He rose, bowed to each of us, sarcastically executed, and turned to leave.

Gearheardt said, "You said tomorrow! And the next time you do that reverse letters crap, I'm stabbing you in the throat."

"Lee you sater."

The Twelfth of Chapters

"**You boys** need weapon?" It was the gent on the bar stool, slurping down his fourth Bloody Mary.

Jack started to answer, but Gearheardt held up his hand. "Need weapon?" he said to the guy. "No, we need *weapons* and its none of your business."

"Not true," bar stool dweller replied. He rose, drained the last drop from his glass and sat down at our table. "Name is Bill," he said, holding out his large hand to be shaken. "Bill's business is weapon."

"Bill is not a Russian name," Gearheardt said.

"Bill is not Russian person," Bill replied. "Bill is Ukraine." He struggled to get his wallet from his back pocket, then extracted a business card, covered with hieroglyphics or maybe Ukrainian writing.

"Okay, let's assume you eavesdropped on the whole damn conversation with that loudmouth. And assume also that you know shit from Shinola about weapons. What's your proposition?"

"Bill get same weapons for you to Jersey at one half price. Plus, extra bullet."

"Well, I will assume you don't mean just one extra bullet, why would I want to buy unknown weapons from an unknown source even to save some money? And where, pray tell, would you get these weapons? At least with the Pentagon guys, I know where the weapons come from."

"Get same weapons."

"I understand. Same weapons. But where…..wait a minute. Are you saying you are selling me the same weapons the Pentagon is selling me?"

"Same."

"And how might that happen?" Gearheardt turned in his chair to face Bill head on.

But Jack jumped in. "Bill," he said, "how exactly would that work?" He was hoping to head off a long bullshit session that Gearheardt almost effortlessly engaged in with apparent bozos.

Bill signaled the waiter that a fifth Bloody Mary wouldn't be rejected. He plopped his briefcase on the table, withdrew a pad and pen, and dropped the briefcase back to the floor.

"Here is how plan work." He drew a circle and carefully wrote *'weapon/America'* in the circle. He drew an arrow to a second circle, inside of which he wrote *'country A'*. On the arrow he wrote *'weapon assist.'* A third circle was drawn named *'country B'*. He wrote *'steal no buy'* on the connecting arrow. Finally, a third arrow was drawn, labeled *'buy for $'* which pointed back to the original *'weapon/America'* circle.

"Pure frigging genius, Bill," Gearheardt said, slapping the smiling Ukrainian on the shoulder.

"Yes, genius," said Bill. Recognizing sarcasm was evidently not the Ukrainian's long suit.

Jack said, "Bill, even assuming your scheme or whatever it is might work, the time it would take to ship to different countries, go through any kind of customs, even ones which are paid-off, the sheer physical movement of tons of equipment would take—"

"Weapons already here."

"Yes, I know, but---"

"Weapons will not leave here. Country A, maybe like Egypt, not Egypt but like Egypt which get free weapons from America, say they receive weapons."

"But they don't?"

"No need. My country, Ukraine steal weapons."

Gearheardt leaned forward. "I think I see where this is going."

"So, the Ukraine steal the weapon, leaving Egypt off the hook. And then the Ukraine guys sell the weapon to us."

You could tell Gearheardt liked it.

"But the Ukraine could be accused of stealing hundreds of millions of dollars of weapons and—" Jack stopped.

Bill said, "What weapons? How can Ukraine steal weapon which Egypt do not have?" He gave a lopsided grin to Gearheardt, then stopped as if suddenly remembering something. "And country A is not Egypt. I say Egypt but not Egypt."

Gearheardt said, "So we can assume it really is Egypt."

Ukraine Bill shrugged and waved his hand, "It does not matter. So, I am to have a deal?"

Gearheardt looked at Jack. It was Jack's turn to shrug.

"Who knows who is to be trusted in a swindle operation."

Gearheardt also shrugged and stood up.

"Let me make a couple of calls. You and Jack can have a few more Bloody Marys."

Jack started to protest but decided he could use a few Bloody Marys and he had absolutely no input on the veracity of Ukraine Bill. Who had by this time succeeded in ordering more Bloody Marys.

Gearheardt left and Jack watched as Ukraine Bill collected the pretzel dishes from the surrounding tables and proceeded to crunch through handfuls of pretzels with reckless abandon. When the bowls were empty, he began meticulously picking the larger pretzel pieces from the front of his shirt. After brushing off the remaining crumbs, he turned to Jack.

"I am also to be *Bill the hostage*. That will make it work right."

"I'm not sure what you're talking about. You mean—"

"I will stay with you for hostage until weapon delivered and you are satisfied." It seemed a directive rather than the answer to an unasked question.

"That's great news, Bill." Again relying on Bill's inability to recognize sarcasm.

Half an hour later, Gearheardt returned. As he approached the table he gave a thumbs up. "You checked out, Bill. We've got a deal."

"And guess what, Gearheardt, Bill here is going to be our insurance."

"Perfect." He sat down and looked at Bill's grinning face and then at Jack's not-grinning face. "You're not kidding?"

"We've just inherited the Bloody Mary king of the Ukraine. And he likes pretzels."

Bill produced a document from his briefcase and held it and a pen out to Gearheardt. Who signed without even glancing at the contract.

Bill said, "You boys need soldier persons, too?"

"I suppose you supply Ukrainian mercenaries for small wars."

Jack couldn't actually tell if Gearheardt was truly interested.

"No Ukrainian. Hawaiian. We have exclusive. Non-traceable."

Gearheardt said, "Let me think it over."

"Okay, Bill should visit relax room. Then maybe we go to eat. Have Bloody Mary."

He left after handing his briefcase to Jack to watch over.

"Charming," Jack said. "How in God's name did you check him out? The guy's half idiot."

"Maybe so, Jack. But the other half is Bryce Roger's partner."

"Didn't you say that Rogers is Mrs. President's---"

"Yes, I did, Jack. And that was the second call I made. I think everyone is covered."

On the street, Gearheardt and Bill negotiated the price of Hawaiian mercenaries and Gearheardt bought two dozen. Jack's head was swimming with information showcasing the rise of a shitter-detail man to a Pentagon-officed arms dealer in cahoots with a Ukrainian alcoholic and the wife of the President.

"Crime, war and profit make strange bed-fellows, Jack."

"Why didn't Rogers, who you say is the cousin-in-law of Mrs. President, recognize the Ukrainian? I mean if they're both associates of Mrs. President?"

Gearheardt chuckled. "Lord, Jack, you know an astonishing little about swindling. They're just trying to get a double commission. Mrs. President let the proverbial cat out of the bag, that's all."

"So, she screwed up the scheme?"

"No, she was trying to get us to cut her cousin-in-law out of the deal and take his share. The Ukrainian is her partner too. She's a pro, Jack."

Chapter 14

(actually 13, but unlucky to have 13 in the manuscript) (Crap, I've put it in) (Forget the 13) (Damn it, no XX, you know what I mean)

The following morning, after ditching Bill the Ukrainian in Georgetown blubbering in Bloody Mary mix with celery poking into his ears, it was decided that Jack would take the Marine helicopter to Manhattan while Gearheardt made sure the weapons were actually available and the money was being transferred.

"Where are we getting this money, Gearheardt?" Jack asked. They were in front of the Hilton, waiting for a cab for Jack.

"I made a deal to sell the package back to the Egyptians." He lit a cigarette and blew smoke over his shoulder. "Originally, it was coming from the presidential slush fund."

"Wait. If we use the package, how can we sell it back to the Egyptians? These are the same Egyptians who were definitely not Country B, right?"

"Yeah, sure," Gearheardt snorted. "That lying Ukrainian bastard. I just know he's cheating us some way. Anyway, the

Egyptians are borrowing the money from a Russian bank, First Moon Bank."

"Gearheardt, we're buying stolen weapons to attack American citizens, so the president can take over the financial system. And you're worried about the guy being dishonest?"

Gearheardt flipped his cigarette into the street. "You don't like this deal, do you, Jack?"

"It gets wormier every day."

"Why do—"

"Gearheardt, I'm with you because I believe that the country has gone bonkers over money, over profit, overpower—which means money—and to hell with everything else. Wall Street is not the disease, but it's damn sure a symptom that needs treating. As far as the president doing anything helpful for the country by controlling the financial system, he probably won't but he can't be worse." He paused. "And I'm doing it because the CIA asked me to do it. At the end of the day, you have to believe in something."

Jack paused and wiped his eyes. "And right now, the Central Intelligence Agency is the only sane voice in the country. They're not afraid to wear their allegiance on their sleeves."

"Right, Jack. Well said."

"You weren't even listening, were you?"

"I've got to get you a taxi, Jack. The Marine helicopter won't wait forever." Gearheardt stepped into the street and waved down a cab. "See you tomorrow evening. You know what you need to do, right?"

"Get a feel for whether or not the investment banks suspect anything or are on to the plan to attack them." Jack felt a bit of guilt at not having told Gearheardt that Edwards was going to accompany him. In their brief chat last evening, Edwards said that he believed he knew the real reason for all the talk of attacks and mortgages and Russians.

Gearheardt shook his hand and started back into the hotel to prepare for his next meeting, a chat with an arms specialist who would handle the logistics of dispersal.

"Wait!" Jack yelled, stepping back out of the taxi. "The Russians have a bank on the damn moon?"

"They're not as dumb as they look, Jack." He gave a thumbs up and disappeared.

Jack arrived at a helipad at Quantico and found the Marine helicopter crew had been waiting for him. The crewchief, throwing a K-Bar at squirrels with the encouragement of the ground crew, came over and assisted in getting him into the aircraft. The pilots, a first lieutenant and a captain, neither of whom looked over sixteen years old, climbed into the cockpit while still playing liars dice—taking turns holding the cup while they strapped in.

Jack asked the crew chief, "Is this the helicopter that flies the president?"

It smelled like diesel, dirty clothes, and sweat. The seats were canvas benches running along the sides of the cabin. Wire and aluminum were the primary decorating motifs.

The crew chief, plugged into the aircraft intercom, laughed and said into the mike, "This guy wants to know if we fly the president around."

He laughed and leaned toward Jack, "Yeah, we're picking him up on the way to New York. You'll have to scoot down to make room for the first lady." He laughed again.

The engine started with a roar and any talk now was impossible except on the intercom or leaning until lips touched ears.

Jack stood up and waved at the crew chief who was hanging out of the door.

"Hey, there's another guy supposed to be here! Edwards! Any sign of him?" Jack had to shout.

"This him running up here?"

Edwards ran from an adjacent parking lot, threw a small bag into the helicopter and jumped in.

"I've been over at the White House lawn since first thing this morning. I thought you said Marine One!"

"That damn Gearheardt did. Not me."

Edwards started to strap in, sitting on the canvas bench next to Jack.

"Scoot down and make room for the first lady," Jack said.

Edwards screwed his face into a question mark.

"Forget it," Jack said. He looked toward the crew chief and gave the signal for 'pulling the chocks.' The crew chief signaled the ground crew. The pilot gave them a quick salute and a few minutes later they were at fifteen hundred feet. Heading for New York.

Where they were deposited, on Staten Island, that afternoon. On the ferry into Manhattan, Edwards queried Jack. "Have you got all this figured out? I'm not sure who to believe. But even worse, I'm not sure *what* anyone believes."

Jack was still not comfortable leveling with Edwards. Gearheardt always had the effect of pulling back the spring and launching the pin ball with a scheme, then watching the ball bounce around between various traps and scoring points. And when the ball started for the final hole, he would hit the flappers and send it back careening around the board.

The idea was first taking over Wall Street. Then blackmailing people with pornography as the basis for the value behind the currency. Then it was using the Marines to fight the Federal Reserve employees who were the infantry. Or were the Marines on the other side? And what about the Russians? And now the Ukrainians. And the chance of losing a few trillion dollars in the derivatives market. But who would lose and who would win?

"Jack?" Edwards finally said.

"Just thinking things over, Edwards." He looked at the man standing next to him at the railing. "What's your first name, by the way? I can't call you by rank because it's changing every day."

"I don't have a first name. That's why I joined the army."

"Are you by any chance related to Gearheardt?"

"Why—"

"Never mind. Look, the fact is that I don't for a minute think anyone is actually going to start a shooting war between the Federal Government and Wall Street. This is all, in my opinion, an elaborate cover for something going on that someone wants to hide from the American people. Either a coup or a distraction from some colossal mistake."

"I'm not sure if that's encouraging or greatly disappointing," Edwards said. "So why are we heading to Wall Street and what are we going to try to find out?"

"I'm not sure. Ostensibly, I'm to find out if Wall Street has learned of the possibly impending attack and if they're preparing any kind of a counter-offensive."

"To the *not-going-to-happen* attack by the Federal Reserve employees?"

"Them, yes. And a platoon of Hawaiian mercenaries and untold battalions of Russian savings and loan owners, mostly not actually Russians."

Edwards wrinkled his brow. "I have to say I'm not completely following all that." He turned to Jack. "How did the Russians get in the middle of all this financial mess? You told me they had purchased billions of dollars of mortgages. They've never been astute inves—"

"But they had North Vietnam plus two. That paid off big for them."

"What does that mean?"

"They bet the spread that North Vietnam would win the war—"

"Didn't they?"

"Well, we thought we had won in 1973 and came home. But the Russians had plus two— years in this case— so they cleaned up."

"I never understood exactly how the US fell for that."

"Well, since the North Vietnamese had only been killing folks in South Vietnam, Laos and Cambodia for a dozen or so years, we of course believed that if we quit and came home, they would stop killing South Vietnamese."

Edwards grimaced. "It seems pretty stupid when you put it like that. Kind of one of those *'What were we thinking?'* situations."

The ferry was pulling into the dock at the south end of Manhattan Island. As Jack and Edwards began to leave the boat, the roar of two artillery shells passed overhead, one close behind the other. Moments later, the wall of a building near the terminal partly disintegrated in an explosion, followed by a similar explosion in the adjacent alleyway.

"I'll bet that damn Gearheardt is test-firing the 105s he bought, "Jack shouted as he dove for cover. "I'll strangle that bastard if I live through this."

After the dust had settled, Jack and Edwards made it to the offices of *Darkman and Darkman* without further interruption by artillery fire. The populace seemed to take the shelling in stride and only when passing the few wounded and slightly maimed were voices of loud consternation heard. New York, it was evident, was not to be distracted during the hours the Exchange was open.

"Charles Bestman, please," Jack said to the receptionist, "Edwards and Armstrong to see him."

With that message passed on, a disheveled gentleman shortly appeared. "I'm Bestman," he said, shoving his hand toward Jack, who shook it, "Gearheardt said you were dropping by. Coffee or anything?"

Both Jack and Edwards demurred and entered the lobby elevator. On the top floor, the three stepped into a glass-walled conference room. The shelves protruding from each of the end walls were loaded with clear plastic tablets containing announcements of merging, selling, buying and financing transactions—most notably in the hundreds of millions of dollars.

Seated at the head of the long table, Bestman spoke, "I assume the shelling just now was Gearheardt announcing the beginning of the siege."

Jack was taken aback, having believed his mission was to ferret out information about the secret planned invasion. Recovering, he said, "As it seems you know Gearheardt, you should know that assuming anything about Gearheardt is at best questionable."

Bestman laughed. "We can agree on that. And by the way, pardon my appearance. Some fist-fighting on the floor this afternoon and I didn't get a chance to spruce up." He laughed again. "You should have seen the other guy."

Edwards jumped in. "I can't remember much actual fist-fighting on the exchange floor in my day. A rival bank poaching or---"

"Oh no, our own guys fighting each other. My Alpha group was dumping mortgage packages and didn't bother informing the institutional boys down on three and they were buying the junk as fast as we could sell it. They lost quite a bit of money. Charged up here and tried to kick ass."

"And the Alpha group is—"

"We're not sure who we work for. We take buy or sell instructions over a wire and just dump, jump, or pump to our heart's content. We only know what the result is at the end of the month when guys are bonused-up or fired."

"Who does the research?" Edwards asked.

Bestman laughed. "Yeah."

Which wasn't much of an answer.

After a moment, Bestman asked, "Tell me again why you guys are here? It's not a very interesting place really. I think a lot of the guys are looking forward to this attack or whatever it's going to be. Most of them are so rich they're bored to tears. Even sex doesn't seem to get them excited."

"What about the chance of losing all that money? It would seem—" Jack started.

"Lose it to who? It never leaves Wall Street. Sure, some folks try to cash out every once in a while. But we get a fee for that and a fee for reinvesting it. And remember, we just trade pieces of paper. Or to be more precise, these days we just mostly trade computer inputs. It's not like we build anything or grow food." He smiled.

"You seem pretty cynical for what—thirty?" Edwards said.

"I'm not cynical, exactly. It's just that I found out after college that I didn't really have any particular skills and I didn't feel like doing a lot of hard labor. Wall Street seemed to be the place to put that kind of situation to work. We're the financial greasers that keep America growing and buildings built and farmers farming and lawyers—." His voice trailed off.

Jack looked partly concerned and a fair part disgusted. "Financial greasers?"

The conference room door opened and a fabulously attired gentlemen entered. "Stay seated, gents!" he said, although no one had begun to rise. The man, looking to be in his mid-forties, with shiny fingernails, a white collar on a light blue shirt, and one hundred percent comfortableness on his countenance, took a seat at the other end of the table.

"I'll handle it, Bestman," he said, the dismissal evident and understood by the soon to depart Bestman. The confident man, palms firmly on the table, began, "So, gents, my pal Gearheardt says I can level with you, and you, in turn, with me. Bestman had the best of intentions, no pun intended, but has only begun making his fortune here at *Darkman and Darkman*. Might be of interest that young men like Bestman are started at a salary which exactly matches the gross domestic product of Mozambique in 1966. We at *Darkman and Darkman* believe it is important that our young men, and a woman or two I've heard, can relate to their relative importance in the financial world."

Jack and Edwards nodded, not sure if nodding, laughing, or being disgusted was the answer to the dangling of irrelevant yet troubling information.

"And you are---"

"Jackson Beanable, Jack. We share that first name of course. The Beanable's were the first investors in *Darkman and*

Darkman. But that's not why I'm chairman of the board at only forty-three. My income last year matched Portugal's GDP."

Jack found himself fervently wishing he had a fortune so that he could not give it to this jerk to invest. "I'm sure that wasn't a factor, Jackson," he said. "Look, let's get down to tass bracks," he knew it would annoy this dolt, "and talk about the attack and your response. To be honest, I was surprised to find that you, and assumedly all of the Wall Street banks, are aware of the action."

"Au contraire. Jack." The guy winked.

"Ah, so the good man Gearheardt has struck some sort of deal with just you."

"You're quick, Jack. Quite—"

"I know Gearheardt like the back of my hand, Jackson. In fact, I should have suspected the fix was in when he asked me to come up here and see Bestman."

"Yes, Bestman was just the cutout, so to speak. If you had been a raving do-gooder or any other kind of asshole, you would have never gotten to me. I was watching and listening on the company watching and listening system."

"Is that the Acme Seven-Ten Series Watching and Listening System, Jackson?" Jack asked as insultingly as he could.

Beanable looked at Jack, then at Edwards, and then turned back to Jack. "You don't like me much, do you, Jack?"

"Is it a requirement?"

"No," he chuckled, "not at all. Very few people like incredibly rich people actually. I would suspect that you are not terribly wealthy."

"I'm considerably less wealthy than Portugal and dropping toward Haiti." After a long moment, Jack spoke again. "I'm not sure what this conversation is about. You obviously know something about a plan I believed was secret. And you know Gearheardt, right?"

"Yes, and yes. And I'm reasonably certain that you and...Edwards is it?...know more than you're letting on. Let's leave it at that., *Darkman and Darkman* is prepared to support the president and we expect to receive our just rewards. You can assure your partner of that."

"What about the derivatives?"

It was a lucky guess on Jack's part. A shock had ruffled Beanable's face for just a brief moment as derivatives were mentioned. He leaned forward, his forearms on the conference table. "I thought that was settled. What do you know about the derivatives?"

Jack glanced at Edwards, who shrugged. He was on his own in a subject far above his financial level. "Let me tell you about the derivative market, Beanable. When I lived in northern Thailand, and don't ask, I used to go out to the racetrack on Saturday mornings. It was a dirt circle, a run-down stable, and a set of wooden stands. The horses looked like they were tubercular and on their last carrot. The betting was handled by a guy who pushed a bicycle cart around taking money and giving out chits."

"I hope there's a point in this story. I've got some money to make today."

"But the betting was not on the best horse, a laughable term in fact. See, the races were all fixed and the betting was on which owner had the last bribe."

"Right, so the bets were on the highest bribe. Great, let's get back to—"

"No, the local samlor drivers, tough bastards who had calves like steel springs, ran the horse-drugging industry and, after the bribes, they doped the horses so that some horses actually collapsed in the starting gates and others flew around the track like greyhound banshees."

"I'm still hoping this story has a point, Jack. Out of courtesy to Gearheardt, I'm still listening. But getting pretty impatient. And a samlor is...."

"A samlor is a three wheel—sam is three in Thai—bicycle which is like a taxi. Kind of like a rickshaw."

Beanable rose and adjusted his jacket, then his tie. "This travelogue is enchanting, Jack. But I've made my deal. I expect Gearheardt and the president to live up to their side of the deal. Forget the derivatives. Way over your head."

Jack rose also. "You're betting on the horses, Beanable."

On the street after being all but perp-walked from the hallowed halls of *Darkman and Darkman,* Jack and Edwards looked for a taxi to hail. Fruitlessly. As they began walking toward the pier, where a Marine helicopter would await them, the windows of 327 Wall Street began to explode. A distant machine gun being the obvious cause. They hunkered behind a hotdog cart, waiting for Gearheardt's test firing to cease.

"What the hell?" Edwards said. "Is everyone insane?"

"In the immortal words of William Goldman—No one knows anything."

"He was talking about the movie industry, Jack."

Jack stood up, purchased a hot dog, and set off down the street again.

"Oh, would that government were as straightforward as the film industry, Edwards."

Chapter Sky

(because I believe we put too much faith in numbers)

"**Because** you're a damn maniac, that's why! There were fifty caliber bullets hitting just above my head. Fired by you!"

"Calm down, Jack. That's not a reason to get all cranky. If I went apeshit every time I had to deal with maniacs like me, I'd never get anything done."

Gearheardt signaled the waiter to bring more wine. Meeting after the ride back in the helicopter, they were at dinner in Blotto's, a drinking, dining, and bribing place near Dupont Circle in DC. The proprietor, formerly a lobbyist, wisely prohibited wearing a wire, and had two private rooms for procurement—Pentagon and Congressional—swept hourly. Everyone felt safe at Blotto's. Gearheardt, not willing to be patted down at the door, had been seated near the window in the *transparency* section.

"Order a steak, Jack. Just relax. I've got everything under control."

"Coming from you, that's not comforting, Gearheardt. What does that even mean?"

Gearheardt

The waiter delivered, presented, and opened the expensive bottle of wine. Gearheardt sipped and declared it drinkable.

"It means, Jack, that the people who have to have guns, have guns. The people who need to be paid have been paid. The people who will win have been notified and are happy as pigs. The—"

"What about the losers? Have they been notified?"

"I don't like that sarcastic tone, Jack. You're on the winning side, you know." Gearheardt reached out and shook the hand of a passing congressman. Jack wasn't sure of his name and the congressman certainly didn't know Jack.

"That was Congressman Woot—"

"I don't care who that was, Gearheardt."

"He would be sad to hear you say that. He's on the House banking committee and thinks he's on the winning team. Mark him as *not-happy-as-a-pig* when this is over."

Jack picked up the no-doubt extravagantly expensive wine bottle and drank from it.

"Whoa, Jack," Gearheardt said, laughing. "That's about twenty bucks a swallow and the raised numbers on the Countrysidecommunity Savings credit card are almost smoothed out."

Jack took another swallow and wiped his mouth on the linen napkin. "So, the poor folks of Anadarko, Oklahoma, are still footing the bill for you and the president taking over the financial system in America. That's just great."

"They're good people down there, Jack. They deserve to be on the team."

"You're screwing them out of their savings, Gearheardt!"

"That's kind of negative thinking, Jack. If the Russian mortgage guys—"

"Don't give me that Russian mortgage guys crap. I don't believe there are Russian mortgage guys within ten miles of this deal."

Gearheardt looked up at the hovering waiter and pointed to the lobster on the menu. "Is this grilled?" he asked.

"No, but it has been questioned harshly and finger-printed," the waiter said, straight-faced.

"Look, pal, we're involved in serious discussions about serious matters. The last thing we need is a wise-ass for a waiter."

"I've been standing here for fifteen minutes, sir. You waved me over to take your orders."

"Now, I'm waving you away. And bring us two lobsters." He looked at Jack as the waiter departed. "Yes, I'm always a pain in the ass. You don't have to say it."

He picked up the now empty wine bottle and looked toward the waiter disappearing into the kitchen. "No chance, I guess. Do you remember Ronald Reagan, Jack?"

"Let me think. Kind of familiar. Wasn't he the president of the United States a few years ago? Hard to think ba—"

"I was being rhetorical, Jack."

"No, you weren't. But go ahead with your story. I suppose you knew him."

The couple at the next table rose to leave and Gearheardt leaned over and grabbed their wine bottle. It looked a quarter full. After pouring a glass for himself, he held the bottle toward Jack. "You?"

"No thanks, I want to be clear-headed when you explain to me how a dead Ronald Reagan is in on this deal."

"Very funny, Jack. But the question was about Russian involvement. The connection is that Reagan knew exactly how to play the Russians. You dare them to challenge you. You are open and forthright with your plans. In his case, he told them that we were going to build Star Wars, a missile defense system in outer space which would render their weapons useless."

"Which we were actually going to build, and the Russians spent themselves broke trying to build their own or harden their targets, etcetera, etcetera. I know the story, Gearheardt."

"Well, that's most of the story. But the backstory is even better. When the Russians met Reagan in Iceland—"

"I'm not sure you have your timing right."

"—the president offered to loan them the money to build their own system."

"*What?*"

"Look, if the president had just played the trump card, leaving the Russians with no alternative, the Russians would have been forced to throw everything at us before Star Wars was completed. By offering to loan them—"

"Even *we're* not that stupid, Gearheardt."

"I haven't told you the genius part. Just hold on. The Russians had to apply for the loan to an American financial institution. The government couldn't be seen to be loaning that kind of money to people wanting to nuke us."

"Of course not."

"Gorbo put a couple of dozen of his top economists to work on the loan application. Getting the damn appraisals alone was a nightmare. Military equipment, the Kremlin, they even tried to get Siberia listed as vacation property."

"I don't believe a word of this crap."

"I was on the loan committee, Jack. I was the CIA representative. The others on the committee were just savings and loan guys. Wore white short-sleeve shirts and white socks every day. Drove the damn Russians nuts going over the paperwork."

"I don't believe a word you're saying. What financial institution would waste its time reviewing a loan application from Russia to finance a missile defense system?"

Gearheardt downed the rest of his wine and smiled.

"Jack, when you were at Countrysidecommunity Savings and Loan, did you ever notice a subsidiary called Countrysidecommunity International? Based right here in DC."

Jack was silent. His face was empty of any positive emotion.

"That was just to handle regulatory issues," he said.

"Sure it was," Gearheardt said sarcastically.

"And I was sent to Anadarko to—"

"Keep the lid on any information that might have leaked back to the dolts running the local shop." Gearheardt finally caught the waiter's eye and signaled for another bottle of wine. "And to made sure that no one in Oklahoma tried to grab any of the ten-million-dollar loan application fee the Russians paid."

"Assuming any of this is true. What happened?"

"The loan committee turned them down. The Russians were mad as hornets. I think a lot of the guys working on the loan were executed."

Loud laughter came from the private Pentagon Procurement room. The door opened and half a dozen smiling, suited, shifty-looking men paraded out. They proceeded to talk among themselves as they wove their way through the tables toward the front of the restaurant. Some of them stopped by tables as they passed, shaking hands and bellowing greetings.

Gearheardt said, "Looks like the Navy got their new submarine."

"Those were Navy guys?"

"Nope. The Navy guys went out the back door. Those were lobbyists. One of them worked on the Russian loan package on behalf of the applicant."

Jack leaned back in his chair, watching the last of the backslapping, cigar-chomping team exit the restaurant. "So, what happened after the Russians were turned down?"

"They pulled out of Afghanistan."

"What?"

"They were actually planning on using the funding to finance the Afghan war. It was eating them alive. They never believed we would actually build Star Wars." Gearheardt was lighting a cigar. After he shook the match out and dropped it into the ashtray, he spoke with a definite didactic air, "You see, Jack, it was a win-win for Reagan and the U.S. What we really wanted was to delay the Russians from spending money on weapons to fight the mujahideen. They were getting bled dry but the chance for us to loan them billions of dollars kept up their hopes of being able to win that war."

"But we didn't loan them money and they quit."

"And we were able to stop spending millions of dollars to support the mujahideen. Like I said, win-win."

"AND," Gearheardt continued, "we're letting them foreclose on millions of American homes. They're pleased as punch. Remember the average Russian eats a turnip every other day and drinks potato whiskey every day. It's just the politburo we have to worry about. The peasants are pulling the oars and the leaders are just pounding rhythm on the tom-tom."

The restaurant was quietening down. The sound of knife and fork scraping china now the loudest sound. Without the lobbyists, most of whom left after seeing the Navy submarine deal evidently taken off the table, the conversations were subdued.

Jack was morose. Seeing his government at work was depressing. Wondering which side he was on was double depressing.

Finally, he said, "And how does this tie into the chaos we're planning?"

"Well, it appears that the Russians went back to Moscow and told the bloody politburo that the savings and loan industry was packaging mortgages on all the American homes and selling the packages."

"And that intrigued the politburo?"

Gearheardt smiled. "That and the fact that the savings and loan people appeared to be dumber than stumps and greedy as starving rats."

"By the way," Gearheardt was saying as they taxied back to the hotel, "I talked to Beanable and he said he thought you might be a bit uninformed."

"That would be an understatement of enormous proportions."

"I like the way you talk, Jack. Hard to believe you went to some cow college."

"Well, I reckon all this time I'm a-spending with you has kinda rubbed off some good talkin' habits, Gearheardt."

"No, I'm serious, Jack. I listen to you even when it seems like I don't. I value your opinion and our long friendship. You have to trust me on this deal."

"No."

After a while, Gearheardt turned from looking out the taxi window—they were passing historical memorials—and said, "Okay, I'll level with you. There are some things you haven't been told."

Jack waited. And waited.

"So that's your idea of leveling with me—telling me you're not telling me everything?"

Gearheardt said, "If you knew everything, Jack, you could be in danger."

"More danger than the Russian mortgage holders trying to have me killed?"

"In addition to that," Gearheardt replied.

"By the way, why is *anyone* trying to kill me?"

"Well, for one thing, you turned down loaning the Russians billions and billions of dollars. That not only pissed them off, their credit rating turned to shit." Gearheardt turned to Jack in the taxi. "And before you tell me it wasn't you, that's beside the point. You were at Countrwhatever Savings of course, and someone signed your name to the letter pointing out that the Russians were not credit worthy."

"I'm going to guess who that someone was," Jack said.

"Whoa, Jack. We've been best friends for a long time, but if you're going to accuse me of signing your name to a document putting you in mortal danger, you better think about that first."

"But of course, Gearheardt, that's exactly what you did."

Gearheardt leaned forward and tapped on the plastic partition from the front seat. "Are we lost? Our hotel is on the other side of the river. Why are you----oh, shit, Jack. Outta here!"

Gearheardt opened the door and rolled out, got up and began running. Jack followed him. They both jumped a low brick wall and sat on the ground on the other side, gasping for breath. Slowly Jack rose his head over the wall just in time to see their recently departed taxi explode in a Fourth-of-July-quality explosion. Taxi parts rained down on the pavement.

"What the hell?"

"My slip-up, Jack. About the time I realized that we were heading into the boonies, I noticed the driver's name—Hatsheput Orisis."

"So?"

"Jack, I hope I'm not lying to you when I tell you the truth."

"It's about time, Gearheardt. You've been.....wait, what?"

"There's more to the story. Pretty sure that Hatsheput Orisis is Egyptian, Jack."

The pair began walking the path alongside the wall, avoiding what was becoming a major scene of activity in the blast area. In the gathering dark, anyone who might have seen them would not connect them the molten mass of taxi and Egyptian on the parkway.

"Let me guess, Gearheardt. The Egyptians are trying to kill me."

"Well, you did sign for ten million dollars in weapons you didn't deliver. I'm not saying I'm on their side. I just saying—"

"Pardon my French, Gearheardt, but Just shut the fuck up."

They walked in silence.

"Does it ever occur to you to consider using your own damn name in these deals?" Jack finally said.

"Jack, I'm not even an officer of Countrysidecommunity International. The banking regulations are pretty clear about authority and lending limits wi—"

"I want to see the president."

"No problem, Jack. Good idea. Let me get it set up."

"No, Gearheardt. I want to see him right now. Before you and he have a chance to work up a story. A guy named Hatsheput Orisis just blew himself up to supposedly try to kill me. And, evidently, you. I think I deserve to know what the hell is going on."

"He may be doing some presidential crap, but we can try. Cut through the park here and I'll try to talk our way in." Gearheardt pushed through the bushes and in five minutes they were rounding the corner to the White House.

"By the way, Jack. I don't think the taxi guy was trying to blow me up. I'm not quite as reckless as you about pissing people off."

They reached the White House guard shack before Jack could reply. Gearheardt glad-handed the guard and signed them in.

"Is the president alone, if you get my drift, Bob?"

"The first lady had the guys do a sweep of his quarters about an hour ago. If he has company, she's disguised as furniture or a pizza man." Gearheardt briefly described what they needed to see the president about—none of which was true—to the guard to pass on to the president. He went back into the guard shack. "He is in a meeting but said to send you up."

As they walked, escorted, to the entrance, Jack began to lose his nerve. After all, this *was* the president of the United States. His anger at Gearheardt and fear of being killed by the Egyptians had spurred him on. But what did he think he was going to demand to be told?

As they left the elevator a buxom pizza man, clearly a woman, was being escorted toward the exit. She glanced back at Gearheardt and Jack thought he saw recognition.

"Jack," Gearheardt said, pulling him aside in the hallway outside the president's quarter, "you don't know anyone in this meeting."

"What do you mean? I know the president. Who else—"

"Okay, you know him, but no one else."

Jack shook his head, getting the message.

Inside the room and recognizing it as the same room Gearheardt described when talking about his meeting of the night before, Jack saw the president, a cabinet member he recognized (but could not remember his name), Jackson Beanable, Mrs. President's first cousin Bryce Rogers, and Marine General Fixture. He nodded to each of them. Each nodded acknowledgement without recognition.

The president, who was watching a female beach volleyball match on the television looked up. "Jack, give me a minute here. I'm thinking about inviting the winning team to the White House." He looked at the cabinet member. "Suppose they'll wear those uniforms to the White House?"

The man at the conference table, who appeared to be the oldest in the room, looked up over the reading glasses he wore to see if the president were serious. "I rather doubt they will wear those costumes, Mr. President. Perhaps we could save the taxpayers some money by just inviting local strippers to the White House. We've cautioned you before about using Air Force One to—"

The president stood and waved the secretary to silence. "Remind me why I keep you around here, Bob. Always the damn party pooper and gloomy Gus. Do you have photos of me in compromising positions?" He laughed and looked around at the half dozen men in the room. "I'll take some wallet sized and an eight by ten, by the way."

The room, a large, well furnished 'man cave' for the president, contained easy chairs for television, a couch, small tables and an eight-man conference table with deep mahogany leather chairs. With the president at one end and the cabinet member at the other, Gearheardt, Jack, General Fixture and Jackson Beanable sat. Bryce Rogers had excused himself, saying he would return shortly.

"Got to see a horse about a man," he said as he left. The president non-verbally childishly expressed his opinion that Bryce Rogers was not particularly at the top of his 'good pal' list.

"Jack," the president said, "Gearheardt says you have questions about the operation. These men can all be trusted. Speak freely and let's get things cleared up. Oh, this is General Fixture, maybe you met him when you were in the Marines."

"Probably not," Jack said. "But, yes, we've met."

"Jackson Beanable is an investment banker. An honest one I've heard."

Quiet laughter around the table.

"And of course, you know our Secretary of the Treasury, Banyon (Bob) Kinkaid. He knows where all the money is, and we think he carries the keys to Fort Knox on his key chain." The president smiled and said directly to the Secretary, "And that reminds me why I keep you around, Bob."

"Mr. Secretary," Jack said, nodding to the distinguished gentleman.

"Okay, Jack. Out with it. Remember, there's no such thing as a stupid question. Just stupid people." The president smiled.

"Thanks, Mr. President," Jack replied with suppressed sarcasm. "The issue is this. I seem to have been tasked with a number of important actions over the next few days and weeks, and—"

"We have a lot of confidence in you, Jack." That from General Fixture.

"—but the truth is that I actually have no understanding of what is going on."

"Not sure about the others, but that gives me less confidence, Jack," the general said.

"Wait a minute, Jack," the president said, holding up his hand to stop the others from speaking. "I've personally briefed Gearheardt and he has assured me that you're both capable and, uh, capable and whatever else he said. The plan is simple, Wall Street has become too powerful in this country. Everyone up there just seems to be trying to get rich. We are going to teach them a lesson. It's time for this administration to regain control of the country's natural resources, it's economic future, and the future of the free world by wresting control of the wealth of America from those few selfish individuals on Wall

Street who do not have America's well-being as a primary objective."

He finished and it was quiet at the table, all eyes on the president. Finally, the investment banker, Jackson Beanable, spoke. "Are you serious Mr. President?"

If Jack had not turned to look at Beanable, he might have seen the president wink, and everything would have turned out differently. At least for Jack. Gearheardt, did see the wink and knew their plans were manipulated at the highest level of government. And that was good enough for him. He knew that the president ran everything by Mrs. President. And if the president knew what was good for him, he didn't cross her.

The president rose and went behind Jack's chair, grabbing his shoulders and squeezing them with avuncular familiarity.

"Don't worry, Jack," he said. "You're going to be taken care of." He squeezed Jack for one last painful time.

As he sat back down, the president signaled for an aide—hidden in the dark corner of the room and unseen before he stepped into the light—to lower the computer screen and standby to assist in the presentation. A map of Manhattan appeared on the screen. The aide adjusted the focus on the computer.

General Fixture carefully placed his unlit cigar butt in the ashtray and rose to his feet. He adjusted his uniform jacket and headed to the small stage near the presentation screen. As he neared the stage he tripped on a wire and fell head-first into the podium which smashed into the back of the aide. The aide grabbed for the podium, dragging it along with him while he slammed into the large presentation screen which fell backward toward the window, effectively providing a slide through the window for the aide. Moaning coming through the open window seconds later assured the conference participants that the aide had at least survived the two-story fall.

The room was quiet as the general took his seat.

Finally, the president asked, "Any other questions, Jack?"

The Washington Post carried a story the next day referring to an armed potential rapist who had somehow gained entrance to the bedroom of the Mrs. President and had been tossed out after a severe thrashing. Numerous women's groups scheduled luncheons and dinners to honor the Mrs. President bravery and martial skills. The soldier in question, in recognition of his agreement to remain silent, was rewarded with a choice assignment training the Tamang military in rural Tibet.

On the way out of the conference room, unburdened by any new information, Jack was called aside by the Treasury Secretary. He put his arms around Jack's shoulders. To Gearheardt he said, "Give us a minute, Gearheardt."

"Son," he said, talking to Jack, "you seem like a sincere fellow. Former Marine officer, right? And some work for the Agency? First, have you run this by Mrs. President? She sometimes puts the kibosh on some of the president's shenanigans. Leaves a lot of good folks hanging."

"Well, I'm pretty sure she knows about it. I've never really talked to her. But Mr. Secretary, more importantly, are you aware of the overall plan?"

"Besides the damn Marine General pushing that guy out of the window?" He laughed. "I think that might BE the plan."

"But seriously, sir. Does the president even—?

"Son, the truth is," he sobered and looked squarely into Jack's eyes," those bastards on Wall Street have gotten into a peck of trouble and are asking the president to give them a hand. A big hand. And the president, I suspect, is extracting a big quid pro quo."

Across the room, near the elevator, a man was trying to attract the attention of the secretary. Who held up a finger of response.

"Look, Jack. There are few people in this town, Washington DC, who know Jack-shit, pardon the expression, about high-level finance. There are people over on the hill who can't balance their own checkbook. They turn to Wall Street to bail them out of some of the dumbest ideas since lighting farts. And Wall Street just nickels and dimes them until they're cross-eyed and th—"

"I wouldn't call it nickel and dimes, the money Wall Street gets from the government," Jack said.

"Hell, I'm not talking about that. Wall Street shows them a dime and when the DC boys grab for it, Wall Street pulls out a nickel and says, 'wouldn't you rather have this bigger coin?'"

The president had come into the anti-room and was squinting over at Jack and the secretary.

"Jack, take my card. If I can ever help, call me. The answer to your questions is—no, I don't know what cock-eyed plan is in the works. If the president and first lady are involved, it is certain to be labyrinthine. Remember, she is thinking beyond his career." He started to leave.

"Sir," Jack said, grabbing his elbow, "they're talking about actually attacking Wall Street and killing the investment bankers!" Jack panicked at perceived sanity leaving the room.

The secretary smiled, looked over at the president standing with Jackson Beanable, and waved goodbye. To Jack, he said, "Serves them right."

Next Chapter

Gearheardt sat at a table in the back of *Dave's Dive*, a little-known after-hours cocktail lounge named after a bar in Rome. It was just after midnight. Jack had been dropped at the hotel on Dupont Circle. The management at the Hilton suggested that a new hotel be found after the maid had reported the damage in Jack's room. They had hinted that a change might be considered by depositing all of Jack's belongings into an alley adjacent to the hotel. Gearheardt had sealed the deal by emptying a .45 clip into the cigarette machine. Umbrage was taken but the assembled police let them leave with a warning and a promise to join Gearheardt for a drink later in the week.

The waiter was placing Gearheardt's drink in front of him and therefore blocked his view of a man wearing a mask of the President striding into the club along with black-suited and embarrassed bodyguards. Gearheardt then saw and assumed it was an attempted robbery until the man in the mask made a beeline for his table.

He pulled the mask off as he dropped into the booth. It was the President.

"Pretty cool, eh Gearheardt? Me disguising myself as me."

"I still doubt it's you, Mr. President."

"Very funny, Gearheardt." The president turned and gave a drink order and instructions to the men who had accompanied him. One offered him a small package and the president waved it away with disgust. "For God's sake, Randy. Gearheardt is straight, man.

"Okay, Gearheardt, let's get down to tass bracks." He grimaced. "Crap, I hate being around the First Lady's relatives. I talk like an Okie for a week. Anyway, what the hell was that with your pal Jack? I've warned you about him before. He just can't seem to get with the program. Is he going to be a problem?"

"Slick," Gearheardt said, "Jack is as with the program as he knows how to be. Keep in mind that only you and I know the overall scenario." He paused. "And sometimes I think you're holding out on me. And you are an Okie, by the way."

"I'm the damn president, Gearheardt. Of course I'm holding out on you. If you knew everything, then *you* might want to run the show." He signaled for another drink, his first still sitting full in front of him. "Bring me up to date. Are the weapons acquired and getting dispersed?"

"Aye, aye, skipper."

"Knock off the crap, Gearheardt."

"Yes, they are, Slick. We had a bit of trouble with the Egyptians, but—"

"Those bastards."

"Yes, sir. But they were concerned, to put it mildly, that they didn't actually get the weapons." Gearheardt realized, watching the president's face, that he was treading deep water.

The president might not be privy to the fact that money was changing hands involving the first lady's cousin. "Probably a missed communication. I'll handle it."

The president wrinkled his brow. "Did they pay money? I thought this was a straight swindle deal. How much money are we talking about?"

"Not much. Maybe ten million."

"Let me tell you something, Gearheardt. Just be careful of the first lady. Like she always says to me—Don't let me walk in and catch you with your pants on."

"Yeah...What?"

"She's got a tongue like a bullwhip. Always snapping at me. She says if I have my pants down, at least she knows what's on my mind. It's those meetings, like last night with all pants zipped up, that worry her. Always afraid she's being screwed out of something."

"To be honest, Slick, I'm learning that you—"

"Whoa, how much money did you say you got from the Egyptians?"

"About ten million less some fees to your cousin-in-law and—"

"And you weren't going to share it with me? You know, Gearheardt, that's what's wrong with this country. Every man for himself. Greed as an admirable attribute. Money, money, money. Let's take this situation here. You know damn well that at least a quarter of that money should go to me. So, I'm out two point five million dollars because my partners are just greedy."

"Mr. President, I didn't even know that you were aware of the transaction. Much less that you were a part of it. I can assure—"

"Assure my ass, Gearheardt. I have to know about every damn thing that goes on or I don't get my share? I'm up to my nipples in government shit and can't be expected to keep track of every deal." He slammed down the scotch and water. "I'm ashamed to be me, for God's sake. Letting everybody screw me." He put the mask of himself back on and slumped back in his chair.

"I'b prefidunt of murryka an at mens everdel too."

"Mr. President, it's hard to understand you in that mask. The rubber lips flap all around. Did you say you're president of America and that means every deal too?"

"Dab brite."

Gearheardt nursed his drink while the president sulked. Every few minutes one of the Secret Service men would approach the booth and ask if the president would sign something for a member of the bar patrons. He grumpily refused. He was silent, arms folded across his chest. An attempt at drinking did nothing to improve his spirits as the booze didn't seem to make it past his rubber lips and could be seen dripping down his neck.

"Mr. President," Gearheardt ventured, "again I can assure you that you will get your share of any deal that is transacted."

The president ripped the mask off his head and tossed it onto the table. "Hell, I know that, Gearheardt. It's just pretty damn discouraging to find out that the plotters and participants in a scheme that 'I' put together have so little respect for the office of the president to try to steal money from me. Damn discouraging. And if the first lady finds out I've been skunked.... well, let's just say that hell hath no fury like a woman who whatever that saying is."

"So, she'll be pissed."

"She will put my gonads on ice. Like little oysters laying there."

Gearheardt shuddered at the image.

"Tell you what, Gearheardt. Give me five million and I'll tell the little First Lady that I out-negotiated folks on a deal that I was only owed two and a half million. She'll like the sound of that."

"I'll see what I can do, sir. I actually think a great deal of that money is always spent up in New Jersey, getting the troops moved in and messes set up—"

"Mess is an eating place for military guys, right?"

"Yep."

"See what you can do. But I can't be expected to just keep running this country pro bono." He stopped and signed a napkin as the Secret Service agent pointed out the recipient—a dynamite looking woman with the Grand Canyon of cleavages. Impossible to notice what else was in the picture.

"Dave," the president said, "take this back to her and ask her if she would be willing to wear this president mask in a more intimate liaison." He grinned. "Whoa, boy, Gearheardt. Would that not be wild. Kind of like—"

"I get it, Mr. President. And you were about to ask about the documentation that was the subject of this meeting. All the

Savings and Loan documents are complete. You will be Chairman and CEO and sole shareholder of Slick Savings and Loan. That entity will replace the Federal Reserve as the, let's say the manager of all the money in the U.S."

"What do you mean 'let's say'?"

"Well, if, as you suggested, you own all the money, it becomes rather worthless."

"Got it. That's what I meant, control, not own."

The president was thoughtful. After a moment, he said, "Gearheardt, do you think I should lead the troops into battle?"

Gearheardt was taken aback. Did the president actually understand his plans? He decided on a non-answer that the president could not completely dismiss or agree to.

"Slick, if I may call you that again, I think you might consider having Mrs. President lead the troops into battle. The sight of her charging up Wall Street, sword in hand—"

"We're using swords?"

"It was just an image that came to me. But the women's movement, the liberals, the gay crowd, all would be thrilled that you gave her the opportunity."

"The gay crowd?"

"I'm just making this up as I go along, Mr. President. I had not considered the notion of a charging, Teddy Roosevelt-type, leader."

"Forget it. Although I can see some merit in having the little First Lady bravely facing machine guns and bayonets." He smiled, and then quickly frowned when he noticed Gearheardt staring at him. "So, what about the transfer of stewardship and me signing the bills? Did you get the Secretary to agree and set that in motion? And taking that damn Egyptian pyramid off the dollar too."

"I didn't get a definitive response, to tell the truth. Secretary Kinkaid seemed distracted. Then this evening, since Jack insisted on coming to the meeting, the secretary got cornered by Jack."

The president sighed and took on the look of a disappointed parent. "Gearheardt, I told you to take along File 371A from the safe. I told George to let you into the vault when you came down. If you had flashed 371A, just the top page, the Secretary would have signed over to his wife and kids. He has a thing for—"

"Slick, I really don't want to hear about what he has a thing for. I'll get the signatures and documents. And have them before D Day. Trust me."

"Okay. I'm counting on you." The President looked around the room, only a few hard-core patrons and the Secret Services in attendance, but he lowered his voice. "And what about you, Gearheardt? What's your little piece of the pie? DCI? A billion dollars in small bills? An office in the White House?"

"Do you have any idea of the size of a billion dollars in small bills?"

"I have a better idea of a wise-ass who is treading on thin ice. It was just a figure of speech. What do you want?"

"The billion dollars sounds good."

Back at the Dupont Circle hotel, Gearheardt knocked on Jack's door.

"Hold on, Gearheardt."

Jack opened the door dressed in the hotel's cheap terry-cloth bathrobe.

"How did you know—"

"Who in the hell would knock on my door at—" he looked back at the clock on the nightstand, "— two thirty in the morning?"

Gearheardt rummaged through the mini bar. "You want anything out of here, Jack?"

"Actually, Gearheardt the only thing I can think of wanting out is you—out of my room."

"Why did you let me in?"

Jack lay back on the bed, pillows propping him up from the headboard. "What do you want?"

"Jack, this hotel room is not near as nice as the one you had before you trashed it."

He opened two small gin bottles and poured them into a glass he brought from the bathroom. Then he sat down at the desk and lit a cigarette.

"Jack, I would feel a lot better if I thought you were really supporting me in this mission."

"This isn't a mission, Gearheardt. It's the proverbial simian screwing a football. We have Hawaiian mercenaries and stolen Egyptian weapons manned by a gaggle of government employees—"

"The Fed Reserve folks actually aren't—"

"—attacking somewhere, sometime, in order for the President to take over a busted financial system." Jack suddenly laughed.

"What's so funny?" Gearheardt asked.

"As I was describing it to you, it all began to seem logical." After a moment. "And what did you need to see me about at two thirty in the morning?"

"I need you to get to New Jersey first thing tomorrow morning and take control of things."

"What things?"

"The not-Russian troops arrived early. The Hawaiians are there. The Marines are due in at oh-dark-thirty, and it's a giant circus. I've put out the word, and the president backs me on this, that you are our man on the ground. Even though the president doesn't really like you."

"That's good to hear. We're known by the company we don't keep."

"What?"

"Never mind. I'll get up there tomorrow." Jack sat up in the bed. "Gearheardt, is there really going to be a battle? I'm going along with all this, but the idea is surreal. Is this just a ruse to—"

"Jack, that's the kind of thinking that kept us out of the Spanish Civil War."

"No, it isn't. You're the most frustrating person in the world, Gearheardt. That makes no sense at all, yet those inane statements always sound almost profound. It's like listening to a guy with a British accent. Gibberish with a polished, Oxfordian delivery."

"You're raving, Jack. You know all you need to know. What you don't know is for your own protection. Or mine."

He drained his glass and stood up. "I think you might want to consider suiting up and getting on the road. Those Marines will be standing tall in New Jersey and, I'm afraid, looking somewhat askance at the other combatants. Could be trouble."

"Looking somewhat askance? Really. Whose feeding you this blather, Gearheardt? That sounds like something you would say about as much as you would sing the Star-Spangled Banner in Urdu." Jack stood, walked to the closet and pulled out his luggage. When he placed it on the bed, he saw that Gearheardt was staring at him.

"You're getting a touch paranoid, Jack. Why does there always have to be someone behind everything? Something that someone is always holding back from you. Someone always trying to attack you."

"I'll give you three guesses," Jack said as he began to put clothes into the bag. "Here's a hint. There are people trying to kill me, according to you. There are mysterious people popping up all over the landscape. And this 'mission' changes direction about once an hour."

"Jack, it's all for a good cause. We have to save the country from the left and the right."

"Yeah, one side is trying to take all our money. The other is all about shoveling it out the door to friends and constituents."

"You're a cynic, Jack. There are a lot of good people in government."

"They need to show up pretty quick or the country is not going to be worth what we paid the Indians for it." Jack stood up and turned around. "What's your cut in all this financial voodoo, Gearheardt? Have you been offered the big bucks?"

Gearheardt paused and dropped his cigarette into the almost empty gin glass. "Not so far, Jack. A stipend of modest proportions maybe."

"Well, I'm off to do battle. Maybe there's a pot of gold somewhere. I owe it to my ex-family to give them something."

"As always, we will share what's tossed our way, Jack."

Jack paused and turned to face Gearheardt. "How did this turn out where I'm leading the troops and you're handling the money? You're the CIA, not me."

"The president doesn't like you, Jack."

Part II
Into the Fray

Phillip Jennings

Postpartum 1

At the Fenton New Jersey airport, the heat hit Jack like a microwaved sponge. Hot and humid. Heavy. A jeep was waiting nearby with a teenaged Marine sitting at the wheel, smoking and tuned into his earphones. He started as Jack threw his bag into the rear seat and plopped down in the front passenger seat.

"You the new boss, sir?" the Marine said, starting the jeep and accelerating off of the tarmac.

"I guess that's what you would call me, Marine. Do you know where to take me? I was told—"

"Guess so, sir. If you're the boss, we best go down to the General's HQ and get you squared away."

"Is that General Fixture?"

The Marine grinned. "Reckon so, sir. We call him General Plumbing. You know, like Plumbing Fixture?" He paused and looked back at the road, making Jack a bit more comfortable. "Guess some guys just call him The Shitter." He smiled, sobered. "But not me, sir."

"Well, let's just head down to the HQ and not worry about that."

The streets of downtown Fenton were crowded. Military vehicles, staff cars, police cars, bicycles and pushcarts selling every imaginable type of trinket and fast food. The stores along the street were newly, and garishly, painted advertising beer, beer and more beer. With women chasers. Young servicemen strolled in groups, noticeably having partaken of the beer with more beer offers. Slatterns decorated almost every doorway.

"Better watch out with that watch on your arm, sir. These little blond-haired, blue-eyed rascals will come up and snatch it right off. I know a guy who lost his whole arm."

"My watch is not even on the arm near the street, Marine. Don't start that—"

Jack jumped back and retracted his hand from an urchin tugging on his class ring.

"Hey, you're pretty much the square root of a hundred, Mister," yelled the urchin as he merged with the crowd of urchins moving alongside the jeep. They wore matching Polo shirts and appeared to be from a private school.

"F you, you little shit," the Marine driver yelled.

At the stoplight, Jack saw a converted Starbucks turning out tee-shirts that read, "When I Die I'm Going to Heaven, 'Cause I've served my time in Fenton, N.J." over a colorful drawing of a BMW M6.

"My God, Corporal, this place is a madhouse. How long have the troops been here?"

"Most of 'um got in last night, sir. There was a few Seabees or some half-assed civilian pukes before us." He stopped the Jeep in front of a ten-story office building.

"Here we are, sir. You'll find the General up those stairs and through the double glass doors. Password today is—" He looked at something written on his wrist, "Blowfish."

Jack grabbed his bag and awkwardly returned the Marine's salute. "Thanks, Corporal. Who do I give the password to?"

"Whoever you don't want to shoot you, sir."

As Jack stood watching the Jeep pull into traffic, a gaggle of sailors came by, kicking what appeared to be a roast pig down the street.

"Tom, Tom, the butcher's son. Stole a pig and away he run," they sang. Drink appeared to have engaged them earlier. The pig bounced to a stop at Jack's feet. Immediately the sailors began to chant, "Give us our pig. Give us our pig."

Knowing better than to start a dialogue with chanting drunken Navy pig-owners, Jack drop-kicked the pig off of the sidewalk, turned and walked up the stairs into the Headquarters of the First Marine Assault Group, referred to as Fir-MAG. Immediately inside he was stopped by the deep gravelly voice of a burned-out-vocal-corded Marine Sergeant Major.

"Come here, maggot," he projected throughout the considerable lobby. He sat at a desk in full combat-oriented sartorial splendor. "You got a shot card?"

Jack strode purposefully to the Sergeant Major's desk. He dropped his bag, placed both hands on the front edge of the desk and leaned toward the man's face.

"We are in frigging New Jersey, Sergeant Major. I don't need my frigging shot card. I don't need to show you anything, tell you anything, or explain anything. I'm going through that door and up those stairs to see General Fixture. Do you have a problem with that?"

"What's the password, maggot," the Sergeant Major said.

Jack straightened up, sighed, and looked back at the Sergeant Major.

"Blowfish."

Now the Sergeant Major sighed, dropping his forehead into his palms. He looked up. "Did that little prick, Corporal Shulsky, give you that password?"

"I guess that was his name. Why?"

"Blowfish is the password for Russian mortgage salesmen. We're to shoot them on sight. The little prick." He stood up. "Look sir, you don't look like an F-ing Russian mortgage salesman. Who the hell are you?"

"I'm the new commander of this entire task force, Sergeant Major," Jack said, realizing he needed to begin exercising his authority if he was ever going to get anything done.

The Sergeant Major pressed a button under his desk and the glass doors opened. A fully armed Marine took a position just outside the door.

"Don't shoot this maggot, Corporal. He's the new boss." He turned back to Jack. "Good luck, sir." He paused. "By the way, new boss, it might help things if we were told what the f--k we were doing in New Jersey."

"I'll get back to you, Sergeant Major." They shook hands. "By the way, Sergeant Major, how in the world did you get desk duty?"

"Someone sober was needed, sir. This is the new Marine Corps."

Jack was welcomed into General Fixture's office. It was the penthouse, with grand views and exquisite furnishings. The general came around the desk and shook Jack's hand.

"Welcome, Captain. Or should I call you boss?"

"Well, General, it looks like—"

"Fine, I'll just call you Captain." He went behind his desk and sat down. "Have a seat, Jack. You don't mind if I call you Jack, do you?"

"I thought you just said—"

"By the way, Jack. You can have the office next to mine. I'll have my aide get you squared away in there. You let him know if you need something special. And I think I've identified an aide for you. First thing to check is loyalty. Next thing is honesty. Then loyalty again. I'll have him report to my aide."

Jack studied his shoes for a moment then looked up at the General.

"Okay, General, here's how it will actually work. Your aide will report to my aide. You will report to me. This will be my office. I, and I alone, will talk to the president or Gearheardt."

The General swung his chair around and looked out the window.

"I hear you, Jack. Kind of like you're going to be in charge. Is that what you're saying?" He surreptitiously put his hand under the edge of his desk.

"I think we understand each other now," Jack said, starting to rise. Halfway up, he was hit by two high-and tight Marines. Flat on his back, he struggled for a moment and then gave up.

The General stood over him. "Jack, this is something that I don't like doing to a fellow Marine, especially one who has served his country like you have. But this raid on Wall Street is serious. Damn serious. I'm not sure you know how serious it is."

"Serious, General?" Jack was not convinced the General would actually do him harm.

"I've found, in the past, Jack, that young men like yourself, strong and patriotic young men, feel more *serious* without a left little toe. A strange but useful fact."

"Oh, for Pete's sake, General. Tell these guys to let me up and let's get serious." He could not suppress a brief giggle. Little toes? What the hell was that all about.

A third Marine entered the office. Pulling an acetylene bottle behind him. Jack watched as the Marine fiddled and eventually produced a white/blue flame spewing from the end of the torch. With one hand, he took off Jack's left shoe and sock.

"The good news is that it's a self-cauterizing action. Not a lot of blood."

"Are you F-ing *serious*, General? What the hell is going on here?"

The pain hit Jack in mid-whine and he embarrassingly but fortunately passed out.

When he woke up, he was sitting on a couch in the General's anti-room. A female Marine was at a desk working on a computer. She looked up and smiled at him. He was still in his suit, white shirt and tie. But missing one shoe and sock. He remembered the pain then, and grimaced. Slowly and with trepidation he looked down to where his left little toe used to be—and still was. He had all his toes.

The Marine looked up again, "I understand you're the boss of us, sir. Welcome aboard."

From the half-open door to General Fixture's office a voice boomed out. "Is our boy up and at 'em out there, Sergeant Miller? Send him on in."

Jack wished he had a side arm. No jury in the world wou— But that was just hogwash. He wouldn't have shot the general if he had had a 105 Howitzer. He rose and limped with one bare foot into the General's office.

"Shut the door, Jack. Let's finish our conversation."

Jack did as he was asked and then sat down in front of the general's desk.

"Dry ice, Jack. You show the weapon. You build the fear, the anticipation of pain. And then the imagination is stronger than the pain. We just put dry ice on your toe." He laughed, but kindly. "You did okay. I've seen men wet their pants and worse. One guy still imagines that his toe is gone and he's looking at a fake toe. He can even hit the 'fake' toe with a hammer and not feel it. To him, the toe is gone."

"Thanks for the compliment."

"You sometimes sound like your old pal, Gearheardt. Kind of a wise-ass."

"Have you tried burning *his* toes off?"

"Matter of fact we have. Tough customer. Turns out the sonofabitch didn't have toes. Every damn one of them burned off." He chuckled at the memory.

"General, I didn't fly all the way up here to hear the history of toes. The president, and he's your commander in chief, by the way, asked me to get this unholy mess of troops and weapons under control."

"It's under control, Jack. I've got it all under control."

"It looks like suburban Danang, General. In less than twenty-four hours we've turned a quiet little New Jersey town into a pit of women, wine and Lord knows what else."

"We've had practice, Jack. You ever see Olongapo? A wise man once said, 'The women of an invaded country often turn to prostitution to feed themselves and their families. Not using them would be a betrayal of all we stand for.' I think, Jack, that what you fail to realize is that we are preparing to invade Wall Street."

Jack was near dumbstruck. That 'quote' (slightly altered) was from Gearheardt. The Gearheardt who could speak insane reality better than anyone alive.

"Jack, may I call you Jack? Let me give you some perspective. You've probably been told about all the shenanigans going on in the financial markets. You're aware that the commander in chief has certain, shall we say, designs on opportunities that have arisen."

Jack was silent. A silence driven by a growing paranoia. Who in the hell knew what?

"Anyway, Jack, when I was in *the Nam*, I had a number of classmates from the University of Minnesota go to work on Wall Street. Did damn well, even the one who was dumb as a turtle."

He paused and lit a cigar butt out of the ashtray. When it was producing sufficient smoke to kill mosquitos in Brooklyn, he continued. "We had a reunion about the time I finished my first tour and was on home leave. Pretty good time. All paid for by the Wall Street boys. Walter Grunning. Bob Beverly. And Henry Muck—yep, he took quite a pounding with a name like that. Towards the end of the evening, they got up on the bandstand and gave a little rundown on their outstanding success in the market.

"Then one of them, Bob, I think, said, 'But the evening would not be complete without showing our appreciation for a special guy. Come on up here, Fixture.'"

"I was in uniform. I always wore those dress blues every chance I got. Had a round of applause while I was hopping up on the stage. So, Walter said, 'Fixture, you're what makes this country great. I went long in napalm, doubled down in Agent Orange manufacturers, made a killing—no pun intended ha ha—in Remington Ammunition. If you and your boys can keep killing communists in India or wherever you are, I'll be a billionaire before I'm thirty.'"

"So, you've always hated the investment bank--" Jack started.

"Oh, hell no, Jack. The investment boys have been making money off wars since Moses had the measles. No, a man has a right to rip off his fellow man to make a buck. I'm just a jarhead. A Marine who does his duty. I leave politics and commerce to those evil enough to choose those professions."

"So, what's your beef?" Jack asked.

The General stood and looked out of the window, squinting against the late morning sun even though the windows were treated. Finally, he turned, sighed, and dropped back into his desk chair.

"I love war, Jack. It's what makes me feel alive. I love the sound of small arms fire, the smell of cordite, the ear-shattering blast of artillery, the camaraderie , the fear, the death screams of your foes, the camp followers, the whores, the booze, the c-rations, the sound of a Phantom pulling off target leaving behind boiling fire roasting little bastards, the heroism, even the cowardice where a man finds out who he really is. I like having a mission bigger than lives, bigger than safety or wealth, and most of all—the satisfaction of defeating the enemy. Just seeing him retreat and bleed makes all of it worthwhile."

The General was focused on some faraway point through the window.

Jack sat silently, not sure what to say. To be truthful, he was not particularly shocked at the General's words. A bit uneasy. But not shocked. Combat was addictive. He knew that.

"And Jack," the General began, startling Jack, "those silk-suited bastards and the pussy willows in DC wouldn't let us win that war in Vietnam. Threw away all those lives, betrayed all those poor Vietnamese, and gave comfort to America's enemies, foreign and domestic—because it might hurt the American economy. Bad for business. No significant return on the investment, they said. They caught Nixon stealing paper clips from the Democrat's office and said—okay, just for that we're not going to recognize our sacrifices and accomplishments in Vietnam. Just so that Nixon couldn't take credit for stopping the damn war, those bastards just surrendered to the communists."

"General," Jack said, tentatively, "I'm not saying I disagree, but there were other factors. The—"

"Are you one of them, Jack? Are you a Marine turned pussy willow?" He rose and came around the desk. "This is our chance, Jack."

"General, if the North Vietnamese were running Wall Street, that might make some sense. But I don't think Ho Chi Minh ever had a securities license."

Jack still hoped there was some *give* in the implied plan to attack Wall Street. In fact, even now he found it hard to believe there was going to be a shooting war in lower Manhattan. The people running Wall Street weren't common criminals.

"The people running Wall Street are common criminals, Jack," the General said.

Well, there went that idea, Jack realized.

"They have abandoned all allegiance to American principles, the American working man, and the heart of America. The dollar sign has replaced the flag as the symbol of the country."

"Sir, again, I'm not saying I disagree with everything you're saying. But—"

"No buts, Jack. Buts are the bane of battle."

"Buts are the….what?"

"Jack, every true mission. Every action. Every task is challenged these days by the but."

The general had sat back down. From a drawer he withdrew a K-bar, the official Marine Corps knife, a foot long killing tool, sharp as a barber's razor.

"Throughout history, Jack, the heroes of civilization have been the men who ignored the buts. *Buts* get men killed. *Buts* prolong misery and exacerbate the horrors of combat. *Buts* inevitably only delay the result everyone knows is the right thing to do."

Jack decided to make another attempt at assertive action. "Okay, General. I think that's enough about the buts. The president—"

"At the gates of Rome, a warrior named Rametheth gave the order to attack and put the entire populace to the sword. His second-in-command said, 'but sir, there are women and children in abundance.' And if Rametheth had given in to the buts, the Italians would probably still be a major power. Pizza would be limp cardboard with tomato paste."

"Sir," Jack said, "that is the most ridiculous story I've heard a sane person tell. There was no Rametheth and you've just made up that, that, dumb example out of thin air."

"Of course I did, Jack. But I know you get the point. The right thing to do is the right thing to do. Politicians are *but-men*. Always putting a wet finger in the wind. I don't do that. America, since Vietnam, has been run by wimps and charlatans. The communists provide the news. The leftists provide the buts. The dollar is the sole mission of America. It has to stop."

Jack stood up. The General was loco and absolutely right. Talking to him was like talking to Gearheardt. All the right goals but Katie bar the door on the methodology.

"General, I need to get into that office you promised me and pull together my plan, and my team. The President sent me here. He asked that I get things under control. Listening to you, I think there is still a way to go on that."

"Okie dokie, Jack. I'll have Sergeant Miller out there get you set up. I know you believe you need to *get things under control*" the General made quote marks in the air, "and by all means, you must obey presidential orders." He smiled. "Just a couple of things. First, you will not discuss my plan with anyone. And I mean anyone. You just talk about your plan. Whatever the hell it is. And secondly, this evening you will accompany me into the ville to walk among the troops and give encouragement to them. Chat with them. Assure them. The boys all need that the night before a battle.

"I have to meet with the Navy tacticians in a few minutes. They're doing some planning for me. Got some smart boys in the Navy. The Army, some good units, but strangely loyal to the president. Can't trust 'em. I like the Air Force. They'd give both nuts to bomb stuff."

"What about the Marines, General? I'm surprised that you—"

"Oh, the Marines are my troops, Jack. But let's face it, not the most advanced of the lot. The Marines are always just one bar-room brawl from spears and rocks. Those pissants on Wall Street won't know what hit them."

"Yes, sir." Jack of course had no intention of sending Marines in to kill investment bankers. And of course, also, he had no clue what his actual plan was.

"Jack, you might leave that shoe off, by the way. Jackson, that young man with the torch, is squeamish about people's socks. Which is to remind you that the boys are more than happy to dissect you like a lab frog if you screw things up. Do we understand each other."

Outside the door, Jack stopped abruptly. He turned around in a panic. "Sir, did you say, 'the night before the battle'? Like tonight is—" But the General slammed the door.

"Shit!" Jack said.

"That's what folks usually say when they leave the General's office, sir. May I take you down the hall to your office?" Sergeant Miller asked.

As he followed the Sergeant, he could not help but fully realize what had just happened. The General talked and acted exactly like Gearheardt. In fact, he also had to realize, more and more people did.

Jack's office was, in fact, very nice, and the few comfort items he needed were provided by Sergeant Miller without hesitation.

"Is this phone all set up, Sergeant?"

"Yes, sir. And yes, sir, it is a secure line, before you ask."

"Thank you, Sergeant Miller. And please close my door on your way out."

The first thing Jack did was sit on the couch with his head in his hands. He took deep breaths and tried to calm himself. He wished he were back in Vietnam. At least in Vietnam there were people trying to put you out of your misery. Gearheardt used to say that life would never get better than Vietnam. Wake up. Eat breakfast. Shoot people. Eat lunch. Get shot. Take the rest of the day off.

Jack rose and walked to his desk. Just as he sat down, the phone buzzed.

"The White House is on the line that's blinking, sir," Sergeant Miller said.

"Mr. President. I was just putting together a situation report and was going to call you."

"Hey, hold the phone out of the window and let me hear that killing going on."

"Gearheardt! You rotten bastard. They said the White House was on the phone."

"White Houses can't talk, Jack. How's it going up there?" Gearheardt asked.

"Not worth a damn, Gearheardt. The town looks like the Russian Navy just finished two weeks of shore leave. The General is batshit crazy. And they tried to burn my toe off."

"Ha. Sounds good." Gearheardt laughed. "I just finished refereeing an hour-long scream-a-thon between the First Man and First Lady. There's a lump in that marriage mattress, I'll tell you."

"Gearheardt—"

"Yeah, I heard you, Jack. Sorry about the toes. Look, General Fixture is not batshit crazy. And what if he is? You're going to tell me, I'm sure, that he's loading up to attack Wall Street at some point and---"

"Yes, like tomorrow."

"—might spill a little investment banker blood. The tree of liberty, remember, is best watered with arrogant young wealthy bastard's piss. You've heard that, Jack." He paused. "Wait, did you say tomorrow?"

"Yes, dumbass. I said tomorrow. The General wants me to visit the troops with him this evening. That 'eve of battle' talk I'm sure he's dying to give."

"Damn, the president is going to be chapped. And the First Lady will have half the White House staff on suicide watch. She—"

"Gearheardt, let's talk about what needs to be done. Not what the president and First Lady's problems are. A lot of people could die tomorrow if we—"

"Oh, I kind of doubt that, Jack. Last I heard the guys on Wall Street are completely unprepared and, for the most part, weaponless. I would think there would be a lot of surrendering. And it's not happening tomorrow anyway." Gearheardt sounded pleased at the situation. "By the way, aren't you supposed to be in charge up there?"

"I thought that was the idea. I'm not sure anyone—like the president—explained that to the Marine Corps. Gearheardt, we've got to put this attack off. If there is actually going to be an attack. The General is right about one thing."

"And that would be?" asked Gearheardt with a fading interest expressed in his tone.

"Since Vietnam we can't seem, as a country, to decide how to fight wars. Sometimes I think we should just give up fighting wars all together. Either win or—"

"Don't even say it, Jack. What would be the point of having a country if you couldn't have a war every once in a while? I know that sounds funny, but if you live in some shithole that you wouldn't defend, move! If some other country is jacking you around, bomb the hell out of them."

"I'm not going to…. Gearheardt, you and the president need more time to work out the financial system takeover. I need more time to stop this insane attack on Wall Street. What do we do?"

"I've given that some thought while you were whining, Jack. Here's what you do. You've got about a battalion of Marines, plus a couple of Army units and Navy guys--"

"They're doing some planning."

"They'll sink the Statue of Liberty given half a chance. But that's not our problem. What you do is late this afternoon, put all the bars and massage parlors off limits."

"I'm not sure there are massage parlors in Finton, New Jersey, Gearheardt. But I'll shut down what I can. If the Shore Patrol is willing to follow my orders."

"They will, Jack. You have my word."

"What the hell does your word mean?"

"I'll not take umbrage at that, Jack. Just give the order. Keep it under your hat until about nine o'clock."

"So, shutting the bars is the best we can come up with for stopping the attack?"

"Like Napoleon said, 'Troops fight for their country when beer is plentiful.'"

"Napoleon said no such thing."

Part 2 Chapter 2

Jack was unable to come up with a better plan. The idea, explained more fully in a subsequent chat with Gearheardt, was to start a near mutiny in the ranks by denying them the pleasures of military campaigns since, as Gearheardt said, 'Hannibal crossed the Amazon.'

At seven thirty, Sergeant Miller knocked on Jack's door.

"Begging your pardon, sir. The General would like you to accompany him to talk to the troops."

Jack, having spent the greater part of the afternoon and evening negotiating the arrangements whereby the Shore Patrol would get everyone out of the bars and bordellos and back to their respective units, all the time spreading the word that the reason was the senior officers wanted the bars and bordellos all to themselves, reluctantly joined the General outside his office.

"General, I think it might be best if, since the men have to get up early to attack Wall Street in the morning, if we close the bars early this evening."

The general, pausing in putting on his well decorated General's hat, looked at Jack as if he was insane. "Good Lord, son, I have to assume you're joking or drunk."

"General, I don't want to get back into the 'who's in charge' argument—"

"Suits me. I am." He strode off down the hall, used the stairs rather than the elevator, exited out the front door of the building where a squad of Marines joined them. Jack followed.

"Good evening, Marines. Let's go down to the ville and have ourselves a beer."

"We can't drink, General. We're on duty." The Marine who spoke, a gunny sergeant, made it clear that he would have preferred having the beer—except for having to babysit a certain General who wanted to walk around town.

Jack fell in with the patrol and marveled again how much Finton, New Jersey now resembled the less genteel sections of Danang. From every store front bar and massage parlor, nuclear-weapon-system-quality sound systems blasted obnoxious music. Sidewalk tables were surrounded by dozens of Marines and Army troops, hats askew, eyes dilated, all mechanically performing their duty as beer filters.

Olongapo, Olongapo

Oh, how I love Olongapo.

It's just a mile outside the gate.

Drink San Miguel and fornicate,

Olongapo, Olongapo

Oh, how I love Olongapo

The General had joined a table and lent his considerable vibrato to the Vietnam era salute to the Philippines. Even Jack hummed along to the familiar tune. It had been estimated that over two hundred million bottles of San Miguel beer had been consumed by the troops in Vietnam and on R&R or survival school in the Philippines. The consensus was that San Miguel tasted like dog piss—which was why most troops preferred it to '33', the Vietnamese beer.

The Marines insisted on toasting the General, leading to an ugly scene when the hapless Army troops did not stand and raise their glasses, thus becoming the first WIA in the War on Wall Street. Jack motioned to the Gunny to move the General along the street. Jack began to attract attention as he was in civilian clothing, a suit and tie. Civilians were good for two things, according to the sergeant who got in Jack's face—bringing them beer and supplying their daughters. "You ain't bringing beer, so where's your daughter?" the sergeant demanded.

The escort gunny sergeant intervened. "This guy is CIA," he said.

The obnoxious sergeant turned to the crowd and shouted, "He's **Sea Eye f--king A**!" To which all the troops whooped and drank more beer. The gunny sergeant looked at Jack and shrugged.

The pattern was repeated multiple times as the General's entourage, including Jack, made its way through the former business center of Finton. At some point Jack began to yearn for the relative calm and quietness of an artillery barrage. Every word uttered by every troop was shouted at the top of his voice.

In the joints where a semblance of order could be had, the General would climb to a tabletop and give his much ignored 'eve of battle' pep talk.

"Men, there always comes a time in every dynasty, empire, or even an uncivilized mob like those I see here (the General could not quite control his anger at not being idolized) that the men, the real men of the day must do their duty, as painful as it might be. We have reached that point in America." A few more of the troops looked up and paused in their shouting and drinking.

"Across that river," pointing east, "lies the wretched well of wealth which withers and wrongfully wrings whole......"

He ran out of the W's he had rehearsed in case his speech became a Gettysburg address to be quoted in perpetuity.

He began again. "The rapacious rascals of ruin have—"

"What's your f—king point?" someone yelled.

The General did not wilt. He stood, hands on pistol belt, for a moment, studying the few dozen men crammed into the small bar.

"Good question, Marine," he said finally. "The point is this—many of you have fought around the world, left your homes and families, lived in squalor, and that's just at Camp Lejeune," he said, getting a laugh. "Now, what I'm going to tell you is sensitive. So, I want all of you who are multi-millionaires to go ahead and leave right now." He paused.

"Come on, you know who you are. If you've got a million or more in the bank, just grab your beer and wait outside."

After a moment, one skinny Marine Lance Corporal stood up and pointed at his tablemate. "Jensen here is holding out, General. I know for a fact he just bought a new pickup." The room laughed. "Says he'll have it paid off by about ten years or if he gets his head blown off the insurance pays it off. Pretty damn good deal, I say." Laughter again and the Marine sat back down.

Jack, standing near the door, between the gunny sergeant and another of the Marines accompanying the General, sensed a change in the atmosphere. The General, it seemed, did also. He shook his head and smiled.

"Gents, across that river, about half a mile from here, are quite a few boys like you. But they could pay off that pickup in about an hour. Maybe less. And we, men like us and those before us, give them that opportunity. We fight the wars." He dramatically patted the .45 pistol on his belt. "And let me tell you about wars, men. They're all about money. About having stuff. Did you know that? Did you ever think about that? Sure, they can be also about God and people who think they're God. We've got those. But at heart, they're about who can own more shit, if you'll pardon my French." A few laughs again. "Now you and me, we've fought the damn communists for as long as most of us remember. In fact, before a lot of you were born. So, don't think I'm throwing in with those bastards. And socialists are just folks who don't have the balls to become communists. They want to drift along in the middle and that's fine with me. Won't work in America because we're wired from the beginning to work toward the top."

Jack was not completely sure if he followed the General. But from the looks on the men's faces, they were picking up the gist.

"Yeah, so what's your f—king point?" someone yelled.

So maybe they weren't getting the gist, Jack realized.

The General turned red in the face, then took a deep breath.

"The point is, Marines, those bastards on Wall Street have forgotten you. They've betrayed you. In plain English, they don't give a shit about you or your families or your pickup payments. THAT'S the point! And tomorrow morning, we're going to cross that river and make them pay the bill they owe. Those rich sonsofbitches are going to share the loot they've ripped off America!"

The Marines and the few Army troops jumped to their feet and whooped and hollered. The General grinned and, catching his eye, winked at Jack.

The troops had begun shouting 'Kill Richie Rich. Kill Richie Rich.' Which, for a moment wiped the smile off the General's face until one of his Marine guards whispered into his ear. He laughed and shouted, 'Kill Richie Rich.'

The chant spread along the street from bar to bar. Most participants had no idea what it meant but were more than happy to chant about killing someone—anyone.

They were tired, homesick, frightened and eager all at the same time. At least that's what the troops who had arrived the night before were telling the new troops showing up now. "When we were first deployed up here, there was only one bar and the barmaid only had one eye," the old-timers told the new guys.

"You guys just got here last night," the unimpressed boot scoffed back.

"What's your f—king point?" the old-timer said, exposing himself as the doubting Thomas of the crowd.

Jack began to urge the General to return to the office. He made up various reasons, none believable evidently, as the General continued along the street, glad-handing the troops, slapping backs, posing for photographs, and generally enjoying the moment. He promised everyone he met that he would be leading the charge. "I just ask that anyone seeing me with my boot stuck up some poor rich bastard's ass, give me a hand pulling it out." Jack was panicked that the Shore Patrol would show up before the General left the area.

Finally, Jack convinced the General that it was necessary to return to the office and confirm the logistics of air support and resupply. After numerous beer and speech stops, they arrived back at the headquarters building. Then, as the General went into his office, Jack excused himself to make a head call and went into his own office, closing and locking the door.

His first call was to the Navy Admiral who had arranged for the Shore Patrol to be deployed in mass to downtown Finton and close up the bars.

"All set, Jack," Admiral McDaniel said, "I've got a full contingent of the Navy's finest."

"I said to use the Marine Shore Patrol, Admiral."

"That wasn't possible, Jack. Don't worry—"

"Don't worry? Admiral, sending the Navy guys into that mob is like sticking your finger up a tiger's butt."

"That doesn't make sense, Ja—"

"Okay, I'm a little anxious here. But maybe it's a genius move by mistake. I'm trying to delay the Marines attacking Wall

Street tomorrow and there is nothing like the Navy shore patrol to make the Marines forget everything but blood and broken bones."

The Admiral paused. "You're probably right."

"I know I'm right. Just get the meat wagons ready and alert the hospital ship."

A stick-it note on Jack's chair had said to call Gearheardt. It took some doing, but Jack finally got through.

"Jack, get your skinny butt back here. I've got an airplane waiting for you at the airport. A car will meet you and get you to the Pentagon. I'll see you there."

"I've never been inside the Pentagon. How will—"

"Just bang on the door. By the way did the Shore Patrol show up and get the bars shut down?"

"I think they're there by now. Looks like that will work at least long enough to delay the attack tomorrow morning."

But Jack was wrong. Fifteen minutes after the Navy Shore Patrol waded into Finton, they were drinking beer and shouting Kill Richie Rich. They even sent a contingent back to see if they could commandeer a battleship to sail up the river providing naval gunfire to soften up lower Manhattan before the attack. They were never heard from again until a brig was opened months later aboard a battleship making a call on the naval base at Yokosuka, Japan, and four dead sailors were found. On the wall of the brig one of them had scratched Kill Richie Rich before he died.

Chapter I Have No Idea

By the time Jack landed at Andrews, however, the pilot had passed on the message to Jack that the earlier news was wrong and that the attack had indeed been postponed. And that General Fixture was also on his way to the Pentagon to 'kick some ass' according to the source.

At the Pentagon, Gearheardt met Jack with the necessary badge and paperwork to get them both complete access to all sections.

"The First Lady actually made the arrangements," Gearheardt said as they walked the long halls. "She still has guys in the shitters who took care of everything. By the way, aside from a screaming paranoia and deep hatred of men, she's not a bad person. That 'whirling dervish' act we saw a couple of times is just insecurity."

They turned a corner and ran into another check station. "Boy, she hates your ass, though. Not sure why, Jack. Just be careful around her." They had their badges inspected and then signed forms which assured the Pentagon they would not perform acts of terrorism while in the building.

Entering an office, Jack said, "Great. I suppose she also joins the legions of folks who want to kill me."

Gearheardt laughed. "Jack, you're in the wrong profession for someone who is always worrying about being killed. Even thought of the Peace Corps?"

The conference room they entered was huge, seating for thirty at the long table. Half the seats were filled. The president sat at one end. He looked up from a briefing book, nodded at Jack, and went back to reading. His lips moved as he read, Jack noticed.

The others at the table included Secretary Kinkaid, Bryce Thompson, the Ukrainian arms dealer (Jack couldn't remember his name) the Wyoming Senator, and an impressive array of military uniforms which he believed were the Joint Chiefs and Joint Almost Chiefs.

Finally, the president closed the book and looked around the table.

"So, who are the Marines tomorrow?"

An outbreak of pissing and moaning, under-breath cursing, and near treasonous countenances erupted.

"Sir, we've abandoned that crap. It was just too damn confusing—not that it wasn't a great idea (giving Jack the distinct impression where the idea came from) but we had units wandering all over the place not sure whether they were Marines or Air Force and—"

"Okay, okay, but I still want the Marine Corps to handle my President's Golf Tournament."

"Yes, sir, we'll have Marines there. And again, I apologize for last year."

Jack vaguely remembered hearing of a Presidential golf tournament at which National Association of Lesbians Against

Golf had attacked the golf course and pantsed the president. The photo of the president putting while nude from the waist down was captioned—President Defies NALAG and Completes Eighteen Holes. The light security force of disgruntled Secret Service Agents had been swept aside (some said the President encouraged the whole affair). The first lady reportedly said she was shocked the president kept his shirt on.

"Okay, okay," the president said, "what say we have Jack give us the latest on the troops in Fenton preparing for the attack, which, by the way, is not going to be tomorrow, right, Jack?"

"The WHAT?" This from an Army general who had rows of ribbons up over his shoulder and down his back which from a distance looked like a colorful serape draped over his shoulder. "What the hell is this about an attack? On WHO?"

The president held up his hand. "Don't bust a gut, Larry. You might have misheard me. Grab a cup of coffee while I have a word with Jack and Gearheardt, the CIA guys for those of you who've not met them."

The president gestured forcefully toward those CIA guys and jerked his thumb at the door. Outside the conference room the president tried the door on two offices before he found one unlocked. "Why would you lock your door inside the goddamned Pentagon?" he complained as they took seats in the office.

"Mr. President why aren't we meeting in the White House. It would—"

"Because you-know-who is having some kind of woman's dick-hate meeting or something. So, let me get something straight—it was pretty damn obvious that the Army

Joint did not know didly about the attack on Wall Street. I'm not going back there looking like Daryl Dumbass again. Gearheardt, who all knows about the plan and who doesn't?"

"Sir, I have no idea of the extent to which you've disseminated the real information and the false information. I have assumed that your direct reports—"

"I don't screw around with my direct reports—wipe that grin off your face, Gearheardt—and most of them wouldn't be—" He paused, passed his hand over his eyes and then looked at Gearheardt, then Jack, and back at Gearheardt. "Is there not a goddamned list of who is involved in the plan?"

"Mr. President, if I may call you that, when the DCI briefed me, he said—"

"And the DCI is---"

"Stevens, sir."

"No, I mean, what the hell is a DCI?"

"Director of Central Intelligence, sir."

"So, he knows?"

"He told me that you briefed him, Mr. President."

Jack was aware that Gearheardt had dropped calling the president 'Slick' or any terms of familiarity. It meant that Gearheardt was distancing himself from whatever plan was in place. He was just a loyal servant now, which bode ill for the success of the plan.

"Oh, yeah, that guy that's creepy as hell? Looks like Sneaky Pete. But did he brief you on the plan where we kill everyone on Wall Street or where I take over control of the financial system?"

"I think that's the same plan, sir. Isn't that your understanding, Jack?"

"Don't bring me into this, Gearheardt. I'm sitting here thinking there's a battalion of Marines sharpening their bayonets looking for Richie Rich's head on the end of a sharp stick."

The president looked over at Jack. "I have not a damn clue as to what that means, Jack." He placed both hands flat on the desk in front of him and sat up straight.

"Look, I don't care whether the plan was to stuff escargot up a dwarf's butt or napalm Disneyland. I want to know who knows what and IS THERE A PLAN to get me control of the financial system in the damn USA?"

The room was silent. The president put his head in his hands. Jack needed to take a leak really bad. Gearheardt was trying to remember if that goofball Edwards still had the Maserati keys.

Finally, Gearheardt spoke. "I think I know what to do, Mr. President."

"I'm all ears, Gearheardt."

"We start a new plan—"

"Oh, for God's sake, Gearheardt."

"Wait, Slick. Let's look at what the situation is. First, we have Slick Savings and Loan. You own it. It's set to take over control of the Federal Reserve Bank. So, we have a virtual money press. Then we have Jack's Marines at our beck and call bivouacking half a mile from Wall Street, raring to go. We have a shitpot full of folks not knowing if the attack is a ruse or if we're kicking ass and taking names in the investment community—I'm for that, by the way—and we've got the whole thing ready to be blamed on the Russians who hold all the American home mortgages which we will force into foreclosure."

"And why are we doing that?" the president asked.

"The Russians take legal possession of half the homes in America. No way to force the residents out. And we send the Rooskies a real estate tax bill that will suck up about eight tenths of their GDP. Of course, we give amnesty to all the homeowners, the Americans, and with no mortgage payments, you'll be elected President for life."

"Damn, the Democrats have been looking for a plan like this for ages, Gearheardt. Do you think it will work?" The president looked hopeful, but a bit skeptical.

"Sir, the ANA will bless this with a perfect score—Clients for Life. That's their top rating. The Russians will be hiring attorneys faster than the tailor killed those flies."

"The what?"

"Never mind. *The Association for Needy Attorneys* has never had a better proposal they said." Gearheardt smiled at Jack.

"As long as I get my money, I couldn't give a damn about the attorneys. And forget that President-for-Life crap. I need room to *operate* when I get that cash." He reached over and patted Gearheardt on the arm. "Okay, let's figure out what to tell the folks, and keep a damn list this time." He started to rise. "What do we call this new plan?"

"Hitler's Plan, Mr. President."

"Jumping Jehoshaphat, Gearheardt!"

"Sir, no one will want a anything to do with a project called Hitler's Plan."

"Not sure I do either, Gearheardt," the president said. He looked at Jack. "What do you think, Jack?"

"I never argue with Gearheardt, Mr. President."

"He's always right, eh?"

"He's rarely right, Mr. President. But it's a waste of time arguing with him. Go along or forget it."

"Hmmm," the president responded. "By the way, what ever happened to the Brits? I thought that we had engaged that toothy guy who runs the spy business over here, Squadron Commander Deedes, I believe it was. Weren't they going to provide some cover for the mortgage fiasco in Europe? Claim they endorsed it or something?"

"Yes, Mr. President, but it's a bit late now. Wall Street has stuffed those mortgage packages into the vaults of half the banks in France and Germany. The Brits are not dumb enough to step into the middle of---," Gearheardt said.

"Sure, they are. Get that jackass on the phone. We need some cover, or we'll end up taking the whole blame for something we did."

A speaker phone was found and Gearheardt punched in a number.

"Aw, Wing Commander Deedes, here. You appear to have my private number. What may I help you with, sir?"

"Dickie, this is Gearheardt. I have the President of the United States here with me."

"Very good, sir. Good afternoon, Mr. President. How may I be of service, sir?"

"Good afternoon, Dick. I believe that—"

"Dickie, sir."

"—in the venture that---what?"

"Dickie, sir. You said Dick."

The president looked at Gearheardt and raised his eyebrows. He mouthed 'what the hell?'

"Oh, my apologies, Wing Commander. Dickie of course. So the question that we are addressing is your continued willingness to support our efforts in the mortgage packages the U.S. banks sold in Europe."

"Well, Mr. President. This is awkward, sir. To be quite blunt, those packages were of a very smelly sort. Quite a row in the financial circles."

"I understand, Dickie. There are few morals on Wall Street. But all we are asking is that your government change its position from being a victim to one which was simply overwhelmed by the upside possibilities of the opportunity."

There was a pause. Then, "Mr. President, with all due respect, sir, that would be much akin to disavowing a paternal responsibility by claiming to be a bloody pederast. I very much doubt Her Majesty would—"

"Oh, for Pete's sakes, DICK, don't bring her into it. Who wears the pants in that gang bang you call a country? Let me tell you—"

A dial tone was heard.

"I don't think we should plan on any assistance from the Brits," Gearheardt said.

A knock on the office room door was followed by a head sticking in. "Mr. President, the gentlemen in the conference room have requested I respectfully escort you back. Impeachment was mentioned."

The president sighed and stepped to the door, waving the messenger to get out of his way. As he left, Gearheardt, who had been scribbling madly, passed a folded yellow sheet into the president's hands. "We need to use this as a place-holder plan, Mr. President."

"Don't worry, be happy, my ass," the president muttered under his breath.

Later, back at the White House, the first lady confronted the President. "Now what have you been cooking up with your pals, Slick?"

"We need you to join in with us, dear. We call it Hitler's Plan."

"I don't see how you feed yourself, Slick. Men and stupidity go together like yellow stains on the porcelain."

The president smiled as she slammed the door. Smart guy, that Gearheardt, he thought.

Back in the conference room, the president wasted no time in regaining control. "Gentlemen, the first lady is on her way over. If we can get this meeting completed, we can be out of here before she shows up." The only sound was the adjusting of ties and checking of wristwatches.

"Okay, I will admit that things got a bit ahead of themselves. Here's the scoop." He pulled the yellow paper from his jacket pocket, smoothed it out in front of him and began to read. "The Republicans have completely sold out to Bangladesh and at this time are drawing up plans to annex Burma, now called that other name, Mayonnaise or Myron or something, to give them a port to drain the annual floods into. I may have some of the facts wrong, but you get the idea."

An Admiral started to raise his hand but was quickly given maximum intimidating looks by everyone else.

"We think that the real threat comes from Egypt—" the president read.

A chorus of 'those bastards' muttered.

"—and their longtime traditional ally, Tasmania."

The president leaned over to Jack, sitting next to him, and whispered, "I'm going to kill that f—king Gearheardt."

The participants around the conference table were studying the note pads in front of them with furrowed brows and bitten lips.

Finally, the Chief Joint cleared his throat, "Mr. President, not everyone here has been cleared for the Solar level information. Accordingly, they may not understand the significance of what you have just laid out. In code, of course. May I suggest that we re-convene this briefing tomorrow in the White House at which time only those participants whose actions are necessary will be required to be in attendance."

At that moment, he became Ambassador to France or an island of his choice upon his retirement.

"A solid idea, Chief Joint, and you are, of course, absolutely correct."

The conference room became a flurry of briefcase stuffing activity and emptied quickly.

Except for the Senator from Wyoming who waddled his bow-legged butt over to the president.

"Mr. President," he began, "I *am* a Republican and I *have* Solar clearance. And I don't have the foggiest idea what in the blue blazes you were talking about."

"Have a seat, Shorty," the president said. "Let me tell you something which, in the words of a former president, is 'how the cow ate the cabbage.' Now everyone knows you keep a dead horse in your office—no, no, don't give me that denial crap—which though he may be stuffed expertly, is against Senate rules. But what most folks don't know, and I'm not saying this is a bad thing—is that you had your late wife, Emma, prepared by that same taxidermist and---don't give me that denial shit again—you have her all gussied up like Dale Evans and you got her on that horse when folks aren't around. Now what you're up to with her is none of my business, but the great state of Wyoming I happen to know has a law against that sort of thing."

"Slick, you and I know both know that is just hogwash. And, by the way, I happen to know the laws of my great state and there aren't any of them that deal with dead horses and stuffed wives. I understand the way the game is played in Washington, Slick. I was sitting in my senate seat when you were still peeing your pants and sucking on your mama's ample breasts. So, you think that just by spreading a rumor you can chase me off the reservation. Well the cabbage I want *you* to eat is this—it's high time that this country got back to honesty.

Just basic damn honesty. And it's got to start right here, right now."

"This is the Pentagon," the president said.

"Okay, well it's got to start over there across the Potomac, then. This country was not based on getting rich as all get-out and to hell with the way you got there. We had a basic God-fearing group of men with integrity and vision and a love of their fellow men."

The president looked at his watch, impatient to get going. "Shorty, I'll give you half a billion dollars and a new concrete culvert in front of every ranch house in Wyoming."

"Now you see, Mr. President, the love for my fellow man just went up a notch. But I need cattle-guards on top of those culverts. That's cow country out there." He reached out his hand for the president to shake. Which he did.

"But here's some more of that *cabbage* talk. You may think 'hey, this Senator from the great state of Wyoming sold out PDQ—that's pretty damn quick for you young men—but the fact is that I'm with you all the way. If this country is going to be run right, we need to take control of those traitorous felons on Wall Street. No one elected them to get so rich they could bribe Washington into doing their bidding."

Jack looked at Gearheardt and was disappointed to see he seemed to be shaking his head in an affirmative motion.

"Senator, if every Republican in Congress felt like you do, we could get this country back to economic prosperity quicker than a coon dog with his ass on fire."

They shook hands again.

"But Mr. President, there has to be some sanity in the new economy. That dot com business was just plain silliness."

"Well, you know technology is—" the president was defensive, and Jack realized that the dot.com explosion must have financed most of his last campaign.

"Yeah, I know it's mostly bullshit, Mr. President. Goddamn coffee makers that start your car and figure out your taxes, so you have time to go pay five dollars a cup for coffee. But here's what I'm talking about. You can't, and I know you'll take some umbrage, but hear me out. You can't just take the money from Wall Street and piss it away on one damn program after another. Free money is the root of all evil. True in Bible days and even more true now.

"And the Democrats seem to want to just dispense the country's cash to every Tom, Dick and Harry that says he needs it. A man goes Gimme Gimme and points to a starving family and wham, you drop a bushel basket of money on him. And the foreign countries—hellfire, you might as well just convert the B-52 fleet to money-droppers. Just fly over and open the bomb bay doors and let-er-rip. Why do we need a state department if our answer to every besotted government is to just send 'em some cash? Ammunition is just the middleman. Drop dollars and save the bombs."

"Well—," the president started, his face becoming a bit red.

"And before you mention all the precious lives of young American's we've spent on foreigners, let me remind you that none of them paid their own way over to the place they died."

The president leaned back in his chair. "Shorty, I haven't a splinter of an idea of what that last thing means."

"It means, President not for life, that every time a basket case country screams about some bully bothering them, you Democrats think nothing of just loading up a few ships of men and guns and sending them off to—"

"Whoa, hold your horses, Shorty, and I don't mean that dead one in your office. I don't remember the Republicans exactly dominating the peace rallies."

"Hell, Mr. President, I'm not saying we never wanted a war. We just wanted to win the ones we started. That dumb SOB in the White House during Vietnam strung together a series of peace efforts sometimes disrupted by a few bombing missions. Oh, and we told 'em where we would bomb so no one would get hurt. No sense in getting the enemy all cranky if you can help it."

"You right-wing sunsabitches just won't let that one go, will you?" The president was on his feet. "We got poor people coming out of our ass here in the USA and you want to send our boys over to stop people without a nickel to their name in a fight that's been going on for a million years and goddamn little democracy has come to—"

"GENTLEMEN!" It was Gearheardt, who also jumped to his feet. "For God's sake. Now you're even changing sides in your own argument! May I respectfully remind you that the Central Intelligence Agency is damn near the end of its patience. We've listened to this Battling Bickersons bullshit for half a century. Does anyone need me to tell you what happens to people who piss off the CIA?"

"Don't make me laugh, sonny boy. The CIA tries any shenanigans in the great state of Wyoming, and they'll be wishing—"

BOOM! The windows rattled and the coffee thermos rolled onto the floor. Gearheardt jumped up and ran to the window .

"Senator, were you driven over here in a black limo by a driver wearing a cowboy hat?" he asked over his shoulder.

"As a matter of fact---"

"Well, the cowboy hat survived."

The senator was visibly shaken.

The President, the senator, Jack and Gearheardt sat silent for a moment. Finally, the President spoke. "Well, that was a hell of a coincidence."

After the "bow-legged bandit" (as Gearheardt called him) left, the president, Jack and Gearheardt stayed behind to tie up a few loose ends.

"First of all, Gearheardt," the president started, "who was that Eastern European potato head who sat next to the first lady's cousin? Sonofabitch looked like he made that suit for himself on the way over here."

"That's the Ukrainian arms dealer who arranged for us sell the Egyptians their own weapons, Mr. President."

"Hmm. So where are the weapons now?"

"I believe, and I'll have to check, the Marines have them. Or at least they'll have them before they attack Wall Street."

"Gee, the Pentagon must have had to do a lot of studying to come up with that plan. Weapons before the battle. What a concept."

"You don't like the military very much, do you Mr. President?" This from Jack.

"Don't start that shit again, Jack or whatever your name is. I had a college deferment, asshole. And the military always thinks they're so damn smart. Bunch of know-it-alls. But guess what—who is it always ends up getting their ass shot off in some shithole county? The military, that's who."

"An excellent point, Mr. President," Jack said with professional-level sarcasm. "And who is it---"

"Gentlemen, gentlemen, let's get to the issues at hand," Gearheardt said.

"I didn't start it, Gearheardt," the president said. "I'm just saying that the military always gets the benefit of the doubt. But..."

"Okay, moving right along, gents. Does anyone know where the Russian mortgage brokers are? They came over to fight as Federal Reserve workers and Savings and Loan officers."

"Arizona," the president said. "Okay, next item."

"Arizona?" Jack asked. "How in the hell did they get to Arizona?"

"Airplane. What's next, Gearheardt?"

Jack was troubled by the attitude of the president but agreed to move on. At some point, however, the question of why the president sent one thousand Russian mortgage brokers to Arizona would have to be addressed.

"So, the Marines will do the fighting on Wall Street? Any disagreement there, Jack? Mr. President?"

"Gearheardt, if you tell me the 'paperwork' is all set for Slick Savings to take over the Fed, I say we schedule the Wall Street attack day after tomorrow."

"I think we've got everything squared away, Mr. President." Gearheardt winked at the president, who smiled.

Jack wondered what was going on. He felt very uncomfortable with all that he did not know. And where was the CIA in all this? What happened to the pygmy? What happened to Eddie Jackson? Did the president now 'outrank' the Pygmy? Is there really going to be a military attack on Wall Street? Was all this just about money?

He unfortunately knew the answer to the last question.

"Let's go down and see what the damage is," Gearheardt said. He sounded happy.

The area around the blackened hole in the ground was ringed with yellow police tape. A number of military and civilian policemen were scouring the area. A disheveled limo driver sat on the curb, a blast-worn cowboy hat hanging on his head in small strips. Evidently he had survived the explosion.

"How in the hell would I know a dwarf from a pygmy," he was saying to one of the policemen. "I heard a click and ran for my life. A three-foot-tall something was running for his life alongside me. And he was laughing. He said that it was the work of the Central Intelligence Agency. That's all I know."

"Hmm," mused the policeman, "looks like this is another case of the laughing CIA pygmy blowing up cars in the Pentagon parking lot." He was being a bit sarcastic.

"F--- you," said the limo driver. "You asked me what happened. I told you."

In the parking lot of the Pentagon, the president shook hands with Jack and Gearheardt and started to walk away.

"Mr. President, where are your security guys? Where's your limo?"

"I'm just going to grab a cab, Gearheardt. I'm not sure I trust those Secret Service guys." He turned and headed toward an exit.

"What the hell?" Jack said, watching the president disappear.

"He's got a date, Jack. That's what he meant about not trusting the Secret Service guys. They would give their life for him. But they won't lie to the first lady for him. That would be painful."

Gearheardt punched Jack's shoulder. "Let's move on," he said.

Another Chapter

The boys began walking toward the Marine Memorial, looking for a taxi.

"Did you—"

"Yes, Jack, I heard them talking about the pygmy. When we meet the agency guys this evening, I promise to bring it up."

"We're meeting with the CIA this evening?"

"Jack, sometimes I think you forget who we're working for. The CIA isn't the shadow government like some people believe. It IS the government. These administration and congressional fools couldn't sell sex on a troop ship. And they come and go with the whim of the working folks, the so-called populace, most of whom couldn't identify their representative if he wore a 12 by 12 *Hi, My Name Is John Doohickey* sign."

Jack stopped dead in his tracks.

Gearheardt stopped a step ahead and looked back at Jack.

"Gearheardt, you know the most depressing thing about what you just said?"

"Sex on a troop ship?"

"No, dumbass, I'm serious. The most depressing thing is that you said it. You've always been so damn upbeat about America and our leaders—not the ones who ran the Vietnam War—and I was the cynical one. But now you sound like, well, me."

"I'm from Princeton, Jack, but I'm not stupid."

"What?"

"I mean the wonderful liberal education hasn't totally blinded me to the mess this country is in. Everybody is so busy trying to make a buck that no one's running the store, the government store, that is."

"Exactly, Gearheardt! Exactly. That's what I've been trying to tell you. 'America, the Best Place to Make a Buck' is the new motto." Jack was excited and sad at the same time.

"I never liked that E Pluribus Unum deal anyway," Gearheardt said. "Sounds like pretentious bullshit."

"Well—"

"The thing is, Jack, and by the way, let's pick up the pace. We've got to be at the CIA before dark. So anyway, the thing is that Wall Street screws the American folks everyday but Sunday. You ever heard of that tulip disaster in Holland? Folks buying tulip bulbs like there was no tomorrow, and—"

"Yes, Gearheardt, we heard about it even out at cow college in Oklahoma."

Gearheardt stopped suddenly and turned to Jack. "You wanna know when you know you're just a damn dollar dispenser for Wall Street? That's when you're driving madly around town looking for Beanie Babies. F__king Beanie Babies. Wall Street convinced millions of people that the next big investment sure thing was Beanie Babies. We're the dumbest people in the world, Jack. Blinded by pure greed. Hell, at least the Dutch could eat the tulip bulbs."

"Uh, I don't think so, Gearheardt. But I'm just flabbergasted that you've come around to my way of thinking. America has gone mad."

"Well, a garage full of boxes of Beanie Babies kind of gives you a wake-up call, Jack. But its more than that. Have you heard of churches that charge admission? Just damn disgraceful and—"

They were within sight of the Marine Memorial.

"Churches charging admission?"

"No. I asked if you had heard of any," Gearheardt corrected.

They approached the huge statue of the Marines raising the flag on Iwo Jima.

"Always a thrill, Jack. No matter how many times I come here. Seeing those Marines on top of Mount Baldy just sends a thrill---"

"It was Mount Suribachi, Gearheardt."

"Suribachi means bald in Japanese."

"No, it doesn't."

And just like that, serious discussion with Gearheardt was over.

There were no taxis at the Marine Memorial. Gearheardt commandeered a tourist bus and demanded to be taken to

Langley. Fortunately, the majority of the tourists on board seemed to relish the idea of being taken to the CIA headquarters, and particularly in the mode of being hi-jacked to the building—given the story-telling possibilities.

The driver, a rather plump black lady with a congenial manner, said it made not a whit of difference to her. And asked the location of Langley, which of course bumfuzzled Gearheardt. We had to stop and call a case-officer Gearheardt knew vaguely and talk him into giving us directions. The tourists closest to the front and within hearing distance more than likely had misgivings about the future of the intelligence community while listening to the phonic disagreements of one-way streets and traffic circles.

At the main gate to the CIA headquarters, Gearheardt said goodbye to each and every passenger, exchanging phone numbers and addresses and promising to try to get together at least annually.

"What the hell was that all about, Gearheardt," Jack asked as they waited for clearance and a guide to escort them into the building.

"Those were good people, Jack. Salt of the earth. I wanted to make the day special for them."

"In other words, you were jerking them around."

"I get my kicks where I find them. Hey, here comes Mary Ellen. Used to work for me in Tortures and Confessions Department."

Jack never knew when Gearheardt was kidding.

"Hey, Mary Ellen, at what temperature do eyeballs explode?" Gearheardt said as the very lovely lady approached.

"Wow, Gearheardt," she said, accepting a brief greeting hug from him. "It took exactly six seconds from the time I saw you until I remembered why you were thrown out of the department with prejudice."

Gearheardt grinned and turned to Jack. "Mary Ellen is an attorney. She knows it turns me on when she talks legal."

"Yes, and before we go further, I'm also reminded why I dismissed your dating propositions with prejudice."

By this time, we had entered the main lobby, traipsed over the huge CIA emblem on the floor, and received documentation allowing us to go almost any place in the building unescorted.

"It's hard to believe the mission you must be on, Gearheardt. Allowing you unfettered access to this building is beyond any security precaution I'm aware of. God help us."

"Thanks, Mary Ellen. By the way, this is Jack Armstrong. My best pal."

"I cannot fathom a more pathetic recommendation." She shook Jack's hand and left.

"I thought all the women swooned over you, Gearheardt. I get the distinct impression that Mary Ellen is not swooning." Jack found he took a bit of pleasure in seeing his friend spurned.

"A bit of a misunderstanding in the application of a device of torture, in which we were trapped for forty-eight hours, has probably biased her judgment," Gearheardt said wistfully as he watched two prefect hips sway themselves down the hall.

Gearheardt

The DCI's secretary finally found Jack and Gearheardt wandering around the halls on the fourth floor and escorted them to the office of the DCI. Who was not there.

"Director Stevens will return in just a few minutes, gentlemen. If you like I can get coffee for you. Or perhaps a cyanide capsule." It was an old CIA joke.

Gearheardt sat down while Jack strolled around the large office, looking at diploma's, photos, memorabilia such as flags and knives, a large number of knives.

"Gearheardt," he said over his shoulder while scrutinizing a certificate in a foreign, unreadable, language, "there's not a single plaque or certificate with the name Stevens."

The DCI came through a side door as Jack spoke. "Quite right, Jack. Over the years, some of us at the agency play many men." He shook Jack's hand, patted Gearheardt on the back as he passed his chair and sat down behind his desk.

"All too many good men actually forget who they really are after so many years as someone else. In fact, I keep my birth certificate here in my desk drawer so I can 'ground myself' every so often."

He opened the drawer. "My God, I'm actually Ralph Durvis!" he said. Then he laughed. "No, just kidding you, boys." He pushed the drawer closed.

"So, what did I want to see you about?"

Jack was not certain he was pleased to find that Director Stevens had a deep sense of humor. The only other CIA officer with a similar sense of humor, Gearheardt, was often bat-shit crazy.

"Gents," Stevens began, his manner close to avuncular, "this mission has been planned for some time. You two were brought in only recently. Of course, you, Jack, had to be buried in Anadarko to have a plausible trail of documentation to show the President. More about that later. But keep in mind that things at the Agency are not always what they appear."

"No shit," Jack muttered.

"But you can be assured that the President is not taking over the financial system, that Wall Street is not going to be assaulted by the Marines, and the true nature of the black hole in the banking system unfortunately dwarfs the potential crisis which those events could precipitate. You see—"

"Sir, with all due respect," Jack said, "I'm not sure the Marines are on board with your position. I can't speak for Gearheardt's promises to the President, but I can tell you that General Fixture is fixing, no pun intended, to kick ass up and down Wall Street."

Stevens chuckled. "I know it seems that way, Jack. However, what you don't know is that we have a man buried so deep in that whole operation that Fixture wouldn't take a piss without us being at the urinal next to him. Our man is as reliable as the sun coming up in the morning. We started him digging in years ago. Only I and one other is even aware of his existence. I think that—"

Jack frowned. "You mean Edwards?"

The DCI glared at Gearheardt and then lasered his glower in on Jack. "Shit," he said.

Chapter Before the Next Chapter

The CIA boys were much more efficient than the Marines and Jack and Gearheardt were both barefoot and secured to their respective chairs before the acetylene tank was through the door.

"I think you will find it less painful to tell us exactly how you found out about Edwards right away," Stevens said. He was behind his desk. Slumped in his chair and sporting a fairly decent evil look.

"Edwards told me," Jack said.

The room was silent except for the acetylene torch hissing near Jack's toes.

Finally, Stevens waved the CIA goons away. "And watch that torch, Jenkins. Dammit, that carpet was a gift from the Saudis. On your way out tell Martha to get those carpet repair guys back up here."

"The bastard ran off with my Maserati, too," Gearheardt said as he was putting on his socks.

Jack looked too late to find out if Gearheardt actually had no toes.

The DCI was surprisingly contrite. "Sorry about that, gentlemen. With all these budget cuts, we've been asking a question just one time and then burning off toes. No long, torturous—pun intended—inquisitions which just cost time, and time is money. And if I might toot my own horn just a bit, that process, called No Talk, No Toes, in the vernacular, is becoming quite popular in the interrogation industry. We discussed franchising it, but…..well, anyway, we need to move on."

"I think I've seen your ads," Gearheardt said. Jack assumed it was just a wise-ass comment. It drew a nasty look from Stevens.

Stevens went on. "The fact is that Edwards is actually in the building. And the current chairman of the Federal Reserve Bank and he are meeting. Assuming they've located the Fed chief. Little bastard took off this morning and hasn't been seen since breakfast."

Jack furrowed his brow. "Didn't the Fed Chief resign not long ago? I read—"

"Well, yes, as a matter of fact. The current chief was handpicked to begin—"

"Handpicked by who?" Gearheardt asked, leading Jack to believe that his pal was not the father of this misadventure as he had claimed.

Stevens shrugged as if the question was of no consequence. "I guess you could say by us."

Jack wanted to ask exactly how that worked, but Stevens went on.

"While we wait for Edwards to join us, let me fill you in a bit. After World War Two, the tendency for a U.S. president was to act as if he ran the government. The country was all about whooping and hollering over beating the Japs and Krauts, so no one took him seriously. Happy days were indeed here again."

"You mean he just ignored congress and—" Jack said.

Stevens laughed. "Ignore congress? Why? Congress is the spittoon in a high-class saloon. Glad it's there or the floor gets all slippery. But it's best not to stick your hand in it. Congress exists so that the people of America feel like 'one of their own' made it to the top and they have a say-so in running the country.

"The interaction between the president and congress is like the Japanese kabuki. All acting, no accomplishing."

Jack had heard more cynicism but couldn't think of where or when.

Gearheardt said, "Hercules once said—Morality belongs to those who wear the crown."

"Hercules?" Stevens asked, brow fully accordioned.

"Gearheardt probably thinks Hercules was a Greek philosopher and that things a Greek philosopher says lend gravitas to his inane remarks," Jack suggested.

Gearheardt smiled. "Thanks, Jack. Couldn't have put it better myself."

Director Stevens looked at Gearheardt. "Hmm," he said, "I understand you're one of the Agency's top operatives." The skepticism was peeking through.

"Sir, in all modesty, that certainly is my opinion," Gearheardt said. "And don't let Jack's humble education from a cow college fool you, he's a hell of a lot brighter than he looks."

Jack pantomimed 'thanks.'

"Uh huh," Stevens said. He looked at his watch. "Where can Edwards be? I would think he's completed his 'discussion' with the new Fed Chief by now."

At which point Edwards, in mufti now, opened the door after a quick knock.

"Never caught the little bastard," he said. "We found spoor everywhere, but he's still on the loose." He shook everyone's hand with a brief greeting and sat down. "So where are we in the plan to save America?"

"Wait a minute," Jack said, leaning forward toward Edwards, "what do you mean you found spoor? Isn't that a term you would use—"

"We're tracking the new Fed Chief, Jack. You know he's been in the building for years. We've found that hiring big game hunters is the most efficient way to ferret him out."

"Are we talking about the damn Pygmy?" Jack was alarmed. "The Pygmy is the new Fed Chief?"

Gearheardt said, "We have a dwarf as the chief financial officer of America, Jack. Quit acting so surprised. It's a new day in America."

"He's not a dwarf. He's a pygmy." Stevens sounded a bit apologetic. Jack assumed it was his idea.

"And the president appointed him?" Jack asked.

"Well, kind of. The president had asked that we find a new Fed Chief that he could control. Since at that time we had Xanalto in a cage in the basement annex, I thought we could assure the president of total control."

"I'm not sure that's the kind of control the Pre—" Jack began.

"Yeah, yeah. We don't split hairs around here, Jack. Let's get on with Mr. Edwards status report."

Edwards cleared his throat. "Thank you, sir. And Jack, I understand your confusion. With permission from the DCI let me give you the background."

The DCI stood. "I know the background. I'm going to take a leak." He left through a side door which evidently was a private restroom. Or he was peeing in a coat closet.

Edwards began, "Jack, you're aware that a few years back, a Pygmy snuck aboard a CIA aircraft leaving Africa, found his way to Langley and has built up quite a following by agreeing to take all blame for any failures the CIA might be involved in."

"The little prick tried to have me killed in Mexico," Jack said.

"But he didn't, Jack. And around here we always say a miss is as good as a mile. Let's say we try to overthrow a small country and instead everyone is killed. A failure? No, the Pygmy agrees that he was the owner of the plan, the execution, the hiring and training of peasants and mercenaries—and never mix the two, Jack—no one's admin jacket suddenly becomes toxic. Yet, a lot of people are taught a lesson they'll never forget. A win-win."

"Except for those killed."

Edwards laughed. "Our record is perfect there, Jack. No one we've killed has ever successfully attacked us. I know that sounds callous, but so is cutting a calf's nuts off."

"I'm not sure there is any kind of moral equiv—"

"Of course you don't, Jack." Edwards rose and walked to the phone, punched in buttons, waited, and then, "This is Edwards. Any update on finding the Fed Chief? Yes, the pygmy guy…..Whose cat was it?.... All paws missing?..... What do you mean roasted?..... Well, stay on it. The guy has a meeting on interest rates in half an hour." He looked at Jack and Gearheardt and shrugged. "I guess you can take a guy out of the Kalahari, but……"

Gearheardt, who had been sitting quietly with a bemused expression, spoke up. "This pygmy guy, always causing trouble, screwing up documents, disobeying orders, eating the pets, why don't you have someone take care of him?"

"Don't think we haven't considered it, Gearheardt. First, we have to catch him. Then we desperately need him to sign some documents. And the flip side is that he's a perfect bureaucrat in many ways. We were going to make some huge hoopla announcement about him being the first Bushman of the Kalahari to be appointed the Chairman of the Federal Reserve. He is scrupulous about not giving a shit who's getting screwed by the government. He is hated by both sides of the aisle. He has an unbridled love of the president who he thinks is God. And he makes his own clothes."

Jack had a plethora of questions, but none tumbled out of his awestruck brain, except, "Does he know jack-shit about the US banking system?"

"Not that we can tell, to be honest. That's why we were caught off-guard when within hours of taking over the reigns as Fed Chief he made a few astounding changes and signed a deal with Gaborone we're still trying to figure out." Edwards was obviously chagrined.

"Gaborone?" Gearheardt asked.

"Capital of Botswana."

DCI Stevens had just stepped back in and took his place behind his desk. "Botswana? Great subject. You must be talking about that damn pygmy."

"Why not fire him?"

"The president actually likes him. He's a perfect bureaucrat in many ways, and he's hard as hell to capture." Stevens retrieved a cigar butt from an ashtray on a side table.

Jack spoke. "That's not exactly the story that Edwards just told us."

Stevens wasn't perturbed in the slightest. "We like to have more than one story about everything we do. If a man is capable of being hated, we can work with him." He lit the cigar. "But let's get down to tass bracks."

Jack inwardly winced. How deeply embedded in the U S government was the First Lady's cousin-in-law?

"Jack, let me be frank with you—"

"Sir, you can be Wee Willie Winkie with me. I would just like to know what's going on, what's the end game, who's in charge, and why am I in the middle of it."

"We would all like to know those things, Jack. And if you weren't in the middle of it, you wouldn't know anything about any of it and you wouldn't be worried."

After a moment, Jack said, "That's an answer?"

"Gearheardt said we could count on you. We need someone who is relatively sane and has some moral guidelines. Someone who is not greedy as a starving dog, and who doesn't need all the money in the world just to be happy. Someone not in the government."

"Why am I feeling pride and dark despair at the same time?" Jack asked rhetorically.

"Edwards, please continue with your briefing," Stevens said.

"Yes, sir." He stood and began to pace around the room as he spoke. "The bottom line is this, dispensing with all beating around the bush, coming right to the point, as it lays right how, in—"

"Damn it, Edwards, get on with it."

"Yes, sir. Jack, you and Gearheardt know the sub-plans by now. The attack on Wall Street, the takeover of the Federal Reserve, and handing a huge part of the nation's banking system to the president, and his wife I would assume." Edwards seemed unsure of himself—unusual.

Jack said, "Generally speaking, yes. We're aware of those plans and we are beginning to understand, if I read this the right way, those are all diversionary devices to avoid the consequences of something more devastating. Right?" Jack held up his palm toward Gearheardt to stop him from interrupting.

"Further, and yes, you are generally correct, Jack, you and Gearheardt are evidently the only two Agency employees who have dealt directly with the pygmy. I believe it was in the scheme to invade and occupy Cuba by faking an assassination of the president of Mexico and blaming the Cubans." Edwards looked up and over the top of his glasses at Gearheardt and then Jack. Both nodded a 'more or less' yes to his question.

"I'm not sure my *relationship* would qualify as being familiar with him, Edwards. He was trying to kill me," Jack said.

Stevens spoke, "Jack, I think you would agree that an action as substantial and potentially serious as having you killed would very definitely quality as a relationship. Wouldn't you agree?" He smiled. "Even in the agency we rarely kill strangers."

Gearheardt nodded his head. "They have a point, Jack."

"Let's get this meeting back on track, gentlemen," Stevens said. "We need you men to work with the pygmy, assuming we can find him, and find out what deals he has made since he became Fed Chief, and help us build a plan to undo them, or nullify them. After that, perhaps just murder him. Don't you agree, Edwards?"

"I think 'murder' gives the wrong message, sir. Didn't we come up with a euphemism like extreme prejudice or something? Or was that just in the movie?" Edwards inquired.

"Okay, okay, let's call it whatever the euphemism de jure might be. But just be sure you murder the little bastard before you let him go." Stevens was firm.

"Sir, could you give us a suggestion as to what actions you fear the Fed Chief has made? That might help a bit if we had to use the toes or talk routine," Jack asked.

"This is confidential of course. And we're trying to get verification. But the rumor is that he bought Botswana and also invested billions in beads."

"Beads?" Gearheardt sounded dubious.

"Yes, beads. It seems that beads are a major stock of the money trade in the lower desert regions of southern Africa. But that problem is working itself out. It's the ownership of Botswana that we're trying to assess just what that might mean," Edwards said.

Gearheardt asked, "Just out of curiosity, how did you manage to disinvest from billions of dollars in beads already? That would seem—"

Stevens smiled. "For payment we sent them two million Beanie Babies and over three hundred thousand Pet Rocks."

Gearheardt was impressed. "Genius. We do have some good bankers in this country."

"Okay. Gearheardt, you and Jack know your job now. The Pygmy knows you're vitally involved in the deception initiatives. We've established that. So, find him. Grill him. Find out what he's done and where the documentation is. Work with Edwards here to come up with a solution for what needs to be done. If Congress needs to be involved, so be it. Steer clear of the President. Keep me absolutely updated. And then, when we've agreed that things are under control, do that…. murder thing. Not murder but that other name for it."

He stood and walked around his desk, shaking hands with Jack and Gearheardt who met a messenger coming into the office as they left. The messenger handed a note to the DCI and left.

Edwards stepped to speak quietly with the DCI. "Sir, why didn't you mention the problem? The one with the capital P?"

"You meant capital D?"

"No, I was saying capital P for Problem. You mean D for derivatives."

Stevens winced. "We don't say that word, Edwards. My financial analysts are still working 24/7 on what the hell to do. Let's find the pygmy and maybe by then we'll have something."

He had been glancing at the message lying on his desk. Now he looked up at Edwards and handed him the message.

Edwards read: *Marines have de-testiclated the Charging Bull bronze statue on Wall Street.*

"Shit," said Edwards. "I thought Jack said the Marines were on hold."

"Is de-testiclated even a word?" asked Stevens. "I'm pretty sure that means they've cut the nuts off the Wall Street bull. That can't be good."

Jack and Gearheardt ducked into an empty office and closed the door.

"Gearheardt, we need to take a step back and sort things out."

"Good idea, Jack. I've got a feeling that the Marines have their acetylene torch crew working on Wall Street. You might want to head back to New Jersey and see what's happening."

"Where are you going?" Jack asked.

"I'm going to find a damn Republican and see if they plan to just stand by and watch the country head into the shitter. You know as well as I do that all this fake war and Russian mortgage troops blather is just another cover-up for a power grab and accompanying vote producer."

"They couldn't keep that quiet, Gearheardt," Jack said. "They could just kill everyone."

"I doubt that Jack, but you get the point. Human misery is God's gift to Democratic fundraisers and vote gatherers. Republicans are just lizards laying on a rock in the sun."

"I'm not even going to comment on that. But—"

A polite knock on the door which opened slightly.

"Is one of you Mr. Gearheardt?" a young woman asked.

"Yes, one of us is," Gearheardt replied, taking a slip of paper from her hand.

Gearheardt read the message and handed it to Jack.

"The Fed Chief formerly known as the Pygmy is evidently on Wall Street," he said. "I think I should cancel my visit to the Republican Rest Home and find the Fed Chief muy pronto."

"I'll see if I can hide the keys to the landing craft and stop the Marines."

Which was not exactly what Jack was really thinking. Given what he had heard, learned and conjectured over the past few days, an attack on Wall Street by the Marines might be just what the country needed. If it was followed up by an attack on the White House and the Congress. A coup. Unbelievable that a coup sounded like the best alternative. But then again, he realized that he actually didn't know the true reason for all the distractions, fake-plans, and threats. It wasn't as if America was in danger of a take-over enemy attack. Or was suddenly broke and a world beggar-country. What was it they called those basket cases—a failed nation state?

Equally surprising, and troubling, was that Gearheardt seemed almost distant. The old Gearheardt, the one who raced Ho Chi Minh in a Corvette. The one who lived in a CIA controlled brothel in Mexico City. The guy that the former president of the US sucker punched in a bar in Olongapo in the Philippines. Where was that Gearheardt? And the worst part—what Jack was having a hard time adjusting to—was that the reality was that Gearheardt had not changed. The people they dealt with were more and more like Gearheardt! His ideas didn't stand out as looney and dangerous. Looney and dangerous were the norm.

And most disturbing. Most depressing. If the love of money was the root of all evil, America was hell bent for leather chasing the devil, not to kill him but to form a joint venture. E Pluribus Unum was now Caveat Emptor. Wearing the Star of David as a badge of shame would pale beside the shame from an edict to wear your net worth on a sign around your neck. Nobel Prize. Pulitzer. Olympic Gold Medal Winner. All were just *Joe Shit the Ragman* unless they had turned the *honor* into cash.

And finally, the question that every man had to ask himself. Though Jack had faced life-threatening situations in the Corps and the CIA, cheating death, defying the possibility of being maimed—did he have the character, the moral courage, the strength, to be not rich?

Jack picked up the phone in the office and got an outside line. He dialed the number on the business card he had in his pocket.

The phone only rang once before, "Secretary Kinkaid's office."

"Yes, this is Jack Armstrong, I talked to the Secretary and he said to call him if he could be of assistance. I could use his assistance."

"Yes, Mr. Armstrong, let me check to if the Secretary is available."

After a few minutes, "The Secretary is regretfully unable to take your call at this time, Mr. Armstrong."

"Would it be possible to talk to him later? I can call--- "

"The Secretary asked me to convey to you that you have his full support. That you seem to be an honest man. But again, regretfully, he cannot take a call. The President has asked him to represent him at the Conference of Leaders and Financial People in Ulaanbaatar, Mongolia, tomorrow. He's leaving shortly."

"The conference of what?"

"The exact response of the Secretary, Mr. Armstrong. Good day, sir."

Jack remembered the President's squinting, beady eyes when he was talking to the Secretary after the White House meeting.

Gearheardt came back from taking a leak. "Jack, we better get our asses in gear. I'll get the Marine chopper to drop you in Jersey and then take me over to Wall Street. I'm pretty sure that the Pygmy is in the Dow Jones building or over at Darkman."

He stood and held out his hand. "Good luck, Jack. Get those Marines under control. Their attack could spoil a lot of well-laid plans."

"For you, too?" Jack asked.

Gearheardt looked surprised, then he laughed. He tightened his grip in their handshake. "We're partners, Jack. Always have been. You take care of the Marines. I'll take care of you." He left.

Jack caught up with Gearheardt outside the building.

"I've arranged for a car to take us to the helicopter pad, Jack. We'll be on our way in a few minutes."

Jack watched Gearheardt light a cigarette. After a moment he said, "What's going on, Gearheardt? This is madness."

"Not sure what you mean, Jack." He turned and looked squarely at Jack's face. "And I might ask you the same question. What's going on with you? I get this feeling that you're anti-everything America stands for—killing bad guys, making a lot of money, ignoring opportunities to gain advantage over enemies. Capitalism! Providing a—"

"Oh bullshit, Gearheardt. Say it. You know damn well that I've always worried that Americans can overdo *breathing*. Anything worth doing is worth overdoing. That's our motto. And we've just elevated net worth above—"

"I've heard the speech, Jack. So, should we embrace Marxism, celebrate the proletariat, and tax ourselves ninety nine percent so that poor people can drive bigger cars?"

"No, Gearheardt," Jack said firmly. "We should keep Judeo/Christian ethics in our capitalism. Our universities should educate us as Americans. We should simply remember the Golden Rule in damn near everything we do. Our—"

Gearheardt scoffed. "Right, Jack. That'll turn things around." He flicked his cigarette into the street. "Our universities are run by old hippies. Our newspapers are run by jerks we used to bully in high school. And our politicians are spineless tweebs who believe they were called to be our perpetual parents."

The two friends stood silent. CIA employees leaving the building pushed past them chattering like magpies. Jack realized he had somehow visualized trench-coated, fedora-hatted, platoons of serious men, averting their eyes, exuding mystery and confidence would be exiting the building. Of course, Gearheardt, much closer to the Agency, had always said that the CIA was becoming the IRS with guns. *"The peanut man started gutting the Agency replacing spies with college chums from the Academy whose 'no harm, no foul' philosophy counted on America's enemies playing by the same rules."* It hadn't worked. [Years later, after the Arabs killed three thousand Americans, the cry went up 'where in the hell was the CIA?" to which the answer was, 'in sensitivity and diversity training.']

Finally, Gearheardt said, "Jack, I'm not saying that the Wall Street crowd isn't a confederation of assholes who are looting the coffers of the unwary. But at least they're not communist bastards out to enslave—"

"Why do I always think you might have a cogent idea bouncing around in your damn head, Gearheardt? The statement you seem to be trying to make is a non sequitur of an admirable purity, rendering it absolute gibberish."

"Lord, Jack, the way you talk sometimes." He laughed. "Your problem has always been you think too much."

Jack looked at his shoes and shook his head, then faced his pal. "Gearheardt, my statement no doubt sounded like the pretentious bullshit it was. But somehow, just saying 'you're full of shit' wasn't enough."

"If you say so, Jack. I just know that we're the best damn country that ever existed. And the left, the liberals, the communists in our schools are trying to destroy us. We have to do whatever we can to—"

"Gearheardt, I get it. Not sure how it applies to Wall Street trickery, but I get it. But remember the old story about the two campers who woke up to a bear rampaging through their camp. The one hunter started to run out of the tent and realized the other hunter was lacing up his tennis shoes. 'My God, Hank, do you think you're going to be able to outrun a bear?' he said. The other hunter said, 'Don't need to. I just have to outrun you.'"

"Yeah, I always liked that one." Gearheardt had spied their ride to the heli-pad and started to walk away.

"Gearheardt! The point is that we can't always just outrun the other guys. Just being less evil isn't good enough."

"Jack, sometimes you just don't make much sense. Of course it is."

"Just staying ahead is not a win, Gearheardt, if you lose your soul."

Gearheardt stopped as he was getting into the car. "Do you ever watch Soul Train, Jack? Damn good music. And by the way, I get your point. You're saying we need to Save the Whales, right?"

Jack had almost forgotten he was talking to Gearheardt. That reminded him. He had no idea what went on in his pal's mind.

Gearheardt

Chapter I've Certainly Lost Track

As promised, Gearheardt was able to commandeer a Marine Corps helicopter to take them to Fenton and Manhattan.

As they landed in Fenton Jack stood to leave the aircraft.

"Jack remember," Gearheardt said, "the most important thing is to keep them out of Manhattan for at least two as they landed in Fenton days. And Jack, keep your head down. I hate it when my friends are shot in the head."

"Me too," Jack replied. He stood in the door of the helicopter and looked back at Gearheardt. Who smiled, then unexpectedly rose and stepped to Jack and gave him a manly hug.

"Take care of yourself, pal," Gearheardt said.

The flight mechanic was busy sweeping peanut shells through the door of the helicopter. The pilots had been munching on peanuts and dropping the shells on the floor during the flight. When Jack had pointed at the growing pile of shells and mouthed "what the hell?" to the flight mech, the Marine pulled the microphone away from his face and shouted over the engine noise into Jack's, "They say it helps to keep them awake."

Now Jack stood in peanut shells on the tarmac as the helicopter rose and departed the Fenton airport. Where the same Marine in the same jeep was waiting.

The ride to the headquarters of General Fixture was even more of a shock than the first time. Fenton now had a GI supported economy of alcohol, loose women, cheap souvenirs and shops to tailor ill-fitting clothing from inexpensive material. Multi-colored taxis wove irregular paths of formerly outlawed driving patterns—sidewalks, parkways, and lawns—carrying half a dozen Marines per car searching for the trouble only they could bring with them, guaranteeing they would find it. Jack saw a sign on a store front announcing the soon to be open "Annie Lee's Bar and Clean Women Establishment." It rang a bell in the basement of his mind.

General Fixture greeted Jack amiably. "Welcome back, boss. If I can call you that."

"Hello, General. And you can call me just about anything. Things are a bit confusing in DC, and that includes the Pentagon. I think I'm still the president's official representative, but there's—"

"You are if I say you are, Jack. I've had no word to the contrary. Here, have some coffee and let's have a chat. Now I got the word that we needed to hold off on the battle for a day or so. That's fine, fine." He returned behind his desk and sat, chewing on an unlit cigar. "I always say, never rush into a fight. Give your artillery time to---"

"General, forget the artillery. We need to talk. Answer this—what are your intentions or instructions after you, for the sake of argument, take over Wall Street? Are you going to then march on DC and foment a coup?"

"Son, you're missing the damn point. Taking over Wall Street IS a coup. How long do you think those bastards in Washington will last without a suction hose hooked up to the American people—that hose being Wall Street? A week, two weeks?"

Jack was taken aback for only a moment. Wasn't this what he had been suspecting?

"And the leader of the country will be……..?"

"Not decided yet, son. But if you're thinking it would be me, that ain't gonna happen. I didn't serve thirty-five years in the Marine Corps to spend my final days as a, pardon my French, f—king politician."

After a knock on the door a young corporal entered and gave the General a sheet of paper.

"Thank you, Rodriguez. I'll buzz back with an answer, Tell Colonel Bovary to give me a few minutes."

The corporal left. The General held up a finger indicating Jack should give him a minute to read. He did and then smiled.

"I've had a team of intelligence officers and the head of the War College holed up practically the whole night. Coming up with an appropriate demand to whoever is in charge over there on Wall Street." He looked up at Jack. "We can't just start blasting away willy nilly."

He tossed the paper onto the desk in front of Jack. The message was elegant in its simplicity: Surrender, you pussies, or you'll all die.

Jack said, "Well that's sure to go down in the history books, General. I can see the War College influence."

"Sometimes I think you're shitting me, Captain."

Jack sighed. "No sir, I think I've just reached the point where we should just get down to tass bracks."

"Heh, heh, you're in the Egyptian arms deal, eh?"

"Sir, I'm in every deal and in no deal. I'm for most things I was against and will probably change again tomorrow. I'm leading the charge and cleaning up behind the parade." Jack rubbed his eyes. Then looked back at the General. "I'll make *you* a deal, General. Hold off the attack on Wall Street for forty-eight hours and I'll be your air officer."

"Welcome aboard, Jack. I thought you might feel that way, so I had a full uniform and 782-gear package put down in your office. New boots, too. Best of all, you have a .45 pistol, not that piece of shit you pilots carried in Vietnam. The pistol that Poncho Via carried." He came around the desk and shook Jack's hand as he stood up. "Since you're technically still my boss, I'll forget that damn girly haircut. But try to do something with it before D day."

Gearheardt called just as Jack sat down in his office.

"Just checking up on you, Jack. You looked kind of lost, standing there knee deep in peanut shells. Doing okay? The General give you a hard time?"

"Doing fine, Gearheardt. Where are you?"

"I've got a meeting with the Pygmy in half an hour. Up at Darkman."

"Whatever happened to—what was the name of that investment bank that Edwards and I visited? That guy Jackson Benabler or something like that?"

Gearheardt scoffed. "Those boys got an idea in their head that they couldn't trust the government or the CIA. They had deals with both. So they changed their names and headed south. But Darkman and Darkman picked up the slack."

"I'm confused," Jack said. "Didn't you set up a meeting for us at Darkman and Darkman. Some guy named Bestman?"

"Yes, Mr. Have To Know Every Damn Thing. Those people you met were not the real people. And Beanable is now Roland somebody. They're trying to screw the president by pretending they haven't been paid. Seems dishonest to me."

Jack gave up. "There Is, at last, no honor among thieves," he said.

"Boy, we're certainly counting on that, Jack."

"Gearheardt, whatever happened to that motley damn mob you had at the Willard the other night? I thought that was the army that was going to attack Wall Street impersonating Federal Reserve employees and Russian savings and loan executives. Or something like that."

"Jack, I wasn't completely honest with you."

"No shit."

"Those guys were just decoys to distract everyone while we got the Marine Corps up there in position," Gearheardt said.

"Why all the—"

"Can you imagine the shit storm it would have caused if folks found out the Marine Corps was taking over Wall Street and, potentially, the U.S. government."

"Caused *which* folks? That's what I don't get about all this fake and decoy and subterfuge, and......wait, did you say that you knew the Corps was maybe taking over the government?"

"They are?"

"Don't pull that crap with me, Gearheardt. You just said that the Corps was potentially taking over the government."

"But they're not going to do any such thing, Jack. Give me the time I need and the Corps will be eating through silk sheets."

"I assume that inanity suggests the Marine Corps will be bought off?"

"Precisely," Gearheardt responded confidently.

"I wouldn't be too sure about that, Gearheardt," Jack said, almost to himself.

"Look, I need to run."

"Wait, what happened to those thugs and the Russian mortgage guys and the Federal Reserve employees and potential Gearheardt Raiders?" Jack asked.

Gearheardt laughed. "Ever heard of Arizona?"

"I've heard it mentioned in board games, yes. Get on with it."

"We gave the whole cobbled-together-army a gambling license on Havasu Indian land and shipped them off."

"Hmmm. And the Havasu Indians?" Jack asked tentatively.

"Northern Michigan cotton-growing land."

"You can't grow...."

"The government buys the cotton intent back from the Havasu farmers or something." Gearheardt was beginning to sound distracted. "Jack, I really have to head out. The last thing I need right now is to get up to Darkman and find the Pygmy gnawing on a secretary's leg or something."

"Okay but keep in touch. I've told General Fixture he needs to hold off for a couple of days, but.... wait, what's *cotton intent*?"

Gearheardt laughed again. "Let me put it this way. How much wood would a woodchuck chuck if a woodchuck could chuck wood?"

"So, the feds are paying the Havasu Indians based on how much cotton they would grow if cotton could grow in Michigan?" Jack was skeptical.

"I think there's a requirement that the Indians have to be honest about their intent. Look, Jack, I'll be the first to admit that I haven't told you everything. The truth is that we need troops, in this case mercenaries, on the California border. We've also made a deal with the Mexicans to have a battalion at the border ready to prevent Americans trying to flee to Mexico."

"Yeah, that's been a real problem."

"Okay, not yet Jack. But we happen to know that the California governor is instigating the first 'Instant Socialism' reform this summer." Jack heard Gearheardt yell 'just a minute' to someone nearby him.

"I hate to ask, but—"

"The governor is going to mandate that each Californian with income above the state's medium income find someone below and split the income evenly. Boy, there's a scramble in the California assembly to find folks with high, but slightly below average income. The public will be left with—"

"Gearheardt, there's no way that's going to happen.
"Jack, in some countries it takes decades to create the economy of the miserable and un-inspired. California hopes to do it in one election cycle."

"I wish I didn't think you're serious, Gearheardt."

"Jack, there's even a legitimate whorehouse, actually a ranch, in Nevada that is nearly on the border with California."

Jack wrinkled his brow. "What the hell does that have to do with Instant Socialism in California, for God's sake?"

"Nothing. I just thought it was interesting."

Jack hung up.

Jack changed into the Marine gear left in his office. The battle fatigues, called utilities by the Marine Corps, even had his name above the pocket. There was a silver star on the collar, signifying that *someone* had promoted Jack to Brigadier General. Putting on the shirt gave Jack a feeling of instant power, even if he found out it was just a mistake.

Corporal Miller knocked and then entered his office.

"This for me?" Jack asked, pointing at the star.

"The orders came from the White House just today, sir. Congratulations."

"I'll play the game. What did you need, Corporal Miller?"

"General Fixture would like you to attend a planning brief at 1730, sir."

"Tell him I'll be there. Thank you, Corporal Miller."

Jack slumped at his desk, trying to take it all in.

His phone rang. "Will you hold for the president" a woman said.

In a moment a voice Jack recognized--at first thinking it would probably be Gearheardt—as his Commander in Chief boomed, "Hey, Jack. That's what I tell the interns. 'Will you hold this for the president?' Ha, ha. So anyways, have you got those Marines under control? I spent half the damn morning trying to get that star for you. Some jackass has to approve it I guess. But you got it, right?"

"Yes, sir. Thank you, sir, I guess."

"No thanks needed, however insincere, Jack. You got that star for a reason. And that reason is so you will do what is needed to be done to accomplish the mission of the United States of America which is to make me the richest son-of-a-bitch to ever live. Ha, ha."

Ha ha my ass, thought Jack. He means every word of it.

"Well, Mr. President. I will do what is needed to be done in order to promote the welfare of the Republic and if that means—"

"Yeah, yeah, blah, blah, blah. Hell, you sound like me on the campaign trail. I get it son, you're a loyal American. But those bastards up in New York have all but emptied the country's coffers. We have to borrow money from them just to bomb some shitass monarchy or get new seat-covers in Air Force One. By the way, did I ever tell you about the time—"

"Mr. President, I would love to hear that story, and I'll bet it involves the women—"

"Damn straight."

"Yessir, but there are things that I need to be doing. If I might ask you, sir, what you had called me about, we can address that."

"Well, Jack," the president lowered his voice and speech speed, "I guess if someone is talking to the President of the United States, then whatever the President of the United States is talking about is most likely the most important thing for the guy who is NOT the President of the United States to listen to. Would you agree with that, Jack?"

"Yes, sir."

"Okay then, and boy you sure ain't Gearheardt. That boy would wade barefoot across a molten lava field to hear about the President's shenanigans with interns. But if you're in such an all-fired hurry, here's the thing. I need you to find that damn Pygmy fellow and hook up with the Marine Corps inquisition team and find out the code on the Fed Chairs personal computer and send it to me. Muy pronto. I got the computer right here. And about a dozen goofy looking computer nerds have been scratching their heads trying to it to fire up. They're worthless. So, you find it out. Got it, Jack? And then, Jack, shoot that little sonofabitch in the head. Multiple times."

"I'll suppose I'll try, sir. But why would I have any more luck—"

"You going to see Gearheardt when you make it to Wall Street?"

"I assume I will, Mr. President."

"Well, that pygmy fellow will be somewhere around that damn Gearheardt."

"Are you sure, sir? I didn't think—"

"I'm as sure as the President of the United States can possibly be." It sounded as if he held the phone away from him. "Evelyn, can you tell that numbnuts Ambassador from Shitland, or whatever African jungle that he represents, that I'll be tied up a bit longer?" he yelled.

"No need, Mr. President," Jack heard Evelyn respond, "you just told him. He's standing right here at my desk."

"Aw shit. Well give him some goat blood or whatever he wants and shut my damn door the next time I'm in here talking on the phone."

Jack heard a door close.

"Mr. President, I hear you about getting rich and all that. The American people have come to expect that of their politicians. But this pygmy thing, What's the big deal? So, he's head of the Fed, you're the president, what harm could he do that you couldn't take care of?"

"Jack, you're a smart fellow. At least Gearheardt thinks so. Do you know anything about Barings Bank?"

"It sound familiar. Some major trouble, but, no, I'm not all that familiar."

The president cleared his throat. "Well, Jack, let me tell you just a bit. They were a merchant bank, over there in London. Started by an old boy named Baring in 1762 or so. Did some heavy stuff like finance the Napoleonic Wars. Put up the money for the Louisiana Purchase. Financed digging the Erie Canal. I remember singing that dang song in grade school. Anyway, there ain't no Barings bank these days. Damn teenager in Singapore bet too big on commodities or derivatives or some damn thing. Lost a couple billion pounds, that's English money, and broke the bank. Shut her down just like a strip-mall furniture store."

Jack was listening and looking out his window toward Manhattan. He could swear there were barrage balloons floating near the World Trade Center.

"So, when I'm talking about losing some money," the president was saying, "I'm talking about a shit-pot full and then some."

"Who lost it, Mr. President?"

"Haven't you been listening, Jack. The damn pygmy bet the Fed's money, our money, into the derivative market."

"How much?"

"All of it. Every last damn penny!" It sounded to Jack like the president had pounded the desk.

After a moment Jack reluctantly asked, "I am assuming from your tone that things didn't go well for us."

"Well, let's put it this way, the check to pay for buying Botswana bounced."

Jack knew he was over his head in terms of global banking, so he was cautious. "Isn't that kind of a good thing? I mean we don't need to own Botswana."

"This is not about Botswana, dumbass. This is about the complete destruction of America's banking system." Jack heard a great sigh of anguish. "Look, if you can get to the Pygmy and get the password to the Fed Chief's personal computer, we might be able to stop this disaster."

"I'll try, sir. Are we broke yet?" Jack asked, not really expecting an answer.

"Good question, Jack. The truth is that no one knows. The derivative market workings are only known to a handful of people, evidently. Figuring out who owes who will take months, if not years."

"So, what's the problem?"

"Think about it, smart boy. We have a Double Indexed Transmogrified Fluctuation Settlement. The DITFS."

"I'm not sure what that is, Mr. President."

"Me neither. That damn Gearheardt and his CIA pals came up with that name. Probably just obfuscation."

Looking closer out his window, Jack was sure that barrage balloons circled overhead in Manhattan. He needed to see General Fixture as soon as possible. Barrage balloons were normally used to prevent air attacks. Of course, they hadn't been used since the First World War, but nothing was making much sense.

"What the CIA guy, Stevens or something like that, and Gearheardt were telling me was that my plan to take over the financial system, printing money and fixing interest rates and things like that, had run full-steam into the reality that we might have bet fifteen or twenty trillion dollars on exotic and hopelessly complicated financial instruments."

"But if it will take months to—"

"Jack, you could do with some serious listening lessons. We can't know diddly until we get to the Pygmy's computer. Right now, there are financial gurus in Burmese villages claiming we owe them billions of dollars. And that damn three-foot moron wants to solve things by printing up new money by the megaton. Just pay everyone off. He'll denude the Northwest timber territory and the dollar won't be worth vulture vomit. It'll take a pickup load of hundred-dollar bills to buy a condom, not that I'm worried about the price of condoms, but that's just an example."

"I think I'm beginning to get the picture, Mr. President," Jack said.

"Are you still there? Get your ass over to find the Pygmy."

"Yessir. And sir, are you still taking over the financial system? I'm trying to understand which side I'm on."

"Not if it's a system that'll make the thirties depression look like the days of wine and roses." The president sounded defeated, or at least desperate.

"Mr. President, I'm not sure how finding the password to the Pygmy's computer—"

"You know, Jack, I remember waking up this morning and thinking— 'I really need to get that Jack fellow to spend a lot of time second guessing me. That's what I really need to do.' That's called sarcasm, cement head. I didn't make you a damn Captain-General so I could have one more wiseass to second-guess me! I guess that's coming as a surprise to you. FIND THE DAMN PYGMY!"

The President hung up.

Corporal Miller buzzed. "There's a Mr. Gearheardt on line one, sir."

"Gearheardt, just the guy I wanted to talk to."

"That President Slick is worrying himself sick over having to tell Mrs. President that the country is broke," Gearheardt said, barely keeping from snickering.

"Were you listening, you jackass?"

"Jack, I think things are a little too serious to *not* wiretap, don't you?"

"I don't even know whether I'm supposed to—never mind. Is what the President saying the real case?" Jack asked.

"Pretty much. I'm not sure that the Pygmy has all the information on his computer that the President needs to be able to stop the money being printed. But it's a good place to start. One way or another, we need to make sure the Marines are in place. That's why I was calling you."

"In place in Manhattan? Or over here in Jersey? And I thought you didn't want the Marines there for a couple of days. Is there a sub-plot to the sub-plot sub-plot?"

"I can neither confirm or deny that, Jack."

"Which means there is something going on that I don't know about."

"Not knowing is a relative term, Jack," Gearheardt said. "You know all the pieces. You just don't know how they fit together. But to answer your question, I would like to have the Marines in Manhattan tomorrow before sundown. Can do?"

"I imagine so, but I'll have to check with General Fixture. I'm meeting with him soon."

"So we're all clear, Jack? Remember, I know you're carrying a lot of the burden, but when this is complete, I'll share all we are going to get."

"You know, Gearheardt, the pornography-backed currency system doesn't seem so insane anymore." Jack was tired and uneasy. "Crap! Gearheardt did you know that there are barrage balloons over Manhattan? And there seems to be people firing up at them. I can see occasional tracers."

Gearheardt laughed. "Yeah, I know, Jack. Those are my anti-aircraft folks and the people shooting at them are some guys from either Botswana or Burma. I'll explain later."

Gearheardt hung up.

Another Chapter

Gearheardt quickened his pace after leaving the docks at the end of Manhattan Island. On his way to Darkman-Darkman, after stopping to call Jack, he worried that things could get out of control quickly when the Pygmy met people who hadn't known he was a pygmy. Pygmaphobia ran rampant on Manhattan Island, often forcing dwarfs and midgets to wear 'I'm not a pygmy' signs around their neck. In a world which rewarded size above all except wealth, the status of 'at least I'm not a pygmy' was important to some people.

THE Pygmy accepted and reveled in his role as the bottom of the food chain. His willingness to accept all blame, even when he was not in any way responsible, made him a favorite in government circles. Even by those who hated him. Those, the Pygmy loved best. He had the perfect bigoted attitude—he was superior to everyone in every way. He remained, he said, in a continuing state of being FDH (fat dumb and happy), secure in his superiority and almost complete ignorance of the world beyond his squinty vision. A solid government employee who could not be fired, in fact who could rarely be found. And now he was the Chairman of the Federal Reserve.

At the Middle-Eastern-Potentate-luxury level Darkman-Darkman building, Gearheardt was ushered immediately up to the top floor and shown into a conference room tastefully decorated in the flamboyant cross-dressing style of an interior decorator married to the Chairman of the company.

"About damn time, Gearheardt," the aforementioned Chairman stated as Gearheardt took a seat.

"I had important things to do, Roland," Gearheardt said. "Where's the Pygmy? I thought he was in this meeting."

"He was under the table when we all got here. But—"

"He didn't start biting ankles did he?" Gearheardt said with a laugh, trying to lighten the atmosphere.

It didn't work. "He was taking pictures up the dresses of Mrs. Laughlin and Miss Covington if you must know."

"Did you discuss the derivatives issue?" Gearheardt asked.

"We chased him out from under the table with a broom and he took off down the hall. Does that answer your question?" The Darkman-Darkman boss was not in a happy mood.

"I told you he could be difficult, Roland. You should have let him stay under the table until I got here. He is, remember, the Chairman of the Federal Reserve Bank."

"I'll remember that the next time a Chairman of the Fed is under the table with a Polaroid. Let's deal with that later. So, what's the word from the President? Do we have a deal or not? We're getting demands from banks in Swaziland. Our people overseas are either hiding under their beds or taking to the hills."

"Just hold your horses, Roland. The President is an honest man and won't go back on his word." Gearheardt smiled at the rolled eyes of those at the conference table. "Not if he wants something. And you know what he wants."

"First of all, it's no skin off my nose if he becomes the next Fed Chief—I assume this is in addition to being president—and becomes fabulously wealthy. Having the investment banks all report to him is fine. I've checked with all the major banks and the only one who wouldn't go along was Marlow and Vermen. They seemed to think they had a private deal. But you don't screw with Wall Street."

"I heard the entire bank skedaddled to the Bahamas or someplace in the Caribbean."

The Chairman smiled for the first time. "Ha, they wish. The whole bank of back-stabbing traitors are on Devil's Island if you call that the Caribbean. Don't ask me how I know." A thin grin. "Marlow sold out their fellow investment bankers. They're paying the price. The first price, I've heard, was about a million insect bites each."

"Serves them right. So, what's the next step?" Gearheardt was already showing signs of getting bored with the conversation. "This, if I understand it, is not a complicated situation. What you're asking the President to do is either A). Tell the global banking and investment world that the U.S. is not paying off on the market losses and to go, pardon me, f—k themselves. Or B). to let the Pygmy go ahead and print up however many trillion dollars we need to pay the losses and let the financial markets do what they will.

"In a nutshell, that's the question. There are, of course, some nuances which Wall Street will have to deal with." The Darkman exec looked concerned but not yet panicked.

"Of course," Gearheardt said, "and one of them is whether or not the Marines are coming over to protect Wall Street from the assault by the legions of stiffed bankers. Or are they coming over to protect Wall Street from the American public when they realize that toilet paper is more valuable than the equivalent sheets of paper currency, no matter the denomination."

"I think that your assessment is over-simplified, but basically that's the case. I would say that Wall Street would prefer the former. A bit of a blight on our reputation but—" The banker shrugged and spread his hands out, palms up.

Gearheardt looked around the table at the other Darkman execs who had silently listened to the exchange. All were sweating and pale. "Roland," Gearheardt said, "do you really think that in either case, the citizens of America are going to let you just go on your merry way, raking in millions and keeping the yacht industry booming? Are you that delusional?"

"Gearheardt, I've been told that you were supportive of the Wall Street position. As a patriotic American, I'm sure you're aware that the growth of the financial markets, led by Wall Street, have enriched—"

"Maybe one percent of the population," Gearheardt finished the sentence.

Before the Darkman exec could respond, the door of the conference room burst open and a burly brace of security men perp-walked the Pygmy into the room. As soon as they let him go, he darted under the table. The female participants in the meeting shifted their legs to the side of their chairs.

Gearheardt banged on the table. "Xuattle-le get out from under the table. The African savage bit is not playing well and is damn sure not appreciated." Xuattle-le was not the Pygmy's real name, which he claimed was unpronounceable. Even his parents could not pronounce it.

Xuattle-le crawled out, straightened himself up, and took the seat at the end of the conference table, opposite the Darkman exec. "Very well, Mr. Gearheardt," he said, "may I suggest we bring this meeting to order." His voice, Oxfordian and deeply resonant, quieted the room.

Gearheardt broke the silence. "Knock off the Cary Grant imitation, Xuattle-le, you're wearing the skull of a small animal around your neck on a chain of finger-bones from.....let's not look closer. And your drape, handsome though it might be, appears to be infested with insects. Or as you have called them before—snacks."

"Yeah, what's it to ya, ya wiseass," Xuattle-le said. "I'm takin' like zero crap from yuz."

"The pygmy, ladies and gentlemen, has learned all of his English watching movies in the janitor's closet of the CIA headquarters, having purloined a television from God knows where. He is a terrific impersonator and a Don Rickles-class wiseass." Gearheardt seemed to take pride in the pygmy's aptitude for languages.

"Whatever you say, pardner. I reckon we ought to get on with this stock tradin' business." Xuattle-le had produced a flask from within his garments and took a manly swig of what smelled like scotch whiskey. He wiped his mouth with the back of his hand and offered the flask around the table. There were no takers.

The Pygmy, standing in his chair, slammed his 'briefcase' on the table and began to rustle through paperwork inside. The briefcase was of genuine leather, evidenced by its mottled hairy exterior and the delicate aroma of fresh kill. The handle was a particular style of dog-collar which caused some consternation in those meeting participants closest to him.

"I ain't the tender-foot that the folks in the White House seemed to think I was. Watched a documentary on the banking biz-ness and other fi-nance info and heard through my pals on shitter-detail the president was lookin' for a dupe (he pronounced it doo-pay) to put in charge of the money operations. Since I may be the only critter in the White House whose brain outweighs his gonads, I figured that position was mine for the takin'."

Much to the stomach-churning disgust of those watching, the Pygmy pulled his hand out of the satchel, held a small blob of something up to the light, evidently determined it was edible, and popped it in his mouth. The ladies, perhaps still smarting from the indignity of the earlier photo-shoot, left the room in what could be called a huff.

After finding and lighting a cheroot, the Pygmy sat down and said, "Gentlemen, let the biddin' begin." His head was all that was visible.

"The bidding for what, Mr. Pygmy?" Roland, the Darkman man, didn't try to keep the disdain from his voice and succeeded.

"Seems like some folks wants to stiff the world. And there are other folks who want me to print up a few trillion bucks to tide us over this unfortunate pile of horse apples. As a wise man once said, I went to Princeton but I ain't stupid."

Gearheardt spoke up. "You went to Princeton?"

"No, I just like the sound of that, Mr. Wise Ass." The Pygmy laughed.

Gearheardt laughed too. "And you're making a proposition?"

"Yep. And it's a fair and easy solution." He consulted a paper. "It's no secret that the President wants to run the money show, either as the Fed honcho or head man on Wall Street. Right? So, I'm willing to just sign over everything, all legal and like."

"What's the catch? Most American's don't give a damn who's running the Fed. And as long as we can stop that million percent inflation you're about to unleash, I don't think Wall Street will give a damn either." The Darkman exec was skeptical but encouraged.

"Well, fine and dandy. I reckon you should call the President and tell him we've made a deal. Oh, and I'll be president."

After a stunned silence, the Pygmy concentrating on a gray blob he extracted from his mouth to study, the Darkman exec signaled to Gearheardt that he should follow him outside.

"Gearheardt and I need a quick conference, Mr. Xuattle-le." His tongue danced around the consonants like a bare foot over broken glass.

Outside, the banker grabbed Gearheardt's lapels. "I thought you could handle this, this, pygmy person! What the hell?"

"I thought his proposal was reasonable."

"Gearheardt! He's a f---king PYGMY!"

Gearheardt peeled the banker's fingers off of his lapel.

"I personally have nothing against the pygmy class," he said.

"This is not a race thing, Gearheardt. And don't change the subject. You told me that the Pygmy was, and I quote, under control. I've been sweating bullets anyway, but always thought that by the end of the day—"

"It's not the end of the day, Roland." Gearheardt patted him on the shoulder. "Hey!" he suddenly yelled, causing the banker to cringe, "look what the cat dragged in!"

Jack was stepping off the elevator onto the floor. He was in full battle garb of a United States Marine. He looked awkward as he made his way through the secretaries and assistants manning the desks and cubicles outside of the boardroom.

"No wise cracks, Gearheardt," Jack said, knowing full well it was a congenital impossibility.

"Hell, I wish I was in the same uniform, Jack. But why in the blue blazes—"

"General Fixture doesn't take no for an answer. And a blowtorch and toe party was hinted at. He felt that expressing my loyalty necessitated full costume. But frankly, what the heck, I'm ready for anything."

The banker standing with Gearheardt held out his hand. "I'm Roland Darkman, Chief Executive of what is becoming an insane asylum. And you?"

"Captain-General Jack Armstrong, special assistant to the President, United States Marine officer, an agent of the Central Intelligence Agency, former banker and Gearheardt's best friend." Jack was pretty sure that Roland had once been someone named Beanable but who cared these days.

"I would suggest you leave the latter off your resume. But seriously, we're more or less in a crisis here," the banker said. "Are you 'adding to' or 'taking from' that situation? I assume, by the way, that the pistol at your hip is real and loaded."

"As are the hand grenades hanging from my harness. The question of my role, however, is a lot more complicated. But I currently take orders from my Commander in Chief, and his preference—I assume this is the crisis you mean—is to *not* print the money and let the pissant, his description, nations try to collect at their peril."

The banker, seeming to take comfort in the fact that the Marines had landed began, "The United States has a long history of living up to its obligations—"

"The Vietnamese will be startled to hear that," Jack interjected.

"—and I think, nevertheless," acknowledging Jack's comment, "that we will survive this market correction with understanding by the world's financial centers."

"I agree, Roland, if that's your name," Jack began, "that those *financial center dwellers* who will not feel the full effect of losing every dime they have, will not retaliate."

The banker's steely eyes lasered in on Jack's face. "I'm not sure what you are insinuating, Captain-General Armstrong."

"My apologies, sir. I didn't mean to insinuate anything. I meant to call you a lying, thieving, crook in plain English. You and that attitude are why this crisis exists. If I had—"

"Gentlemen, gentlemen, let's not fight over money." Gearheardt took Jack's elbow and gently led him away from the banker. "Jack," he said, "there doesn't have to be winners and losers, here. We're all Americans, wanting what's best for America."

"Wow, Gearheardt, you can actually stand in the offices of a plutocrat and believe you believe these guys get up every morning concerned about the welfare of the American citizens."

"Maybe not as individuals, Jack. But they worry about Americans in the abstract."

"I'm shooting myself. I've lost the ability to think, evidently. That actually sounded like you said something meaningful."

"Jack, you're always so dramatic. Good Americans don't sit around and worry about who's screwing who in the financial world. No, they worry about how to get a piece of the action. That's what—"

"Okay, I'm shooting you. It's the same as shooting a mad dog when you realize the damn thing is beyond help." He grabbed his friend by the shoulder. "Gearheardt, I know its melodramatic, but you and I used to risk our lives for this country. Vietnam. Mexico. Do you really feel that way about Roland Darkman and his gang of thieves?"

"You're being melodramatic, Jack."

"You asshole, Gearheardt. Get serious. Whose side are you on?"

"I am being serious, Jack. Name the sides. You want this to be black and white. Which side is black, and which is white?" Gearheardt smiled. "Take your time answering. And by the way, when are the Marines coming? Did you bring them with you?"

Jack mentally gave up talking sense. "Just me and my driver this wave, Gearheardt. The rest of the troops are awaiting the go-ahead from the President. I came over to find the Pygmy and—"

"He's inside."

"—do the President's bidding. I'm still a Marine, Gearheardt. At the end of the day, I follow orders."

"And you made Captain-General, that's pretty impressive." Always time for sarcasm.

Even Jack had to laugh. "Remember when our orders were lost, and we were 'Almost Captains' for a couple of years? Anyway, General Fixture thought one star and one railroad track on each shoulder solved his reluctance to follow the President's orders. The President can't actually approve promotions." Jack sighed. "And you have for the millionth time got me off track. I need to see the Pygmy." He started toward the door to the conference room.

"Jack, I'll have to ask you for your gun."

"Do you have a gun, Gearheardt?"

"Not at the moment."

"Well then, you're not getting mine."

"Fair enough. Please don't shoot the Pygmy until you've heard him out. I know the Pygmy tried to have you killed in Mexico. And he can be damned irritating. But he does have a plan."

"Just so you know, Gearheardt, I plan to go in there and get the Pygmy, march him right out to that elevator," he pointed over his shoulder, "and take him someplace where I can have a few words with him. And I lied about coming alone. A crack team of Marine toe-burners came with me. But I will listen to his plan, okay?"

As he started toward the conference room, ignoring the Darkman people staring at him like he was Atilla the Office Crasher, his backpack radio buzzed.

"Armstrong. Hello Corporal. Of course. Of course. Hello General. Yessir. Go ahead...........Who the hell, sorry sir, who is that? Who? Where is...? Do we have any reason to.,..? Yessir. At what time, Sir? Troops also?.......................I understand. Yessir.... I'm at the Darkman building now, sir......Right away, sir."

Jack faced Gearheardt. "Both Transnistria and Guinea-Bissau have declared war on us."

"What?"

"I just got the bare bones. Evidently there's a lawyer already taking clients for the massive lawsuit against America and he's convinced some countries that it's first come, first serve in the payout waterfall." Jack started into the conference room again. His phone buzzed once more.

"Armstrong.... yes, sir..............Got it, sir........You're shitting me. Sorry sir.... I will be talking to him within the minute, General.....Yes, sir, they're in the corporate dining room."

Gearheardt was in his face. "Now what?"

"Evidently the Transnistrians have sent troops to attack New York."

"Damn, how many? When?"

"I think he said there were eleven, and they're booking flights now."

"Not shaking in my boots yet. They're actually flying commercial?"

Jack shook his head. "No air force. But there's a more serious threat. The Guinea-Bissauans have purchased a nuke from the Pakistanis---"

"The bastards."

"—and are negotiating with FedEx to deliver it."

"This might be the first war squarely in the Twilight Zone, Jack." Gearheardt was laughing. "But you're serious?"

"I'm sure the Guinea-Bissauans will face a moral dilemma about lying on the declaration as to the package containing hazardous material." It was hard for Jack to take it seriously also. He sobered. "But this is the harbinger of things to come."

He opened the door and entered the conference room, followed by Gearheardt.

The Pygmy was squatting in the center of the conference table, waving Polaroid photos and trying to get the table to guess the thigh owner. He saw Jack and froze.

"Well, if it isn't the gringo fake assassin. Que pasa, Jack?" He jumped back down into his chair. "I will accept your congratulations for becoming the jefe of the American banking system, yes?"

"You were appointed because the President thought you were too stupid to do anything, Pygmy. Not for any brilliance or ability."

"And who turns out to be stupido, mi amigo?" The Pygmy's laugh was a childish giggle.

"Let's go," Jack said. But he didn't unholster his sidearm.

"Creo que no, Jack." (I don't think so)

"Creo que si, Pygmy."

Roland Darkman broke the impasse by entering the room like he was on fire.

"Gents, knock off the bullshit. I just got word that the President and First Lady are on their way."

"That'll help things," Jack muttered. He pulled out his sidearm, aiming it at the Pygmy's head. "Let's vamoose, Pygmy."

At this point the employees of Darkman, who had remained frozen in their seats during the bizarre happenings, bolted for the door. Only Roland, Jack, Gearheardt and the Pygmy remained.

Gearheardt spoke up. "Before we go shooting each other, let's assess the situation. All those in favor of stiffing the world and just toughing it out, raise their hand."

Darkman and the Pygmy raised their hands.

"All those in favor of printing a stack of money reaching the moon, raise their hand."

Jack and the Pygmy raised their hands.

"Well that didn't help much. Just shoot him, Jack."

"Wait!" It was Roland. "No shooting in here."

The Pygmy evidently took umbrage. "That's your objection, Darkman? No shooting in here!"

Jack's backpack radio buzzed again. He handed his .45 to Gearheardt. "Don't let him get out of here."

"Armstrong...Yes, sir.....Yes, Sir...should I write that down?..........Got it. And sir, I just got word that Disaster One and Two are on their way over. Any instructions?.......Well, Gearheardt actually has it right now, but....... Oh, you were?......Got it, General. I'll check back."

Jack asked for, and received, his .45 from Gearheardt.

"What's the update, Jack. We're among friends, you can—" He looked around the room. "Well, I guess we're among deadly enemies, but tell us what you can."

"The FedEx office in Bissau got nervous when they saw the guy mulling over the hazardous materials question and turned them away."

"Great. I mean it wasn't a serious threat, but you never know." Gearheardt exchanged smiles with a clueless Roland.

Jack continued. "The bad news is that they took the package to *Aitijah Wahid Air* and they accepted it."

"Who is—" Roland and Gearheardt spoke at the same time.

"It means *One Way* in Arabic. The Agency guys think it's a contract airline for delivering arms to terrorist organizations. They call it *Bombs Away Airlines*," Jack said.

Gearheardt laughed. "Kind of a clever name." He paused. "Hey, I know it's not funny, but you know the old saying, if you can't take a joke, stay out of the kitchen."

"Mr. Darkman?" The conference room intercom came on.

"Yes, Denise, I'm a bit busy at the moment. Can Bestman—"

"He's the one who said to call you. There are two men on the lobby. They said you owe them eight million dollars."

Gearheardt turned from where he had been looking out the window at the barrage balloons. "Oh shit, that sounds like Tweedle Dee and Tweedle Dum."

"Who?" Jack asked.

"That damn Ukrainian arms dealer and the jackass cousin-in-law of Mrs. President."

"I thought you said you paid them."

"I kind of paid them." Gearheardt was exceptionally evasive if that was possible.

"Gearheardt, in the matter of paying, there is little grey area. Did you or did you not pay the Ukrainian eight million dollars for the weapons?"

"If you put it like that—no. Jack, are they going to go repo the weapons? I don't think so," Gearheardt continued.

"Okay, boys, what do you want me to tell them? Wait a minute. Why are they asking me for the money?" Darkman demanded.

"Why didn't the Marines have their own weapons?" the Pygmy asked.

Jack and Gearheardt both shrugged.

"There aren't any weapons. It was a swindle operation all along. I thought everyone knew that. It had to look like we were giving weapons to the Federal Reserve Employees who were going to attack Wall Street. No one would believe that they just had anti-tank weapons and fifty caliber machine guns lying around." Gearheardt thought that would satisfy everyone.

"I'm still a bit confused, Gearheardt. Why am I being asked to pay for weapons that didn't get sold?"

"I seriously doubt if Darkman Bank has a license to deal in arms, Darkman. If there actually were weapons being delivered, you might find yourself in deep shit with the ATF boys." Gearheardt looked at Jack. "Can you believe someone thought it was a good idea to have a bureau of Alcohol, Tobacco, and Firearms? Boy, talk about a dangerous mix."

"You amaze me with your gnat-like attention span, Gearheardt.
"Thanks, Jack."

"I'll just pay the damn bill and shift it to something else later," Darkman said disgustedly.

"Mr. Darkman," the intercom said.

"Yes, Denise."

"There's a Ukrainian peeing in the lobby flowers."

"Damn it!" Then apologetically, "Not you, Denise. Would you please tell Bestman to get a check for eight million dollars out of the Hoover Dam syndication account and give it to the men in the lobby? Please get their names."

"Sir, they're on their way up."

"Well, that's great news," Jack said. "Just what we need."

"Can someone get an ETA on the bomb flight?" Gearheardt asked no one in particular.

Denise called again from the lobby. "Mr. Darkman, there is a Secret Service man at the reception desk wanting to secure the building."

"Let him." Darkman shrugged. He looked at two men and a pygmy. "Must be for the President."

"You don't have another gun on you, do you?" Gearheardt asked Jack.

"I'm in charge here!" The Pygmy was standing in his chair again. "I may be only the head of the Fed right now, but I'm going to be president soon. And I'll darn sure remember who-"

"Oh, shut up," Jack said. "You're not going to be the damn president." He leveled the pistol at the Pygmy's head and made a show of jacking a round into the chamber. "Give me the password to your computer. This printing of megatons of money is going to stop. The banks are going to have to face the music and not the American people. That's the way the President wants it. That's the way it's going to be."

Gearheardt sat down. "Jack, Wall Street has pissed away all of America's money. Giving more to the world's banks won't save the American people."

"He's got a point there, Jack," Darkman said. "As much as I hate the thought of not paying off on our bets, we really have no other choice. And besides, only a few small countries have declared war on us." Darkman lit a cigarette with a gold lighter.

"When the President gets here, he can order that *bombs away* aircraft shot down in a mini-second," added Gearheardt. "And I'll personally meet that flight of Trininestrians or whoever they are. Of course, I've got to find a gun." The last as if it were Jack's fault he had no gun.

Jack dove and shut the door just before the Pygmy escaped. After he had walked him back to his chair, he looked at the three co-conference room dwellers. Not people he wanted to die with.

Denise on the intercom: Mr. Darkman, there's a Mr. Stevens here to see you. He won't tell me what it's about. Oh, no. Mr. Stevens and the Secret Service man are fighting, Mr. Darkman. The Secret Service man says the building is secure but Mr. Stevens…. oh my, Mr. Darkman, the President and First Lady walked in. Now they're in the fight. They've knocked over the vase where the Ukrainian man…..Oh, my. What should I do?"

Darkman was calm. "Very good, Denise. Please send them up."

Summit Chapter (not the end)

The conference room of Darkman and Darkman was packed. The President was at one end of the long, 24-person, table and, after much elbowing, muttering and inappropriate grappling, the Pygmy at the other. Mid-table the Chairman of Darkman sat opposite Jack and Gearheardt. The Ukrainian gun-seller, the cousin-in-law of the first lady, the Director of Central Intelligence, and the head of the Presidential detail of the Secret Service, who sat glaring across the table at the DCI.

"Welcome, Mr. President," said Darkman, eager to be the first to be on the wining team. "I was told that Mrs. President, I believe that is her choice of title, was to be with you."

"Yep, exactly right, Darkman. The Mrs. President is visiting friends on the third floor. As you know, she has a consulting business pertaining to the storage of files. Evidently you have a great many which should not see the light of day."

"No idea to what you refer, Mr. President, but anyway welcome to you both."

"Mr. President," the director of the CIA began, "I should point out before we begin, that the Ukrainian (he pointed to the Ukrainian who was fiddling with his name badge) is not cleared for any information beyond that which is already public knowledge." He was in a foul mood as the head of the Secret Service had pulled his chair out from under him as he began to sit down. He had plopped heavily to the floor on his butt, striking the chair with the back of his head. Which wasn't as painful as the laughter which filled the room and stole a bit of dignity.

The Ukrainian wasn't cowed. "Mr. President, You Excellentcy, it is me who is sure of resentment and not eight million dollars. I have provide, as a weapon dealer person, the means to the end of trouble with bank. And all secret, even big secret, will be with me and me only. Unless I tell someone, no one will know." He sat back and smiled around the room.

Bryce Rogers, sitting to the left of the Ukrainian said, "I second the motion," to the befuddlement of all as there was nothing to second.

Finally, the President said, "Thank you, Ignatz, or whatever your name is. I believe we can all take comfort that anyone you tell a secret to has little chance of knowing what the f—k you're talking about. Thank you." He looked at Stevens, the DCI. "Does that work for you, Mr. Stevens?"

Stevens was holding his head in his hands. "Oh, just perfectly. A new level of security seems to have been achieved."

When Stevens sat down at the conference table, Jack asked about Edwards. "I would have thought you would have Edwards here, Mr. Stevens. We've been working with—"

"Edwards is dead, Jack. After you told us he was telling all of the Agency's secrets, we put him back on Waterboard Training, ST—that stands for Self-Taught. Edwards drowned himself."

"That actually seems kind of unlikely, Mr. Stevens." Jack felt a bit of guilt. He had liked Edwards.

"Try it sometime, Jack," Stevens said, his tone suggesting the conversation was over.

"Mr. President," Darkman began, "it might be in order to actually put on the table an agenda for what needs to be decided. I think many of us might be somewhat in the dark as to what is going on, and what the proposed solutions might be. Would you agree to the appositeness of that, sir?"

"Jesus, Darkman, is appositeness even a real word?" the President responded. "Down in Oklahoma, we used to judge a man by his ability to talk plain on difficult subjects. 'Course when I was at the *Sorbornne* (he looked at Gearheardt) that was not the rule, but the Frogs don't talk, they murmur, and God knows what they really mean." He paused. "Where was I headin'?"

No one spoke.

"Oh, yeah, you were asking about an agenda. I'm all for that. Here's mine. First, we need to save the American banking system from collapse due to betting its entire damn kit and kaboodle on derivatives and options for goat meat or whatever. I've been told there are two ways we can go about that—"

Jack interrupted. "Sir, there was talk of a mortgage deal with Russia. Didn't we sell them a few trillion dollars of home mortgages and—"

"That's taken care of, Jack," Darkman said. "They're happy as clams thinking they own what the President refers to as 'shit pot full' of mortgages. Step two, the real estate tax plan, is in the works. Unfortunately, the derivative debacle takes precedent. Isn't that right, Mr. President? And please understand, I'm being as obsequious as I know how to be."

"You're doing just fine, Darkman. I'm glad we had our little talk earlier on the phone. Yes, gentlemen, the impending disaster of being wrong on approximately 100% of the market positions we took has put a damper on some financial strategies. And before Mrs. President finds this conference room and begins to kick some ass, I suggest we get to the solution and quit beating around the bush."

"Gentlemen, since I seem to be the only one with a gun," Jack said loudly, "I would like to do a basic gut check. Who wants to print enough money to pay off the derivative losses, and who wants to not print money and stiff the roughly fifty countries, according to a recent message from the Pentagon, who have declared war on us?"

"Anybody big?" the President asked.

"Everybody big," Jack answered. "I do have some good news, though. The *Aitijah Wahid* airliner hired to deliver the Pakistani nuke purchased by Guinea-Bissau was just diverted to bomb The Hague instead."

"Whoa, Betsy!" the President said, "all kindsa good news there. But what in the—"

"The World Court in The Hague put out a global appeal for all countries to bring their legal issues in this case directly to them. Evidently the Guinea-Bissauians translated that to mean military attacks also. I'm getting this second-hand through a Marine corporal at General Fixture's headquarters in New Jersey." Jack pushed against his free ear with a finger while pressing the handset to his other ear.

"Darkman, you suppose you could get one of those pretty little ladies out there to bring me some coffee?" the President said.

The Secret Service man jumped up. "I'll be happy to get it, Mr. President."

"Well, since I might need your bony little ass, I'd kinda like Darkman to handle this." The President smiled at Darkman as the Secret Service guy gave the finger to the CIA chief who was laughing.

Darkman punched a button on the intercom. "Denise," he said, "can you get coffee for the President?"

Gearheardt asked as he hung up, "You're asking the receptionist in the lobby to get coffee?"

"We ask all our girls to change their name to Denise when they join Darkman, Gearheardt. It saves us the effort to learn names and eliminates our embarrassment from calling someone the wrong name."

"Even in Ukraine, women treated with more polite," the Ukrainian said. "In special if she have big tits." The standards certainly seemed higher.

"Okay," the President said, "I think the consensus is that we stop printing money and tell the sore-winners that they need to pound sand. We've done a lot of favors for the world. It's time they paid us back." He grinned.

"When was that consensus achieved, Mr. President,?" Gearheardt asked.

"It's the consensus of what I want done, Gearheardt. I've not gone to all the trouble of becoming president to just take advice from other people who haven't."

"But it's the opposite of what you asked me to get you-know-who to do and then shoot him." Gearheardt was uncomfortable talking frankly in front of the Pygmy but was getting fed-up with the bullshit.

Jack was trying to remember if the President had mentioned shooting the Pygmy.

"Mr. Darkman, could you ask Denise to have some guns sent up?" Gearheardt asked.

There was hesitant laughter in the room.

The door opened and a disheveled young man ushered the Mrs. President into the conference room.

"If you call me Denise one more time," she was saying, "I'll cram you back into your mother." She turned and started toward the end the table where the Pygmy sat.

Who jumped back under the table, taking his real-skin satchel with him and knocking over water bottles and empty coffee cups.

The Mrs. President sat down, a 'yikes' was heard from under the table, the sound of a head hitting the underside of the table was heard, a stunned silence was heard thereafter.

"Honey," the President started, "we were hoping you would join us. We were—"

"I'll bet," the Mrs. President said.

"—just discussing the issuance of a proclamation denying any fiduciary responsibility for the adverse results of the derivative market which was caused by an attempt by a country like Egypt, and we're not saying it was Egypt, but a country which could very well be Egypt, manipulating the derivative technology platform." He smiled. "How does that sound?"

"Like a whine from a spineless politician explaining to his constituents why he was photographed in bed with a naked albino hooker doing research on suntan lotion." She cracked her knuckles and then spread her hands on the desk in front of her. "If you're not paying, just tell 'em to go to hell."

"Yes, dear, but I think—"

"Somebody ask you to think? Wasn't me," the First Lady Mrs. President said.

Jack spoke up again. "Latest is over two hundred countries and organizations have declared all-out war on the United States."

The President held up his hand. "Wait a minute. *We* haven't even decided what we're going to do. How in the hell are these countries finding out they've been screwed?"

"I told them," came from under the table.

"Get up here, Xuattle-le!" the CIA chief said. "You weren't supposed to—"

Bryce Rogers said, "Hey, that sounds suspiciously like you had a deal with Xuattle-le (he pronounced it *qua idit laly* with a great deal of spittle flying). That wasn't the way that the Mrs. President told me to—"

"Shut up, Rogers," the First Lady Mrs. President snapped. "Cousin-in-law or not, I don't pay you to open your pie hole."

Bestman crept silently into the room and handed the Ukrainian arms dealer what appeared to Jack to be a cashier's check with plenty of zeros, mouthed 'pardon me' to the group, and crept back out.

The Ukrainian gave a thumbs up to Darkman who frowned and gave him a modified Italian salute—disguised as scratching his forehead while holding his bicep.

Jack slammed his pistol onto the conference table.

"IS THERE ANYBODY IN THE ROOM WHO DOESN'T HAVE A SIDE DEAL ON THE DERIVATIVE PROBLEM? ANYBODY?" he demanded.

Jack went around the table, pointing his .45 at each person in turn. "You? You? You?"

No one spoke except the President, who took the fifth.

"Not appropriate, Mr. President," Jack said. "Folks, there are some serious attacks on the U.S. brewing. And that's just the—"

"Ukraine brew beer better all the time."

"Someone shut potato-head up," Darkman said. "He's dumber than a stump and—"

"Eight million no stupid." The happy arms dealer waived the check.

"—not even American."

The President put his hands together, tips under his chin, and assumed an authoritative aura. "I think I should just pull this all together, friends. There has been enough diversions, false propaganda, blind alleys, and—"

"Get on with it, chubby," the first lady said, sounding exasperated. Those in the room who had seen Mrs. President transform into a Tasmanian Devil on speed, held their breath.

"Yes. The reality is that to avert a serious implosion of the U.S. economy, and I've talked to many experts, we cannot simply double the money supply overnight."

A series of explosions rattled the windows, even on the fifty-first floor. Talk stopped while the motley group stared cluelessly at the window.

"Jack, you might check with General Fixture. See if he knows the origin of those explosions."

"Yes, Mr. President." Jack turned away from the table, donned headphones, and spoke into his mike. "Patriot 6, this is SpyBoy. Patriot 6, this is Spyboy, do you read?"

Then, "Yes, sir......General Fixture, we're receiving a number of mortar rounds in lower Manhattan.....Yes, sir, could be artillery, but not a lot of damage being done.....Yes, sir.....I beg your pardon, sir....... No, sir.....the President is sitting not three feet from me......Who? Sir.... Yes, she's here also. No, she didn't hear that....."

The first lady lunged toward Jack. "Give me that mike! I'll tell that bastard—"

Jack leaned away, "Yes, sir.....right away, sir." He took off the headphones. "Hold on!" Jack stood, the .45 in his hand again. "Listen up, for God's sake. Things are spinning out of control. We need to do something about it."

"The question is what, Jack?" Darkman looked worried now. "And what were the explosions?"

"Evidently the Southern Poverty Law Center is protesting the anti-Guinea-Bissau bias of Fed-Ex by planting bombs near their headquarters in New York." Jack looked down through the window to see if more bombs were exploding.

"The FedEx headquarters aren't in New York," Darkman said.

"The SPLC release mentioned their fear of retaliation by red-necks in Tennessee, so the protest was moved," Jack said. "Oh shit! Mr. President, grab the Pygmy." Who was duck-walking from under the table and out the door.

An unseemly wrestling match ensued between the President and the Pygmy, with much gouging, biting, and gonad-crushing knee work. Mostly by the President. Who emerged the victor when the Pygmy threatened to hold his breath until he died— the fervid wish of everyone in the room. He turned blue and was rolled back under the table.

"He'll be okay," the President assured everyone. "No President in history has ever strangled a pygmy and I don't intend to be the first."

"No one would ever strangle on *your* pygmy, that's for sure," the First Lady commented. Rather crudely, Jack thought.

"With all due respect, Mrs. President," said Jack, "can we just move on? The world is turning against us. And we've actually done nothing to address that as yet. We seem at an impasse, with the same number of people in this room voting for more money as there are people voting for defaulting on the obligation. And they're the same people!"

"Who put you in charge?" demanded the formerly thought to be sleeping CIA chief.

"His forty-five, Mr. Stevens," Gearheardt answered. "It seems sanity is an uncommon virtue in this crisis. We started with the simple concept of killing all the investment bankers. A false beginning, true. But a good, reasonable start to any government reorganization."

Gearheardt got to his feet. "The fact is, and I'm not sure why she's reluctant to present it, the First Lady and I have the solution to the current crisis created by the Pygmy, with the acquiescence of Wall Street, whereby the entire net worth of

America was bet on what could best be described as a toss of the coin."

"I think you lost me, Gearheardt," Jack said, "but the important thing is this solution you mentioned."

Gearheardt turned to the First Lady who was filing her nails. "Ma'am, do you want to tell them what we've worked out?"

The Mrs. President held up her hand, palm out and studied her nail work. "I would love to, Gearheardt, but am constrained by the concept of plausible deniability. I have to worry about the probability that I will be offering to run for the presidency myself in the future and cannot risk tainting that opportunity by having a failed financial restructuring hindering my ascent in any way."

"Thank you, Mrs. Current President. A truer patriot America has never suffered," Gearheardt said.

The first lady and Gearheardt exchanged eye arrows.

Watching, Jack thought the 'strange bedfellows' comment could never fit more appropriately. But surely Gearheardt hadn't---his mind refused to go there.

Gearheardt faced the group. "The solution is simple, legal, and was right in front of us, or behind us, to be completely accurate. We will—"

Denise of the intercom interrupted. "Is the President of the United States available for a phone call?"

The President grabbed a phone and punched a blinking button.

"This here's the President," he said. It was always best to start out folksy. It was easy to upgrade to intelligent leader if need be. "How can your President be of service, Major?"

The President bolted upright. "What! How in the hell? Really? Really? Well you can tell that sonofabitch that California is on it's by-God own. And as for you, Major, there will be no reinforcements at all! None. Zero. *You* figure it out!" He slammed the phone down.

"Well, Mr. C.I. *Smarty* Ass. The Russian mortgage bankers we shipped to Arizona to close the California border have just plumb gummed up the whole damn plan we had for that bastard state. Wise-ass California National Guard was too pussy to fight. They just sent a few busses to haul those crazy Russians up to the Mustang Ranch and they're holed up there for damned eternity. And they want me to send more women!" He stood and kicked his chair. "Is there not one bless-ed person in the entire government of the United States who can just do what I ask them to do?"

The head of the President's secret service detail jumped to his feet. "Mr. President, I hope you don't think of my men that way. We are always available and always loyal to our commitment."

The President tilted his head, deep in thought. "Well that's great, Smitty. Maybe you can get the coffee that Darkman can't seem to scrounge up. Hopefully, someone will try to shoot *me* and you can jump in and save my life."

As the Secret Service man searched desperately through his training history for the correct response, the First Lady snorted. "Oh, grow up, Slick. No one is shooting anyone. Let Gearheardt tell you the plan, and then let's enjoy gridlocking

New York by driving around like tourists from Cedar Rapids. You always get a kick out of that. You can point out where your girlfriends live."

The President actually smiled at the First Lady. "Can I wear my mask of me?" he asked.

"Creo que no," Mrs. President answered. "Get on with it, Gearheardt."

"Right. Gents, in the 80's the entire savings and loan industry went on a lending binge that was based solely on a borrower's desire of wanting money. There were few other requirements. Of course, the law of gravity applies to all things, and the debt load was no exception. Everything collapsed. The FSLIC was broke, the borrowers were broke, the savings and loan owners were in hock to their lobbyists and attorneys for billions and billions of dollars. So, the government asked Wall Street to dive in and help save the economy. Wall Street said, why not just loan them more money, guarantee it, we will issue it for a small fee, and you'll not have to face any real political fallout while you're in office."

The politicians said, 'Hey, that sounds like a super idea. And by the way, what about something that looks like money but is not money, to just pass out until we can get to the border, figuratively speaking.'

And the banks came up with 'wish paper.' A promise to pay which looked like real worth to prop up the banks but which paid off sometime around the sun burning out. The politicians were incensed that Wall Street thought they were that stupid. Then they realized they actually *were* that stupid and the whole thing was passed on to the public by amending the banking laws to allow scalping and usury."

The room was silent except for the First Ladies nail file.

Finally, the President spoke. "Is there going to be a test on this?"

Gearheardt laughed. "It's complicated, Mr. President. Here's all you have to know. Using a Series B issue of money—and we can get someplace like the Pitcairn Islands to agree to float it—we print about thirty trillion new and basically useless dollar look-alikes. Pay off all our debts with it. And keep using our real money to make us richer."

"Okay, that sounds better, although I didn't get the Pitcairn Islands reference."

"We just make them the first payee. They go apeshit over how grateful they are---we only owe them a few billion dollars—and then the other countries all scramble to get theirs. Bingo." Gearheardt sat back down. "And by the way, every Republican in office is going to wake up with a certificate in their mailbox guaranteeing a new concrete culvert in a place of their choosing. With a steel cattle-guard. The lawyers are working on language which would allow them to be exchanged for silverware or time-shares."

Jack was back on his radio. "Yes, sir…. Are there threats that I should alert the President to?..... We're seeking a solution, sir…..I appreciate your skepticism sir, but what is the alternative……I beg your pardon, sir?..... I,..I…I'm not sure what to say…..Yes, sir."

Jack turned back to the room, looking flustered. "The Yap Islanders just bombed Pearl Harbor."

The CIA man, Stevens, was the first to say it, "The Yaps bombed Pearl Harbor?"

Jack shook his head. "It was a single aircraft and they only did minor damage to a pickup in the PX parking lot. But the newspapers are going to have a field day."

"How long will it take to get this plan into full operation, Darkman?" The President was energized.

"It is already underway. Just waiting the okay from you-know-who, the idiot," he pointed downward toward the table.

"I know who you're talking about, Darkman," the Pygmy said from his nest under the table.

"And your proclamation on television and through the press wire, Mr. President."

"Wait," Jack interjected, "aren't we doing just the same as not paying our obligations?"

"No one will know for some time, Jack. It's the same principle as a tree falling in the forest. I doubt there's ever been an uproar by people who didn't realize they were being screwed." Gearheardt sounded convinced but avoided Jack's eyes.

"And you're good with that?" Jack asked.

They were standing just outside the circle of loud, argumentive and cajoling, threatening and comforting, over-talking cacophony of people who largely made their living doing just that. The theme generally being maximizing the apex of personal risk versus personal reward. That is, the point at which those two lines cross on the chart of 'greed vs. prison'. A chart which, of historical note, had replaced the 'greed vs. shame' of early, unsophisticated years.

Denise of intercom fame said: Mr. Darkman, there's a man here who says he's the landlord and….."

"DAMN IT, DENISE, CAN'T YOU LEARN TO HANDLE A SINGLE THING WITHOUT…" Darkman stopped and realized the entire contingent of plotters and planners was watching and listening.

"I'm sorry, Denise. I thought you were one of the other Denise's…."

"Bullshit," the First Lady said. "You're just a prick."

Darkman recovered. "Please inform the gentleman that I am tied up and that he should come back another time. WITH an appointment. And if he would be so kind as to leave a note referencing the context of the meeting, I would appreciate it." Darkman smiled at the room.

"Yes, sir……………Okay. He says you should come to his office. He calls it a done deal. And he wants to know why you have a Russian meeting with the President in your conference room."

"I AM UKRAINIAN," the now un-happy arms dealer exploded. "Do not keep with calling Russian of me. Ukrainian is honorable people, not Russian. I will give back eight million check if you think—"

Bryce Rogers, sitting beside the Ukrainian experienced a quick heart stoppage, recovered, and grabbed for the eight million check.

Jack noticed that the Secret Service guy grabbed for the check also, as did the first lady, Gearheardt, and a small, pygmy-sized hand from under the table. The Ukrainian, however, stuffed the eight million check back into his coat pocket and smiled as he knocked away the outstretched paws.

"Ukrainian is a joking people," he said.

The President spoke. "Okay, folks, I'll take it from here now that I know the plan. If you will just give me that eight million check, eight-million-*dollar* check, I will start an immediate and thorough investigation into who instigated the transaction that produced the apparent payoff, you can call it a commission, which smacks of an illegality."

"Go f—k, yourself, Mr. President," Bryce Rogers of cousin-in-law-to-first lady- background said.

The first lady Mrs. President snorted again, "Ha, the dream of all narcissists. But in this case there is no reach or chance."

"That is not helpful, darlin'," the President said. "Okay, we'll forget the eight million check as Mr. English-is-not-my-first-language Ukrainian man calls it."

Jack watched as everyone began talking again. Even the Pygmy climbed up on the table and began demanding he be made president. The Secret Service guy tried to get Gearheardt to have guns sent up. The Ukrainian began choking the Pygmy for no apparent reason, the First Lady and President decided to air vivid and licentious marital-related charges against one another, the CIA chief pushed back from the table and observed with a bemused smile, Bryce Rogers sided with his cousin-in-law adding even more lurid details of interns and references to Alabama football, and Gearheardt whistled a happy tune.

Jack fired the .45 through the ceiling, hoping no one was sunbathing on the roof.

As he had expected, the noise stopped. What he had not expected was:

The intercom had been on the whole time, with Denise and her lobby guests listening.

Jack's radio had been open to General Fixture's headquarters the whole time.

"Shit," the room said, as Jack pointed out those two facts.

The intercom Denise was the first to break the silence:

"Mr. Darkman, the landlord said that shooting holes in the ceiling is against the lease agreement. But he was personally willing to serve as a mediator to make a deal between the politicians, the military, and Wall Street. Fee waived just to save the country."

General Fixture's radio response was just two words: **Broken Arrow**.

Which would have precipitated a much more destructive assault on lower Manhattan if anyone in the military had had a clue what that meant.

Those in the conference room were silent, looking at each other with various degrees of suspicion and hate until, from under the table, the Pygmy said, "Jeff Chandler and Debra Paget."

Chapter Penultimate (I think)

But General Fixture was resolute. Waiting impatiently for the signal to send in his Marines, he and his staff had been playing word games. "Best Jimmy Stewart movie?" his adjutant had asked. *Broken Arrow*, he had replied, then lurched to his feet. "Let's knock off this lollygagging around and get this show on the road. I think there's a good chance that we're the only troops who haven't been captured by Russian mortgage brokers. We're on our own."

And he was fully prepared for what he had to do. Take the United States from the hands of idiots, charlatans, foreigners, and rotten bastards—the last a catch-all for those he had not identified specifically.

His men, fifteen or twenty of his most senior, stood in front of his desk in the New Jersey office building penthouse. All, including Fixture, were armed to the teeth and had camouflaged faces. The Marines were the finest of the finest. Hand-picked by Fixture for the most sacred mission of their careers—saving their country from itself.

"Gentlemen, I need not lecture you on the gravity, or propriety, of our mission. You've heard the leaders of the two main branches of government, executive and banking, betray their duty and fidelity. We're all aware of that part of our oath concerning enemies, foreign and domestic. In that room were both. Yesterday, I was quite frankly struggling with the idea of using my men to protect Wall Street from angry Americans. I don't care about the fools overseas who bet on how many fingers Wall Street was hiding behind it's back. They all deserve to lose their money. I will not, however, stand by and let the American people be led by the criminal class. And that's what it seems gathered in that room."

"Yes, Marine, you have a question?" He pointed to a lieutenant in the back row.

"Sir, should I tell my men to fix bayonets?"

Fixture took a deep breath. "Son, you'll get the final briefing from your company commanders when it's time to push off. I'm just giving you the background."

"Do we have time to short our personal stocks, General?"

Fixture wasn't sure who had asked it. He put his hands on his hips and sighed.

"No. Okay if that's all the questions, you can expect an ops plan within the hour. Get your men ready. We will prep the zone an hour before. And we'll have plenty of CAS throughout the operation. Good luck, men. Semper Fi."

"Semper Fi, Sir," the Marines shouted while breaking away from the desk and heading to the door.

"Who the hell are we attacking again?" a major asked a captain.

"Who gives a shit, sir? We're back in business and the weather is not hot and solid mosquitoes. I'm ready to fight."

"Hmm. Well, I'm not sure I'm ready to kill Americans, even for America," the major said.

"I think they're investment bankers, sir."

The President was on the line with General Fixture. "Well, dang it, Fixture, that would be a coup if you went ahead with that kind of action. Coups aren't even legal in the United States. I know my constitution, General." He covered the phone with his hand and sotto voiced to Darkman, "Didn't I order some coffee about a hundred hours ago, Darkman?" He went back to the General.

"Besides, a coup has to be down in Washington. You can't just pull a coup wherever the hell it's most convenient." He listened. "Yeah, well that's just your damn opinion. Wall Street and the White House are NOT the same thing.....No, you listen to me. If you persist in attacking Wall Street, I'll have the Army on your ass so quick......They are? Who said?.......Well, mother love a goat." He put his hand over the phone again and spoke to Mrs. President. "The bastard says the Army is full up behind him. Have you ever heard the Army back a goddamn thing the Marines do? Should I believe him? Anyone have a number for the Army?"

The sum total of those listening to the President was zero as they were gathered around the opposite end of the table trying to give final wording to the proclamation, adding various personal 'riders' and sucking up to the Pygmy who was still head of the Federal Reserve prior to being murdered later—although everyone knew not to refer to it as murder. Gearheardt's suggestion of *urdermay* was as good as any.

The CIA chief, a political appointee, had embarrassed himself out of the discussion when he was caught talking into the heel of his shoe.

"That was just on television, you jackass," laughed the Secret Service guy.

"Jack, this country is doomed if we don't get true Agency guys running the intelligence services. Look at that idiot taking a penknife to his heel. He was teaching history and coaching badmitton in a junior college before the numbnuts President brought him in to run the CIA."

"It's badminton, Gearheardt." Jack was waiting for further orders from General Fixture.

"You mean that game with a peacock?"

"It's a shuttlecock. And just shut up for a minute."

And at that moment a horrendous explosion shook the building and rattled the window. It was followed by two more of the same, although sounding not quite as close. Jack and Gearheardt ran to look out.

"Whoa, Nellie, Jack, that was artillery. "Angry brown and gray clouds were rising from the street in three locations.

"I think the General is making a statement, Gearheardt. Did you notice that those three rounds marched right up the street? They had to have been oriented to pass right through the building corridor. Great shooting. I'll bet Cox is the AO."

The boys turned back to the room where all had frozen, looking at them.

"Was that what I think it was, Jack?" the President asked.

"The General is dead serious, Mr. President. In my opinion, the Marines will be landing within the hour. May I suggest that we vacate this building and meet with the General as he comes ashore."

Everyone seemed to think that was a good idea except Mrs. President, Darkman, the Pygmy, and Gearheardt.

The first lady spoke up. "I, for one, am not going anywhere and certainly not to meet a smelly old Marine general to negotiate a coup."

The Secret Service man approached her. "If I may, Mrs. President, point out that the safest way to—"

The first lady cold-cocked the man with a left and managed to punch him with a wicked right on his way to the floor.

"Now honey, that isn't helping things, "the president said. He put down the phone he was holding and walked to her end of the conference table.

He dropped her with one blow, but chauvinistically caught her and lowered her gently back into her chair.

"Everybody saw that she threw the first punch, right?"

"Uh, yessir," the CIA chief said, "but actually it wasn't thrown at you."

"Hey, I'm the f—king lawyer here," the President snapped. "Don't answer questions before someone asks them.

"Anyway, she had it coming." He seemed embarrassed. "She can be meaner than a damn snake, you know."

"Mr. Excelently President of America," the Ukrainian started, "if maybe I can offer a suggestion of considerable merit. We can, and this would be very careful to be done, say this General that we will have shot to death Mrs. President if he does not stop coup. It is my suggestion."

The President put his hand to his chin as if he was carefully considering the Ukrainian's suggestion.

Finally, he said, "Mr. Ukrainian, it illustrates my dilemma almost to a tee that someone with, as you call it, eight million check—while I have jack-shit—can make such a startingly stupid suggestion. I do appreciate your willingness to exhibit moron-ity in the hope of saving your profit. I salute you, sir."

"Thank you, Mr. President of American."

Things seemed to go downhill after the knock-out of the first lady and the aftermath of the Ukrainian suggestion—who figured out the President was being sarcastic and began pouting. It was immediately evident that no one had the foggiest idea about how to write a proclamation of the Fed Bank issuing money roughly the equivalent of a year's pay for everyone in America and still protect their own interests. Bickering and outright accusations of venality peppered the discussion. Waking up the only one who had the cleverness, audacity and selfishness to write the document was discussed and abandoned due to extreme fear of what a recently knocked out first lady might wrought.

"Gearheardt," Jack said, "I'm heading out to join with the Marines. I have no idea what is going to happen, but I know which side I'm on. Are you coming with me?"

"Does a pig miss his knuckles? Of course, I'll come with you. No reason to stay here unless I was just in it for the money." He was looking at the President when he answered.

More explosions shook the room. The President finally reached a White House attorney and was hammering questions at him.

"Well, if it IS a coup and it's successful, do I have to leave the country or what? Don't we have a damn coup expert or somebody that knows more than you? They don't have to shoot me, do they? I mean for a completely successful coup?" He listened. "Okay, just for example, and don't pass this on, I want to run a suggestion by you that a foreign agent came up with……No, but he seems pretty knowledgeable about coups and arms deals and anyway, here's the idea."

The President ran through the scenario of shooting or claiming to shoot the first lady. Would that suffice? What are the repercussions? Who covers burial costs? The Ukrainian gave him a thumbs up. His partner, Bryce Rogers, seemed to be flummoxed.

Jack stood up and put his backpack radio on. He shifted his .45 on his pistol belt, then settled his helmet on his head. No one noticed. He motioned for Gearheardt to follow him out of the door.

Passing by the intercom box he heard Denise say "Mr. Darkman, there's a man here who says he's Senator from Wyoming. He has a horse that looks kind of dead. But he—"

"Send him up, Denise."

Jack heard yelling about the lease agreement and animals and punched the intercom off.

As he turned back at the door to say goodbye, he saw the Queen of Close Air Support, an A1-E, fly by the window. Its engine vibrating the glass more than even the artillery barrage which continued in the near distance. (He later heard that the A1 had napalmed Central Park, which commenced the lawsuit of all lawsuits from a coalition of muggers, homeless and 5th Avenue matrons who had witnessed flaming people exiting the park, disrupting cocktail hour).

Outside the conference room Jack grabbed Gearheardt and shoved him into an adjacent office.

"Gearheardt, I'm not sure where you stand in all this. Was the funny money really your idea?"

"More or less, Jack. But the first lady's rotten cousin-in-law screwed me out of a deal I'd made with Milton Bradley. How low of a scumbag do you have to be to cheat someone out of a scam?" His smile bounced back, the good thing about Gearheardt.

"Hey, did you see that dipshit in the A1? The damn Air Force started strafing and bombing while the artillery was still pounding away. How many times did we see that happen in Vietnam? Do the bastards at the Air Force have watches? If you'd give me your .45 I'd shoot him down myself the next time he flies by."

"Calm down, Gearheardt. Look, we've been pals a long time. Through thick and thin—"

"And Olongapo, don't forget Olongapo," Gearheardt reminded him.

"—but you're scaring me. You're evasive…..shit, you've always been evasive, but just answer me—is there a deal going on that I don't know about? I'm heading over to join the Marine Corps invasion of Manhattan. I'd like to think—"

"Jack, I know what you're trying to say. We're partners. But the people in that next room don't like you. You've just never been able to tell people what they want to hear. How do you expect to get ahead with an attitude like that? If we wanted truth, we'd serve sodium ethanol with our pancakes. We would—"

"Do you mean sodium pentothal?"

"Jack, you have always had this problem of basic honesty. You live in a world found only in Golden Books and Dr. Zooage or whatever his name is."

"I can assure you it's not Dr. Sewage."

"Okay, but my point is, by recognizing reality, by accepting reality, you can help reality become more real."

"That is the dumbest thing you've ever said to me, Gearheardt…No, let me finish. I believe your heart is in the right place. But the world you want me to accept is Gearheardt-centric. Your actions have reactions that might not…..why am I standing here discussing this with you? You will never change. You're the best guy I've even known and a menace to society."

"Thanks, Jack."

They shook hands and held for a moment.

Gearheardt said, "Do you remember that time in Bangkok when you were in the hot tub with all those naked women and I threw a monkey in with you." He laughed. "You were so darn mad I thought you'd kill me."

"The monkey bit my nuts, Gearheardt."

"He was a monkey. That's what monkeys do." Gearheardt laughed again,

Jack was sober. "Maybe there's a lesson in there somewhere."

When they stepped back outside of the office they saw the rear-end of a stuffed horse stuck in the door to the conference room. Two men were pushing on the horse's butt. Through the glass wall, they could see the Wyoming senator and Darkman pushing against the horse, trying to get it back outside.

The noise was overwhelming any hope of communication. The first lady, obviously recovered from her husband's sucker punch, was screaming at a distraught Pygmy.

"You're not even a Pygmy, you damn imposter. You're just a short Bushman. Don't think you can—"

"The two are NOT mutually exclusive you shrew. And I never said I was a pygmy. That damn Gearheardt started that rumor. And WHAT DAMN DIFFERENCE DOES IT MAKE? There are no restrictions on eligibility for Fed Chief and anyway, the press referred to me as a Bushman from the Kalahari. What cave were you sleeping in when that news—"

Jack winced even before he saw the blow the first lady struck. It was inevitable. The pygmy dropped like a sack of cement.

The president was still on the phone with the White House lawyer. "What about pension benefits? Still good after a coup or should I resign?"

The CIA chief was examining his belt buckle. "Hello base. Hello base." He moved the post back and forth, pointing it in different directions to get the best reception results.

The Secret Service man sat beside the president, pointing to himself that mouthing 'what about me?' ask him what about me?

Darkman, pushing too hard, tore the ear and right jaw off of the stuffed horse. The Senator was not pleased and mentioned a series of committee investigations the Darkman firm would suffer through.

Darkman pressed the intercom: "Denise, would you come get this asshole and the horse he rode in on?"

Jack and Gearheardt watched. Finally, one of the men pushing on the horse's rear stuck his head into the butt of the horse and said, "Hey, look, I've got my head up an ass."

A number of the Denise's in the room looked ill. "How gross."

Jack shuddered and said, "I'm out of here, Gearheardt. These are the kind of folks you can deal with. I can't." He shook Gearheardt's hand once again. "And keep your head down. General Fixture isn't fooling around."

Gearheardt pursed his lips, shook his head sadly, and turned back to the conference room. "Hey, get your head out of that ass," he said, slapping the guy on his butt. He grinned at the roomful of Denise's and ducked under the horse's legs back into the room.

CHAPTER WHAT DIFFERENCE DOES IT MAKE (2)

As the artillery barrage ended and the 'corrected' Air Force bombing closed the thoroughfares in and out of lower Manhattan, General Fixture had called his key men together on the riverfront docks. Jack, having just made it back in time for the launch, stood in the back row. The General had acknowledged him with a nod and smile.

"Men—I don't believe we have any women yet, do we Sergeant Major? Men, in a few moments we will envelop the general area of Wall Street. It is not foreign soil, nor is it the home to Nips or Krauts. It is America, complete with Americans and, yes, there may be a few Nips and Krauts in there, but you get my point. I know that many of you feel that the slaughter of Americans, even investment bankers, would be rebarbative. I don't use that word lightly. I use it because it bedevils the network news folks when Marines go beyond two syllables." He paused. "Okay, that wasn't as funny as a certain lieutenant on my staff thought it would be."

The General took a deep breath. "Listen up, men. This is important. The most important thing. We are NOT going to attack lower Manhattan with all guns blazing. The United States Marine Corps does not slaughter civilians, particularly American civilians." He let that sink in.

"I do not expect any significant resistance. Our scouts, including Captain-General Armstrong back there, report seeing no weapons, no military equipment or vehicles. We will simply move ashore, post security at the points enumerated on your maps, and let the President know that he must quit double-dealing with Wall Street to the detriment of the American people. All finance related laws and regulations will be fully disclosed and enforced by the United States Marines. The Security and Exchange Commission will be a department of the Navy. I have already briefed the Navy on what the SEC does, and they are in agreement. I have a call in to the Army, but so far have not heard back. Scuttlebutt at the Pentagon says they wanted to run the SEC."

The General looked at a sheet of paper, seeming to check off what he wanted to cover.

"Some of the staff officers have raised the issue of a military-run government, often associated with Banana Republic countries or brutal Communist regimes. Gentlemen, I can assure you as your new President, that will never happen in the United States."

A sort of buzz ran through the two dozen or so Marines. "Did he just say—"

"No, gentlemen, this is not a military coup. A select group of men from the Pentagon, however, will assemble to ascertain if there is a sane politician available to run the country. At that time, we will call for an election or put him in office at gunpoint."

"Sir," a voice from the Marines called out, "just to be certain, are you saying we can't shoot anyone? And, to take that one step further, what if we're fired upon?"

"The Rules of Engagement still apply, Marines. Just because these are investment bankers, that doesn't mean that we cannot protect ourselves. In this case, we are applying the same rules that the nation's defense attorneys have used so effectively in criminal proceedings—that is reasonable doubt. If you have reasonable doubt that someone is not going to shoot you, you may fire at will."

After a moment, a JAG officer who had wandered by the formation raised his hand.

"Yes, Jagoff," the Marine's term for Judge Advocate General officers, "your question is? And I need to remind everyone that we're due at the attack launch in just a few minutes."

"Yes, sir," the JAGOFF said, "doesn't the rather confusing double negative give a Marine pause on the battlefield? It would strike me—"

The JAGOFF got his wish as a number of Marines *did* strike him. Thus, ending the confusion discussion.

"One last note of good cheer, Marines. I've just received word from the team of Marines sent to the airport to intercept the Transnistria infantry. By the time they arrived, the entire Transnistrian army was hospitalized or on their way to jail. They had been caught shop-lifting in the Disney store at the terminal and were beaten silly by two teenagers dressed as Mickey and Minnie Mouse."

The Marines roared their approval. "And by the way," the General continued, "the last word I got The Hague looked like a giant Chihuly exhibit." But no one caught the reference, not even those who knew that Guinea-Bissau had purchased a nuke from Pakistan.

The General raised his hands and his voice. "SEMPER FI, MARINES! GOD SPEED!"

As Jack waited his turn to board the landing craft, he looked at the Lower Manhattan skyline, wondering what was happening with Gearheardt. On his right, he saw the U.S.S. Ike and Tina Tuner steaming up the river to provide support to the Marines. Although Stansfield Turner claimed otherwise, the ship was not mistakenly named. The vote for dropping Stansfield and adding Ike and Tina was unanimous in the Navy. As he watched, the mighty ship became lodged under the Brooklyn Bridge. Liberty- hungry sailors were jumping off the ship onto the bridge in rabid packs. An A-10 Warthog on a shallow dive toward Manhattan shot the hand off of the Statue of Liberty.

Tears came to Jack's eyes. America was turning to crap. Could the Marines save it?

The first wave of Marines came ashore near Battery Park. Young investment analysts were lounging, picnic baskets catered by "21" sat by crates of Dom Perignon White Gold. Half of Cuba's last tobacco harvest was afire between the lips of youthful millionaires, behind five hundred-dollar sunglasses, out to see the Marines do what Marines do best. A few held small flags, hastily made by an enterprising son of a Vietnam refugee, saying 'Go Marine Dudes.'

The first Marines to reach Battery Park were the squad of Corporal Vincente Morales of El Paso, Texas. They shot every one of the investment bankers, dragged their lifeless bodies into a huge pyre of humans, pissed on the pile while standing behind it smoking the Cuban cigars they confiscated. An attempt to light the pile of bankers failed due to the incredible amount of the aforementioned piss that soaked the expensive clothes.

Within an hour, the entire *army* of investment bankers, advisors, fund managers, Ponzi schemers, and the legion of their support staff had surrendered. White flags fluttered like laundry on a Hong Kong apartment building up and down the skyscraper corridors. A rumor quickly spread that the bankers must turn in their cars, leading to any number of young Lance Corporals screaming around the streets of New York in yellow Lamborghinis. A score of Marines were taken to hospital ships suffering broken limbs after driving at high rates of speed into bomb holes.

High above the fray, the President continued his conversation with the beleaguered White House legal staff. "Okay, let's say I appoint him President and promise to do the paperwork later. Then the Marines shoot him. Can I come back as still the President?"

The President leaned back in his chair, the phone still to his ear. His free hand shielding his eyes. "Why don't I just shoot myself and save all the trouble." He bolted upright. "Who said that? Who shouted……Damn it, I heard him. Don't tell me what I heard!" He slammed down the phone.

The Ukrainian's 'eight million' check lay on the table, cut into four pieces. The First Lady, the Secret Service guy, the Ukrainian and the First Lady's cousin-in-law each had a piece. It was decided that all would have to visit the bank together in order to cash, or deposit, the check. No other plan could be devised which satisfied the mutual mistrust. Now, the four of them sat watching the check and each other.

The Senator's stuffed horse, now in two parts, was put on the elevator along with a wildly drunk Senator armed only with a signed declaration from the President that the concrete culvert certificates were good at Walmart.

Quiet contemplation ensued.

"Sir?" It was the CIA chief. "I think my boys have come up with a plan that gets us through this crisis." He began smoothing a faxed spread sheet on the table. "You do know, sir, that the CIA keeps tabs on the global economy to the last dollar. My guys are good."

"Okay, C.I. Asshole, what do you have?" The President's mood was not the best.

"Sir, the bottom line is this," he ran his finger over line after line of numbers and footnotes. "We can pay our losses to every country whose name ends in a vowel."

The President opened one eye and looked through his fingers at the CIA chief.

"That's the f—king analysis? We pay, what was that?, countries whose name ends in a vowel?"

"Yessir. My team thought it would be unwise, assuming we're not going to pay everyone in funny money—which I'm still in favor of—we should have a plan rather than look like we're playing favorites. Early on we rejected the idea to just pay countries predominately white. Even though that seemed to be the safest and most economic. We've given this some real thought."

"And by God, it shows, Stevens, if that's your real name." The President's sarcasm cut through Steven's anti-sarcasm shield and he hung his head.

The President looked defeated. Gearheardt was at the window looking down at what seemed to be combat troops driving Lamborghinis. "What's your idea, wise-ass who got me into this mess?" the President asked.

"Mine, sir? I think the Marines are just here for show. If we just ignore them, go about doing the country's business, we just move on. We use the 'wish paper' idea. Maybe just to the 'end in a vowel' idea, I kind of like that, and figure out how to get re-elected and solve the problem then."

"In other words, deny everything, blame someone else, and hold our heads up high."

"In a nutshell."

"Do I get to be president?" the Pygmy asked.

"Haven't you been listening, jackass? The plan of taking over the financial system has been scuttled by the damn Wall Street investment bankers losing every damn penny you told them to put into the derivatives market." The President seemed particularly angry at the Pygmy.

"What's your opinion, darlin'?" the President asked his wife.

"Well, for starters, although none of you gentlemen seem to give a hoot about me, at least with the U.S. Marines leading the coup, I don't have to worry about being raped and left for dead."

All the men in the room kept their eyes on the table in front of them, not daring to look at one another.

Finally, the President spoke up. "We are blessed."'

Denise on the intercom: "Mr. Darkman, there's a Marine here. He says they just killed all the investment bankers in Battery Park and are looking for women to rape. Should I send him up?"

Denise again: "Mr. Darkman, he says he was kidding about the rape part which is prohibited. The slaughter is evidently true."

There was silence. Then the President said, "Friends, I think it's time we did the honorable thing. Something for the country."

All but Gearheardt then changed their name to Denise, took clothes from the real Denise's where needed, and were among the Darkman staff herded out of the building and told to go home. Brazil was evidently home to what became known as the Darkman Conference Room Clown Committee, the DCRCC.

A last-minute deal between the Congressional legal staff and the White House legal staff gave the acting presidency to

Gearheardt, along with the Chairmanship of the Federal Reserve. Darkman was appointed actual president to add confusion while cockroaches headed for shelter. The Pentagon agreed to investigate and potentially prosecute the Marines who actually stole the Cuban cigars.

Gearheardt, as Fed Chief and Co-President, printed so much funny money that housing starts were down for the year as lumber was in short supply. Fortunately, China bought most of the funny money in one form or another, not quite understanding the *worthless* concept, and became the main poster boy to encourage rapacious success and whipping boy for miscalculations in the American economy.

Two weeks after the **Fall of Wall Street**—a description written by Wall Street investment banks and promoted heavily in the press and swallowed whole by those who wanted to *teach those bastards a lesson*—a photo had appeared in the New York Times showing a grinning Gearheardt presenting Darkman with a huge "key to the country." A congressional committee agreed to investigate that legitimacy until, since the committee chair was from Iowa, the cows actually came home. Roland Darkman was indicted for non-payment of taxes, but successfully counter-sued the government for tax evasion by not enforcing the tax laws and remained President.

Former President Slick successfully built Slick Savings to a major financial institution. Mrs. Former President leveraged herself with reckless abandon. And the Pygmy disappeared into the bowels of the government—awaiting the opportunity to plumb the depths of corporate and government non-accountability—if non-accountability were to ever happen again. And Jack survived on lizard sandwiches.

MSNBC:

"President Darkman, what changes will your administration make to the policies and practices begun under General President Bulldog Nelson?"

"No Pygmys," he said.

"And how successful do you believe that your administration will be in implementing the major campaign promises you made."

"I believe all of my campaign promises will be followed to the tee. I'm proud of that."

"Sir, you promised on many occasion 'Free Money' to every American. Do you—"

"That was taken out of context and misunderstood. By Free Money, I didn't mean Free Money."

The Dow Jones Index soared to 300,000.

Epilogue or Epitaph?

With no one sane at the helm, the country survived, even prospered for almost one percent of the citizens. Gradually the insidious monster of government came back. From Brazil. From communes. From tenured idiots. From California. From Babylonian-trained businessmen.

Late one evening while walking back from trying to stop graffiti artists from redecorating the Washington monument, Jack ran into Gearheardt. They ducked into the best bar on Capitol Hill where Baseball Billy, the bartender and a baseball trivia genius. The small crowd around the bar was silent as the challenger, Taylor, a gentleman from Georgia was miraculously ahead on points.

Jack had sourced two beers and sat down across from Gearheardt. "For old times' sake I got Singha. Shipped from the Pat Pong brewery.

"So, what's up now, Gearheardt? Still with the Agency? Or have you decided on politics?"

"I'm a rancher now, Jack. Got a place out in Wyoming."

"Where did I miss you wanting to be a rancher?" Jack asked.

"Oh, just kind of popped up in a deal. You know, just all of a sudden…. You know—"

"All of a sudden you had a ranch?" There was a trace of bitterness in Jack's voice that Gearheardt caught. "How did it turn out on getting your billion dollars?"

Gearheardt laughed. "Well, there's no honor among thieves, they say."

"I've trusted you all these years, Gearheardt. Saved your ass. Loaned you money. Fought for you when you pissed off everyone up to and including the Pope. I thought you were solid."

"And you were right, Jack." He started to put his hand across the table on Jack's arm, but Jack moved away. "But I think you can see that I need a partner who can smell out the deadbeats and sharks before that happens to me. See what I mean?"

Gearheardt grinned wickedly. "You mean part of President Slick's all the money in the world scheme? That's dirty money, Jack. You said so yourself. If you took dirty money, how could I respect you? Or trust you?"

"Well, you have a point there. I can see the problem that would give you."

"Exactly, Jack. How could……"

"I was being sarcastic you rat bastard."

"So, you're keeping it? Leaving me poor but honest?"

"The Arabs don't like you, Jack."

"What in God's name does that have to do with it? And who are these Arabs who for some reason don't like me?"

Gearheardt would not look Jack in the eyes.

"Guys from Saudi Arabia, Jack."

Jack stared at Gearheardt who was focusing on some distant thought.

"No shit?" Jack said finally. "Some Arabs that I don't know, from Saudi Arabia coincidently, just don't like me. And that's why you're not living up to our 20-year brother to brother fifty fifty deal?"

Gearheardt turned his head to look into Jack's face.

"Its not that simple, Jack."

Jack started to speak and then stopped. He had almost foolishly decided to mention trust, honor, friendship, and loyalty. Gearheardt would have laughed.

"So you're screwing me out of what we made on that deal?"

"Jack, that money came from the citizens of America and other folks, Arabs and Asians, people like that. It's not like the Jack I know to be wanting to---"

"So you're keeping it? Keeping me poor but honest?"

Gearheardt winked and Jack finally understood.

Gearheardt, at the end of the day, was the lucky one, the smarter one. He lived comfortably in his skin, with chameleon ease. Jack struggled on in both worlds, until he found himself in the hidden one, the deep one, the black hole of hell-bent society. Where everything was redefined. Where entering was a lifelong commitment to narcissism and everyone was superior to everyone else. Where *honest* and *best* were words without definition. Like infinity.

The major industries in America were mostly just rearranging words and seeing how fast the new formations would travel.

The new revolution was all about passing on information. And when everything was already passed to everybody, the industry leading companies simply began buying old information and reselling it faster. The Black Market for information was larger than eighty percent of global production of actual things. The Artificial Intelligence programs began turning out information so fast and vast that Google, Facebook, and all online 'news' programs vanished. Remarkably for months no one noticed those companies had stopped operating.

Near mid-century a visiting Euroafriarabian reported back to the Euro Elites (who, it turned out, were better elites than America could produce) that America was a model for producing nothing from nothing.

And the reality for Jack was that Gearheardt hadn't changed. the country had changed. If greed, power, and personal success fed the world, it was World Without End. Amen.

Every man for himself.

The country became incredibly rich over the next years. As one "elite eastern college" grad said, "This country is so wealthy, no one should have to work." Which made some people hate America even more and some people proud. The root of all evil was so ingrained in the populace that it must mean the country is evil, they thought. So half of the citizenry decided to tear down the system that gave them time and wherewithal to tear it down. The other half knew that God wanted, *demanded* that they all be killed or at least re-hated.

Having coffee on his porch one quiet morning, Jack perused *The Craptown Currier [sic]*. Mostly recipes and an occasional story about someone doing something of little interest stuck in amidst football team schedules and breathless reports of two ladies who made it back from the harrowing twenty-five-mile drive to Wichita and back safely. The back page of the "newspaper" reprinted stories which had been in the New York Times days or sometimes weeks before. It was there Jack found two stories of interest.

The first was the filing of a lawsuit against the City of Not Portland by a man who was hit by teargas when he was trying to burn down the Federal Building and, as she had recently become a woman, the teargas interrupted her menstrual cycle. Hopefully $22 million would teach the Not Portland Police a lesson and get her menstrual cycle back on track.

And a gentleman named Gearheardt announced he was running for president. The accompanying photo showed him holding an American flag, a goat beside him on a leash, and the rising sun photogenically shining through his bright red hair. The banner above his head read <u>Let Me Finish the Job</u> And beneath the photo it said <u>*It's Time for Gearheardt*</u>.

It probably was. But there was considerable discussion about what he meant. Thousands of people were burned out of their homes during the discussions. Seventeen hundred and eighty died in the debate in Baton Rouge, LA. Alone. No communication at all from California for days.

Jack dropped his hand over the side of his porch lounging chair and patted his twelve-year-old Welsh Terrier.

"Lord help us, Max. We are doomed"

Acknowledgment

Thanks first of all to my longtime pal and compadre John O'Melveny Woods, one of the most versatile and widely talented guys I've known. This book would never have been published without the support of John and his lovely and gracious wife Judy. And I have to thank a guy I've never met, don't really know, and who might never realize his contribution. His name is Joshua Grenrock, who also has numerous talents and first among them is an intelligent humanness. A fellow questioner of the times and the proclivity for venality among our leaders (leaders in the purely technical sense), Joshua read an early draft of the book. Actually, liked it. And expressed the same to me in a time I was in writer's hell. He lifted me out. And speaking of that writer's hell, I'm pretty sure all novelists reach a point when reading what they've written think "this is crap." And well it might be. I remind myself that the morning I found out that Nam-A-Rama (my first novel) was named as a book of the year by the LA Times and Washington Post, a reviewer in London gave the book a 'pure dung' review. And both might be right. John and Joshua provided an emotional platform at the right time.

And as usual in my novels I thank the innumerable morons who pass through the hallowed halls of our Federal

Government. Among many other achievements you have made writing satire almost impossible, ya bastids.

It has been friends like John and Judy who (besides my family) who have made life worth living. I've been blessed in so many ways. And I've been in a few scrapes.

At least I didn't die.

Yet.

About The Author

Phillip Jennings won the Pirates Alley Faulkner Society first prize in 1999 for his short story Train Wreck in a Small Town, leading him to believe he might be a writer. He's still  trying to find out. He's flown helicopters in combat in SE Asia for three years managing to expertly lose five aircraft from enemy gunfire and poor decisions, chased spies and radicals for various intelligence agencies, created three companies reaching a billion-dollar market cap in industries he knew little about (including one NYSE company he founded in Beijing), consulted for a Saudi Arabian bank in the jungles of Colombia, drank tea with a king and had breakfast with Muhammed Ali. A Mensa member for years he is desperately trying to find the savant part of being an idiot/savant.

Phillip Jennings

Phillip Jennings other works:

Nam-A-Rama (Forge Books 2005) is Phillip Jennings best-selling satire on the venal looniness of the Vietnam War (in which he participated and supported)

Goodbye Mexico the hilarious sequel to Nam-A-Rama (Forge Books 2007) has the protagonists, Jack and Gearheardt, after escaping their failure to stop the Vietnam War, plot to take over a country (or two) with prostitutes and CIA agents providing the support to avoid being assassinated by other CIA agents and retired Russian sharp-shooters.